RANDOLPH SCHWABE

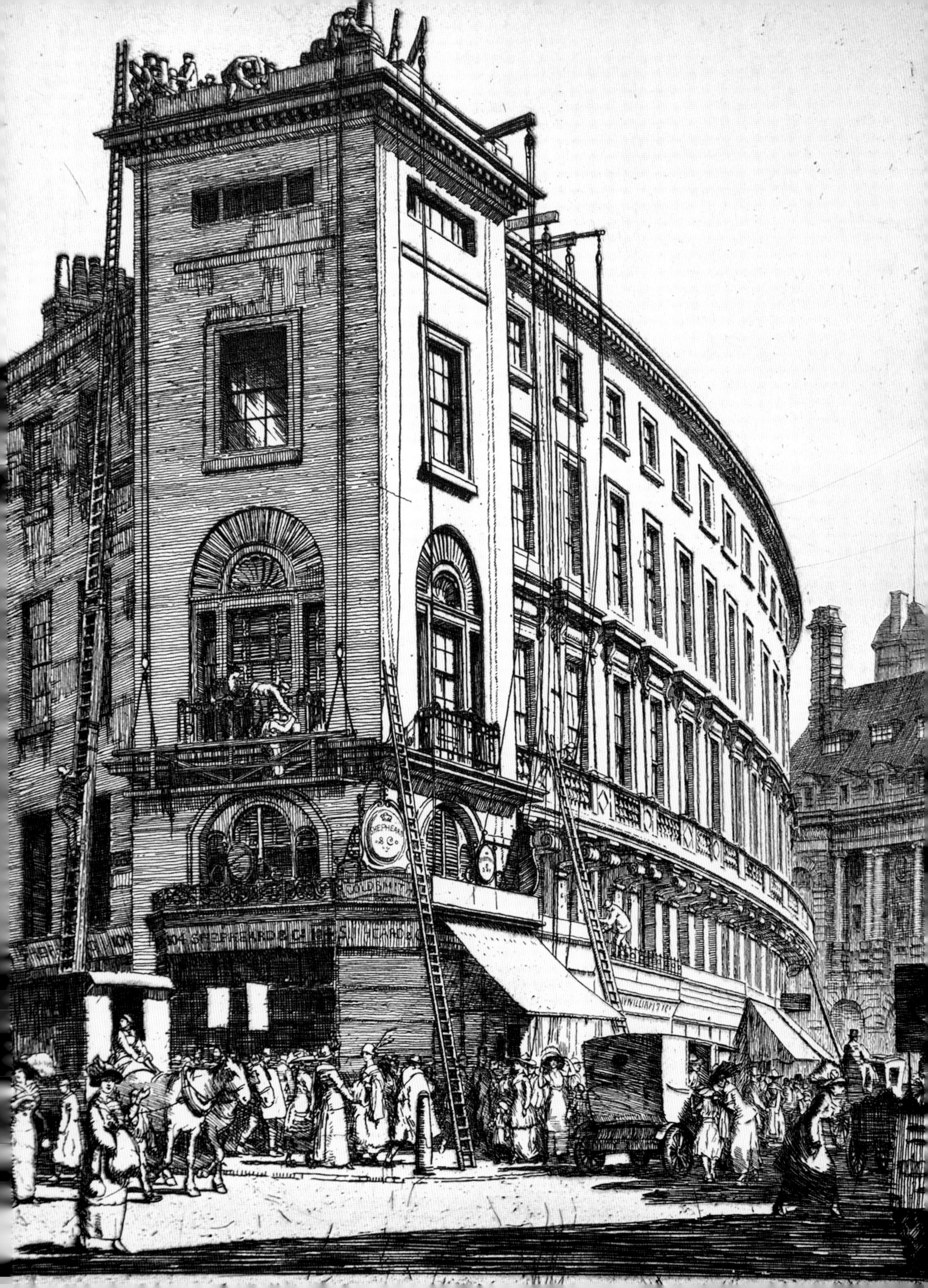

RANDOLPH SCHWABE

Gill Clarke

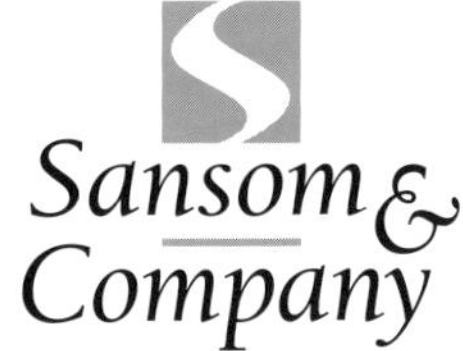

Sansom &
Company

First published in 2012 by Sansom & Company Ltd.,
81G Pembroke Road, Bristol BS8 3EA
www.sansomandcompany.co.uk
info@sansomandcompany.co.uk

MARC FITCH FUND

Published with the support of the Marc Fitch Fund

ISBN 978-1-906593-80-3
British Library Cataloguing-in-Publication Data
A catalogue record for this book is available from the British Library

Design and typesetting by E&P Design, Bath
Printed by Cambrian Printers Ltd.

Front cover: *Bank Holiday — The Swings*; COLLECTION JANET AND DI BARNES
Rear cover: *Randolph Schwabe* by Francis Dodd; COLLECTION JANET AND DI BARNES
Title page: *The Quadrant, Regent Street*; COLLECTION JANET AND DI BARNES

CONTENTS

ACKNOWLEDGEMENTS 6

INTRODUCTION 8

**EARLY YEARS AND
THE DEVELOPING ARTIST** 11

TEACHER AND SLADE PROFESSOR 43

SLADE AND THE RUSKIN 91

WAR ARTIST 115

ILLUSTRATION AND DESIGN 131

DRAWING TO THE END 162

SELECTED REFERENCES 165

INDEX 166

ACKNOWLEDGEMENTS

In researching and writing this biography there have been many people who have provided advice, encouragement and support. I am indebted first and foremost to the family of Randolph Schwabe and in particular to the late Alice, Lady Barnes for her enthusiastic encouragement of this biography of her father and who generously shared her memories of him and his contemporaries. I also owe a special debt of gratitude to Janet and Di Barnes, daughters of Alice and Harry Jefferson Barnes for allowing me access to their grandfather's diaries and letters and for permission to quote from, and reproduce, extracts here. They have kindly loaned materials and answered my many questions. Their friendship and hospitality has been much appreciated. Margaret de Villiers, niece of Randolph Schwabe has provided invaluable help transcribing her uncle's diaries and providing insights into his life in London and Oxford. George MacBride has expertly advised on textual matters for which I am most grateful and where possible his helpful suggestions have been incorporated.

I would also like to thank the former Slade School of Art students I interviewed during my research including: Philip Brown; Keyna Emerson; Paul Feiler; Biddy Picard; Cecil and Joan Riley (née Batty) and Margaret Thomas.

There are many people who have assisted me throughout this research and to whom I extend my thanks. While space precludes my naming them all I am particularly grateful to my good friend Mary Pearce who meticulously deciphered and transcribed much of the correspondence to Schwabe including the many letters he received from his friend and fellow artist Francis Dodd. Liz Lim generously carried out research at the Art Gallery of New South Wales, Sydney and transcribed several of Schwabe's diaries from afar. The following also kindly assisted with transcription of the diaries: Matthew Perry, Caroline St John and Sue Sherwood. Valuable assistance with transcribing letters was also provided by Bobbie Cozens; Isla Duncan and Hester McDonald.

The following also assisted in various ways throughout the genesis of this biography: Bill and Dee Bourne; Emily Gwynne-Jones; Neil Jennings; Paul Liss; Richard Lowndes; Harry Moore-Gwyn; Joyce Poynter; Andrew and Diane Sim; Robert Upstone; Ida Webb and Karen, Louise and Michael Yden.

I gratefully acknowledge research grants received from The Paul Mellon Centre for Studies in British Art and the Marc Fitch Fund which enabled me to undertake interviews and visits to various archives in pursuance of my research. The latter also generously supported the publication of this biography. The Association of Art Historians, UK provided a grant towards reprographic and copyright expenses.

Any biography but particularly one which is accompanied by an art exhibition requires assistance from archivists, curators and librarians, amongst those who have provided invaluable help are: Hannah Hawksworth, Royal Watercolour Society; Caroline Palmer, Print Room, Department of Western Art, Ashmolean Museum; Neil Parkinson, Royal College of Art; Jane Pritchard, Curator of Dance for the Theatre & Performance Collections at the V&A. Staff at the Bodleian Library; British Library; British Museum; Courtauld Institute Library; London Library; National Art Library; National Portrait Gallery; UCL

Special Collections, University College London;
Jenny Treagust, Lesley Durnford, Lindsay Jerome
and Margaret Sawyer, Emsworth Library. Hannah
Jones, Oxfordshire History Centre; Julia Carver,
Collections Officer, Fine Art, Bristol Museum &
Art Gallery; Amanda Stoner, The Cooper Gallery,
Barnsley; Martin Roberts, Herbert Art Gallery and
Museum, Coventry; Kristian Purcell, Collections
Assistant, The Higgins Art Gallery and Museum,
Bedford; Jenny Lund, Curator of Fine Art, Royal
Pavilion & Museums, Brighton & Hove; Patrick
Bourne, The Fine Art Society; Pamela Robertson,
Senior Curator, Hunterian Art Gallery; Sarah
Richardson, Keeper of Art, Tyne & Wear Archives
& Museums, Laing Art Gallery, Newcastle; Andrew
Moore, Keeper of Art & Senior Curator, Norwich
Castle Study Centre, Norwich; Timothy Morgan-
Owen, Curator, Renishaw Hall; Helen Bottomley,
Collections Officer, Russell-Cotes Art Gallery &
Museum, Bournemouth; Barbara Dixon, Manager,
Swindon Museum & Art Gallery; Melanie Gardner,
Keeper of Fine & Decorative Art at Tullie House
Museum & Art Gallery and Laura MacCulloch,
Curator of British Art, Walker Art Gallery,
Liverpool.

Thanks are also extended to Ulrike Smalley, Jenny
Wood, Pauline Allwright, Sara Bevan and colleagues
at the Imperial War Museum, London; Andrea
Fredericksen, Curator, UCL Art Museum, University
College London; Philip Athill, Abbott and Holder Ltd.
and Chris Beetles, Chris Beetles Gallery.

Any errors of fact and/or interpretation arising
out of these various communications are of course,
all mine.

It has been a pleasure to work once more with Steve
Marshall, Director, St Barbe Museum & Art Gallery,
Lymington. I am grateful to the staff at St Barbe
for their help and especially Carole Hawkins for
translating letters and other materials and Lianne
Warner for sourcing the images and photography.

The exhibition has been generously sponsored by
clarke willmott. It would also not have been possible
without the cooperation of the following lenders:
The Ashmolean Museum, Oxford; British Museum;
Hunterian Art Gallery, Glasgow; Imperial War
Museum; Laing Art Gallery, Newcastle; Manchester
Art Gallery; Norwich Museums; UCL Art Museum;
V&A Theatre & Performance Collections; Janet and
Di Barnes and those private lenders who preferred
to remain anonymous.

Finally, I should like to thank Sarah Gilroy who has
again been unfailingly supportive during the lengthy
course of my researching and writing Schwabe's
biography, generously reading and commenting
critically and insightfully on numerous drafts of
this text. As ever I continue to gain from both
her scholarship and partnership.

Dr Gill Clarke
Visiting Professor, University of Chichester, September 2012

INTRODUCTION

Randolph Schwabe (1885–1948) was much 'respected by artists of both the older and newer schools, and while conservative rather than revolutionary in his aims and ideals, his work has a quality of vital distinction which must win the admiration of all who understand the essentials of good draughtsmanship and good design.' So wrote Frank Rutter the long-serving *Sunday Times* art critic, author and museum curator in 1933.[1] Moreover, it was observed that 'In a period which too often neglects good drawing… [Schwabe] stands firm for the classical virtues.'[2]

For Schwabe, drawing was 'as natural as breathing'.[3] Such was his ceaseless delight and interest in all that surrounded him that he was seldom without a sketch book and sharp pencil poised or pen charged with his specially made brown Stephens' ink. Whatever the medium, whether it was oils, watercolour, pencil or pen and ink his approach was one of thoroughness and acute perception. Whether his subjects were gentle bucolic landscapes, country buildings, portraits, Land Girls in the First World War, bomb damage in the Second World War, costume design or imaginative decorations for book illustrations he tackled them all with intense concentration, profound understanding and sensitivity. Schwabe saw a calm beauty in the past – it was not all squalor or cruelty[4] – and his painstaking attention to detail and feeling for composition and tone place him in the lineage of the great watercolourist and engraver Paul Sandby (1731–1809).

A distinguished artist and influential teacher, Schwabe exhibited widely including with the New English Art Club from 1909, the Friday Group from 1913 and the London Group from 1915. He was appointed as an official war artist in both World Wars. From 1919

Schwabe taught at the Camberwell and Westminster Schools of Art and later at the Royal College of Art where he was Drawing Master under William Rothenstein. He was therefore well qualified to accede to the post of Professor and Principal of the Slade School of Art following the retirement of Henry Tonks in 1930 and to maintain the reputation of the Slade and its tradition for good draughtsmanship. Schwabe was a sympathetic and kindly teacher who was well liked by colleagues and students who appreciated his advice, genuine interest, encouragement and the time and trouble he took to help them progress in their careers.[5] He remained in post until his death in 1948 and during that time he influenced a generation of art students.

Schwabe's expertise in art matters meant that he was much in demand to serve on juries and national committees, including representing the art schools on the War Artists' Advisory Committee in the Second World War. He had a wide circle of acquaintances in both the art and literary worlds. Schwabe was a particularly close friend of Charles Rennie Mackintosh and his wife Margaret Macdonald, and also of Francis Unwin, Albert Rutherston, Francis Dodd and Muirhead Bone.

To date, little has been written about his significant contribution to the practice and spirit of twentieth-century British art.[6] This authorised biography redresses this lacuna and in so doing focuses on Randolph Schwabe's career as artist and teacher. Enriched by interviews and conversations with members of his family, including Schwabe's daughter the late Alice, Lady Barnes, her daughters Janet and Di Barnes and Schwabe's niece Margaret de Villiers (née Cobbe), unique insights into his life have been gained. Reminiscences from a number of his former students illuminate life at the Slade pre- and post-Second World War, including its war-time evacuation from London (1939–45) to share premises with the Ruskin School of Drawing in Oxford. Unprecedented access has been granted to an array of family documents, including Schwabe's diaries[7] (1930–48), photographs and previously unseen artworks, which has enabled a vivid portrayal of events, the people he met and his family life in Chelsea, Hampstead and beyond.

The opening chapter traces Schwabe's early forays into the art world of the 1900s. From an 'inglorious and unhappy' three months at the Royal College of Art he transferred to the Slade, where he was taught by Frederick Brown and Henry Tonks. On leaving, Schwabe followed in the footsteps of other British artists and went to Paris where he studied at the Académie Julian. This account of his development and growing reputation as an artist is followed by a close examination of his teaching to supplement his income from the sale of paintings and support his young family post-First World War through to his appointment to the Slade in 1930.

Schwabe spent nearly two decades as Principal at the Slade and it is the years from 1939–48 which are detailed in the third chapter. The focus is on perhaps his greatest achievement – steering the Slade through the difficult war years and its evacuation to Oxford; his collaboration with his lifelong friend Albert Rutherston, the Ruskin Master of Drawing; and the challenge of the Slade's return to London in an age of austerity.

Chapters 4 and 5 reveal further important aspects of Schwabe's working life and demonstrate the expertise and breadth of his artistic achievements. His work as an official war artist, producing a series on 'Women on the Land' in the First World War, and portraits of home-front heroes and drawings of bomb damage in the Second World War are the subject of the fourth chapter. Given Schwabe's mastery of all kinds of media the fifth chapter is devoted to his work as an illustrator, especially with the Beaumont Press and the specialised books on ballet and the seminal books he wrote and illustrated with Francis Kelly on historic costume and armour 'which combine grace and charm with perfectly clear and unambiguous information about doublets and crinolines and periwigs.'[8] Attention is also directed to his period costume designs for the theatre, his scholarly work for various art journals and his editorship of *Artwork*. The biography concludes with an intimate picture of Schwabe's final term at the Slade and his long illness and untimely death in September 1948.

1 Rutter, F. (1933) 'The art of Randolph Schwabe', *The Studio*, p.379. Rutter (1876–1937) wrote for the *Sunday Times* from 1903.

2 Holland, G. (1931) 'Appreciation of Randolph Schwabe', December, *South London Group catalogue*.

3 Tennyson, C. (1951) Introduction, *Randolph Schwabe Memorial Exhibition*, The Arts Council of Great Britain, p.5.

4 Schwabe diary 1933.

5 See for example the letter to Schwabe from Hector McDonald Sutton (1903–92) on being appointed the first Principal of the County School of Art, Mansfield, Notts in 1937. Private Collection. Schwabe taught McDonald Sutton at the Royal College of Art.

6 Grigson, G. (1941) 'Samuel Palmer: The politics of an artist', *Horizon*, IV, 23, p.314.

7 Schwabe's diaries together with his extensive correspondence are the subject of a forthcoming publication and exhibition to be curated by the author.

8 Anon (1951) 'Professor Randolph Schwabe', *Manchester Guardian*, 11/1/1951, p.3.

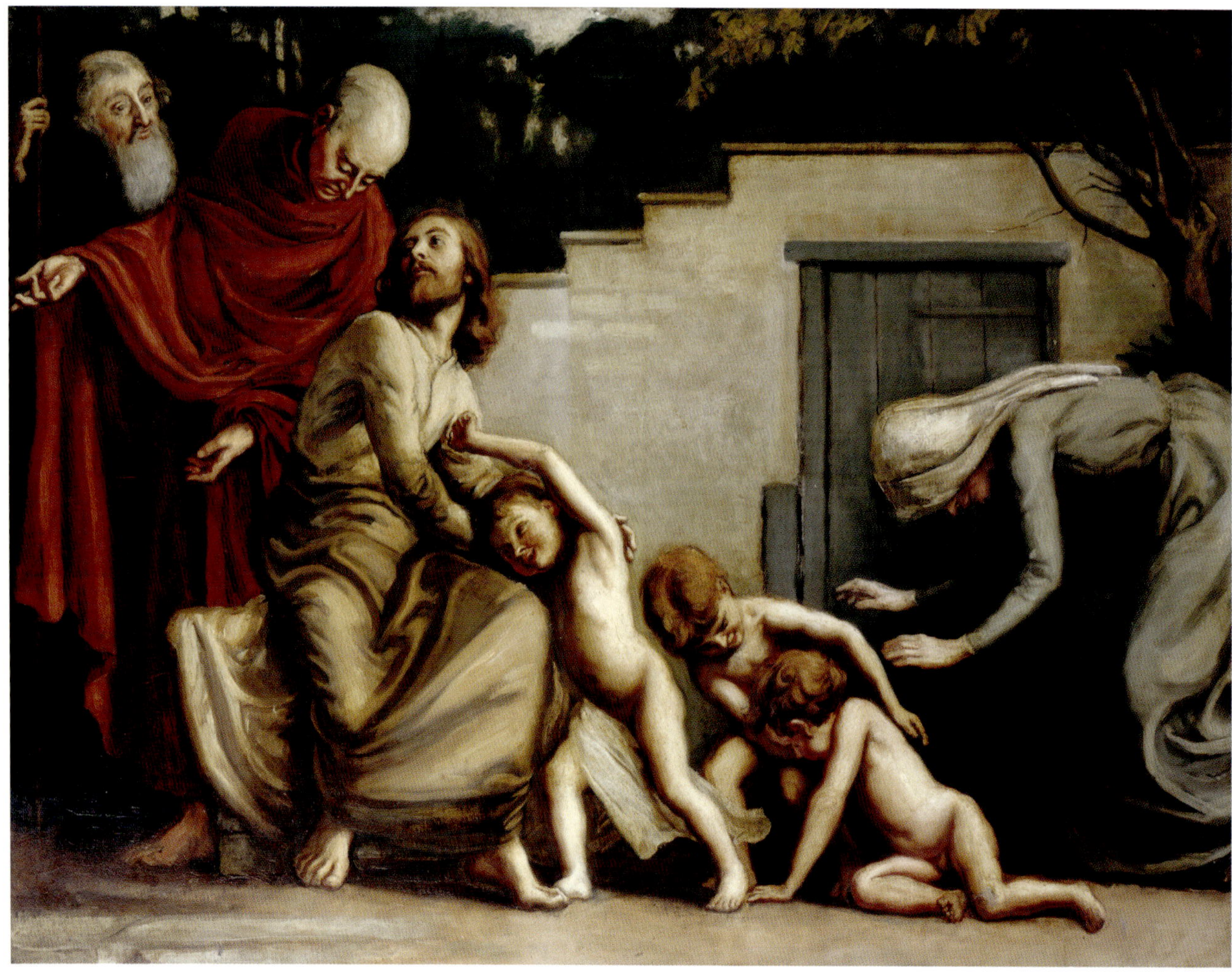

Suffer Little Children to Come Unto Me
1905 | oil on canvas | 91.5 x 122 cm

EARLY YEARS AND THE DEVELOPING ARTIST

Randolph Schwabe was 'a scholarly artist',[1] a meticulous draughtsman and an influential teacher. He was born on 9 May 1885 in Alsbach House, 4 Cambridge Grove, Eccles (in the registration district of Barton-on-Irwell), some five miles from Manchester. He was the second of two sons of Lawrence Schwabe and Octavie Henriette Ermen; his older brother, Eric Anthony, was born on 5 February 1883. His paternal grandfather, a cotton merchant, had emigrated to England from Germany in 1820. Randolph's father Lawrence was the youngest of thirteen children. His mother's family was also in the textile trade. Although his mother was born in Cologne, Germany, her father, had been born in 's-Hertogenbosch in Brabant, Netherlands and later settled in Manchester where with his brothers he established a number of cotton-spinning mills. The Ermens were partners with the Engels[2] family in cotton-spinning factories both in Manchester and in Engelskirchen in the Rhineland where one of the brothers had lived in the village of Alsbach. The family were not only financially enterprising; they had taken out several patents for new processes in the textile industry.

Randolph, following his father's death in February 1933 at the age of 77, recalled him fondly, describing him as a 'good father in many ways when we were boys but his manner about money was his own undoing.'[3] Indeed, Lawrence Schwabe's business venture in Manchester and London manufacturing cotton was less than successful. The *London Gazette* and the *Liverpool Mercury* reported on 19 November 1888 that his partnership with Robert Clay had been dissolved by mutual consent and that all debts owing would be paid by Robert Clay. Shortly after this the Schwabe family moved to Buxton, Derbyshire where his

grandparents and aunts and uncles lived.[4] Randolph remembered his grandmother Ermen being pulled in a bath chair with a Skye terrier in her arms.[5] The family did not stay there long before moving to Bromley, Kent, where his father was involved in selling general cotton goods. By 1892 he had become highly indebted, perhaps ruined, having spent his wife's marriage settlement and having borrowed money from his brother Charles.[6]

Lawrence, Octavie and the two boys moved again, this time to Hemel Hempstead where, with financial help from his wife's uncle Godfrey Ermen,[7] he opened a business as a letterpress printer and stationer in Bath Street. Randolph was educated privately as a day-boy at the nearby Heath Brow School, Boxmoor, a 'classical and commercial Grammar school',[8] run by Walter E.H. Dowling. This small boys' school occupied a private house in Heath Lane and admitted boys aged between 6 and 17. While the majority came from London, a few came from overseas, including Burma, France and Spain. Randolph in one of his few extant light-hearted 'epistolatory communication[s]'[9] to his school friend Saunders in c.1899 pointed out that there were nine new boys, school numbers had not dwindled but risen to 50. This he ascribed to the magnetic attraction of his person: he told Saunders when he read this, to cough slightly.

Dowling, or 'Old Beefy Tooth' (Old B.T.) as Randolph called him, was much respected as a teacher, taking pupils through to school-leaving age and beyond and preparing them for the civil service and business careers.[10] In addition to taking school examinations, for which certificates were given to the boy who was top in any subject, pupils were also entered for the College of Preceptors Examinations.[11]

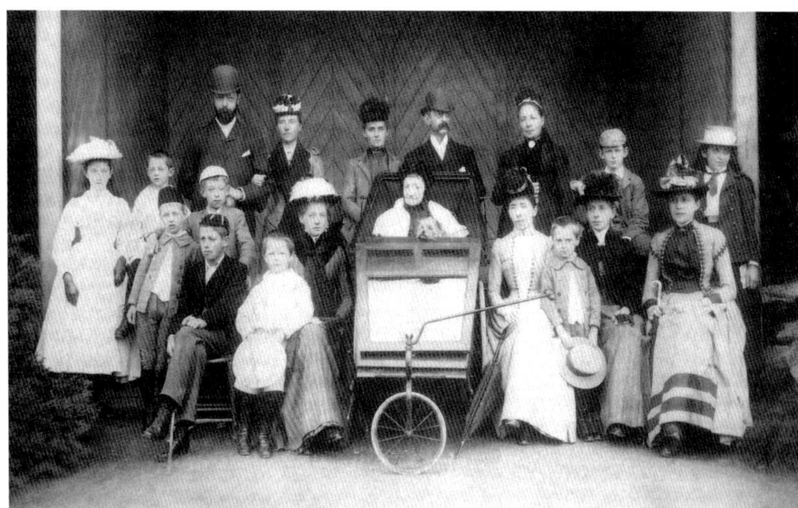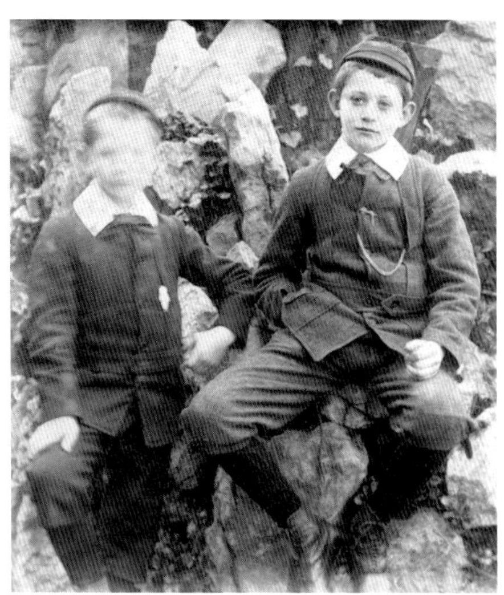

Randolph's talent for drawing was apparent from an early age and evidenced in numerous illustrations for the weekly school magazine *Heath Brow Chronicle* which was edited from the outset by his brother Eric. Naturally left-handed, he was made to write and draw with the right; the pressure allegedly led to his slight stammer.[12] The six-page *Chronicle* contained school news, wit and wisdom – wherein schoolboy humour abounded. Randolph submitted several pieces of wit including:

> *Present day: 'I don't believe in prophets'*
> *Self-Made: 'Don't yer? I do, or I shouldn't be what I am'*
> 18 October 1897

> *Mrs Circle, the boarding-house keeper, felt very hurt when she heard a boarder say that a circle was a plain (plane) figure.*
> 26 February 1898

> *If a man swallowed hot coals and burning lava, would he have an eruption of the skin?*
> 30 April 1898

Reports on school football and cricket matches regularly appeared. Randolph while not particularly interested in sport was expected to attend home matches and cheer the team on.

The *Chronicle* featured original stories and poems, although the Editor informed readers that 'we cannot always be answerable for the originality of the jokes'. Randolph contributed several short stories including *The Invention of Gunpowder*, *The Blowing up of the Bank* and *A Parrot Story*. Dowling encouraged production of the *Chronicle* and afforded facilities for printing, providing in November 1897 an 'Auto-Copyist', which enabled copies to be produced with greater certainty. The Editor made it clear to readers that the cost of 1d. was not for profit but to defray the cost of paper and parchment for the Auto-Copyist.

Studies included Latin and Greek or, as Randolph referred to it, 'that dead-alive language'. English grammar and literature was taught by Dowling, an Associate of the College of Preceptors. Schwabe told Saunders who was at home in Hampstead due to illness, 'We are doing *Merchant of Venice*. The first lesson, Old B.T. read 5 lines; the rest was a lecture on jaundice, hour-glasses, and the Doges of Venice, etc (he spelt it "dog").'[13] Dowling would also read at the school concerts which provided opportunities for budding musicians and vocalists. A reading by Dowling from Mark Twain's *The Jumping Frog* was described in the *Chronicle* as 'an ever-fresh and enjoyable piece'. Randolph gained much pleasure from reading, being able to do so from the age of four, and he would often take the opportunity to spend time partaking of his passion 'on a fine summer's afternoon, in what was called the "Working Men's Institute" (though no working men ever came there, and nobody read the books except [him]) in the Town Hall at Hemel Hempstead'.[14] His brother preferred the gentle art of fishing which, according to Randolph, he patronized with some success.

The summer term heralded the much awaited annual school 'beano' when 'the al fresco meal "neath the spreading trees"' was much enjoyed by the boys. The contents of this had been transported on heavily laden wagons across the river Gade to the Coombes – the boys had to walk the 10 miles or so and arrived about noon. Fortunately the weather was favourable and there were many attractions on arrival, including

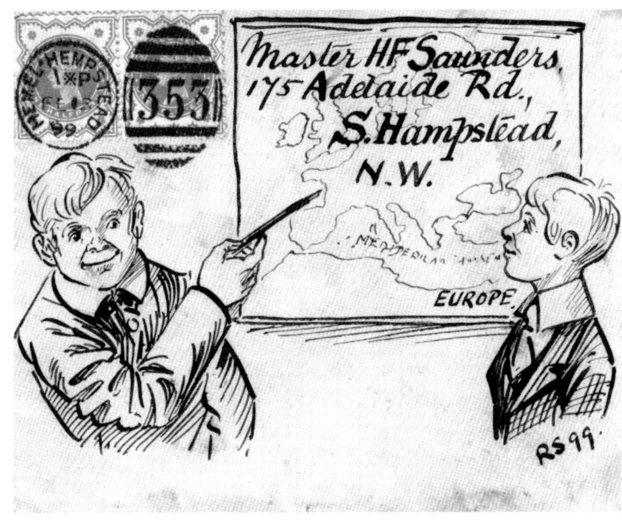

the visit of an itinerant vendor of refreshments who pitched his camp just by theirs – which was just as well as the boys had cleared out the surrounding shops. The end of the summer term was marked by the singing of 'Dulce Domum' and attending services in the parish church in Hemel Hempstead.

During the school holidays the brothers undertook many 'long walks' in the beautiful, unspoilt countryside around Hemel Hempstead, including the 'quaint' village of Ivinghoe with its fine examples of Tudor architecture.[15] Randolph amused himself by making brass rubbings within the limited range of country that was accessible to him, either by walking or short train journeys. He recalled visiting St Albans Cathedral and Watford Church, where he particularly remembered the brass of Hugo de Holes, Justice of the King's Bench, of which he took a rubbing. These amusements foreshadow much of Schwabe's later artwork and his profound interest in historic costume which had been roused by the illustrators of his boyhood (Paul Hardy b.1862, Seymour Lucas, 1849–1923, and Gordon Browne) and his fascination with old buildings.

The Schwabe family travelled to the south coast for their summer holiday in 1896, staying near Portsmouth. It was a memorable holiday for both boys. Eric described in vivid detail in the *Chronicle* over a year later their steamer boat trip on the Solent from Portsmouth Harbour jetty round the Isle of Wight and their subsequent visit to the dockyard to see the *Victory*. The same edition of the *Chronicle* announced that in honour of Trafalgar Day (21 October) Mr Dowling had kindly let the boys off all impositions (lines) and failures. Randolph's drawings, *Some memories of Trafalgar* were certainly not failures; these included, *In the mizzen-*

top of the 'Redoubtable';[16] *Before Trafalgar; The 'Victory's' Wheel*; and Nelson lying fatally wounded on the deck.

Not all summers were memorable. Randolph found Hemel Hempstead a 'slow hole', in which there was nothing to do; and he was greatly disappointed when the family did not have a summer holiday in 1899. He wrote to Saunders to tell him 'The Schwarby (correct pronunciation) household, worse luck, has not yet left its country-seat the address of phwich [sic] is to be seen above [40 Marlowes, Emily Empstead, Herts] – and doesn't intend to.' However, he did record that the family had 'purchased a bathing key early in the holy days and disported [them]selves daily among the waters' and attained a remarkable proficiency, and moreover that they would have excelled, had they had a sufficiency of fine weather.

> But, alas for the vanity of human hopes! on Tuesday last the sun shone not, and scarcely had we entered the element when the rain descended in torrents, and when the downpour had reached its climax, we decided to retire, and effected a masterly retreat amidst a storm of hailstones. The next item on the programme was a plentiful display of electric fireworks, accompanied by the discharge of the celestial thunderbolts, the effect of which was not ba-a-d, but the bathing place [Boxmoor Baths][17] being surrounded by timber, and the iron roves (sic!) above our heads suggested strongly that a few lightning rods, as they are vulgarly termed would not be amiss… since then we have been but once, when the temperature of the water recalled to the mind visions of the North Pole.

With little to do in Hemel Hempstead, Randolph spent considerable time drawing. He produced a series of illustrations for the *Chronicle* entitled *England's Soldiers from 1066 to the Victorian Era*, the first of which was a Saxon Thane. He also contributed a series of contemporary

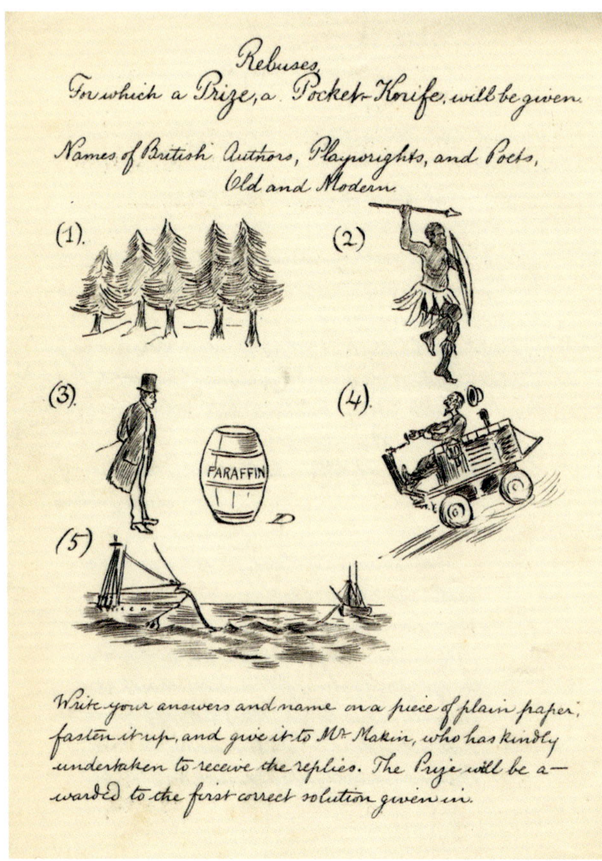

Rebuses
12 February 1898
COLLECTION JANET AND DI BARNES

Soldiers of the Queen. Most successful were his illustrations of the celebrations that accompanied the granting of a royal charter by Queen Victoria to Hemel Hempstead whereby it was created a municipal borough.

Randolph's pen drawings of 'the doings' surrounding the granting of the Charter were reproduced in the *Hemel Hempstead Gazette*. The Editor of the *Chronicle* apologised on 16 July 1898 for having taken up all five pages with illustrations, and explained that, as it was 'a special occasion and one not likely to occur again, and our artist having run wild, we have decided to defer once more the School News till next week, when we hope to make amends for some preceding issues.' The cover of the *Chronicle* portrayed a rather portly man pushing a barrow with the rolled up charter poking out under the caption *Enter the Charter*. The following two pages were titled *In the Procession* and comprised various people in the procession including a mounted soldier from the 'Herts Yeomanry'; a 'Fruiterer'; and a 'Cyclist'. The fourth page – *Unrecorded events* – included several small vignettes: a policeman about to strike another with a truncheon and dignitaries in a carriage passing the Heath Park Hotel. The final illustration was a full-page drawing of the assembled crowd listening expectantly to the *Reading the Charter*. Randolph also drew rebus puzzles. The subject matter varied from the names of boys in the school, including his friend Saunders, to towns in England and British Authors, Playwrights and Poets, Old and Modern. Shortly after this issue owing to a lack of support from fellow pupils the *Chronicle* ceased production, or as Randolph pithily put it 'The paper (H.B.C. I mean) is awfully dead.'

In his final year at school Randolph received the Second Prize in the Fourth Form. This, he told Saunders, was

In the Procession
16 July 1898
COLLECTION JANET AND DI BARNES

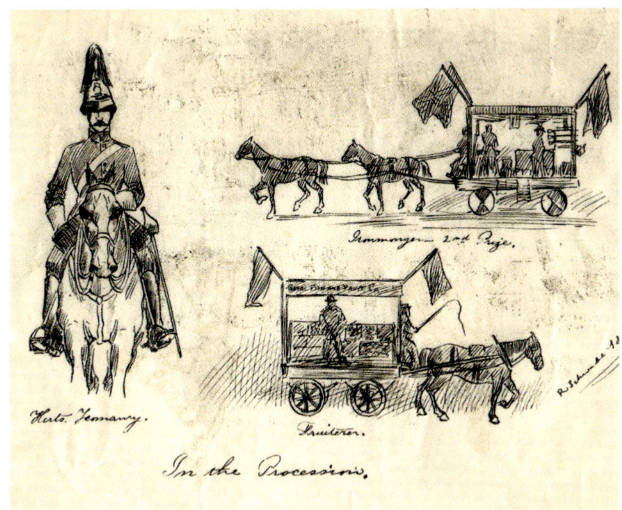

'a remarkable achievement, as there are only three boys in the form. Mr D. [Dowling] evidently expected me to get the First Prize, but I explained everything to him "My dear sir", said I, "I always was the sort of fellah to hide my light under bushel – the bushel in this case consisting of my fellow scholars"; and I pressed his hand in a fatherly manner, while the tears sprang to his eyes (should this scene affect you over-much, you may take it with a pinch of salt).' In the same letter he told Saunders:

> I am not at all as certain as you seem to be about going to Germany this year, though it hath been spoken of. I am slightly more certain that I shall leave school in March [1900], and go to South Kensington every day. This will be a bore; but I always was a martyr to circumstances – Fox ought to have made a note of me.[18]

THE ROYAL COLLEGE OF ART

Schwabe did indeed find South Kensington 'a bore' and studied for just three months, a period he referred to as 'inglorious and unhappy' largely owing to the teaching methods; having to imitate the plaster cast of a foot was for him 'interminable'.[19] He recalled that difficulties had arisen about his entrance to the Royal College of Art as the timing of trains from Hemel Hempstead were such that he could not arrive before 10.05 a.m. – five minutes later than the official start time for his studies. The time-table was rigorously adhered to and it was only at his father's insistence that he was allowed this small grace. The Registrar, Schwabe recollected, was a military man and, not entirely inhumane, consented to condone the irregularity.

As Schwabe was not yet 15-years-old a senior student was appointed to look after him. He advised him to purchase an arsenal of black French chalk in test tubes and stumps made, some of leather, some of paper, with which to spread 'this stuff' on his drawing. He remembered that he was taken to a lavatory, where, with sponges and paste, he was initiated into the mystery of straining without a wrinkle a sheet of Whatman paper on a drawing board – an art he never practised again.[20]

Contact with fellow students was virtually non-existent and Schwabe found the large room where he worked empty. His salvation came in the form of the regularity and timing of the lessons which enabled him to escape to the British Museum where he found entertainment and material for notes in his sketch book. His absences were not noticed nor the fact that he had made no headway on the plaster foot!

Schwabe had a chance meeting in South Kensington with a former pupil from Heath Brow School who was an art student. Schwabe explained to him his un-happiness at the College and he suggested that Schwabe go to the Slade, where he was studying.[21] Although Schwabe had not heard of the Slade, a transfer was swiftly arranged and he commenced his studies on the same day in 1900 as Francis Kelly (1879–1945) and the two sat side-by-side in the crowded Antique Room. Kelly, the first man who spoke to him there, had come down from Balliol College, Oxford, as he had insufficient money to stay up for his degree. The two discovered very early on that they had tastes in common, in the direction of armour and costume.[22]

THE SLADE SCHOOL OF ART

The Slade was founded in 1871, by the art collector and benefactor Felix Slade (1788–1868) who had left

£35,000 to found professorships of Fine Art at the universities of Oxford and Cambridge and at University College, London. Edward Poynter (1836–1919), the first Slade Professor, who had trained in Paris, announced in his inaugural address that 'The superiority of foreign artists… is undoubtedly due to a habit in the schools of thoroughly following out a course of study from the living model…'.[23] The course and methods of study subsequently adopted was similar to that of the French *ateliers* and was one that Schwabe together with other gifted students before him welcomed, especially as he had never seen a model at the Royal College of Art. Poynter's approach was endorsed by his 'appointment to the influential position of director and principal of the National Art Training School at South Kensington… administering the government art system, [where] he again took on an agenda of reform.'[24] His successor at the Slade in 1876 was his friend, the distinguished French artist Alphonse Legros (1837–1911), an associate of Courbet, and friend of Whistler.

When Legros took over at the Slade there were some 220 male and female students who attended classes together except for those for the nude model. He spoke in French when teaching, his remarks being translated by assistants or students. For Legros drawing was the cornerstone of artistic practice; he said:

> I wish to impress upon you more and more strongly the necessity
> of studying your models with such a thoroughness as to get them
> by heart. To that end persistent drawing must be kept up. Drawing,
> and drawing, evermore, should be the student's motto (and the
> true artist is ever a student). The Old Masters made a practice
> of drawing, and drawing much, and with a pains and earnestness
> which, if imitated by us, would give us more of their power…[25]

Referring to a reproduction of Michelangelo's study for the figure of Adam in the Sistine Chapel, he pointed out to students that every stroke, every line was indispensable and that nothing was without its use; even the least stroke he informed them was put in with certainty in the right place. This approach to constructive drawing and the power of line was the genesis of the Slade tradition of high standards of draughtsmanship.

Following Legros' resignation in 1892 after nearly twenty years at the Slade, Frederick Brown (1851–1941), the far-sighted teacher and head of the progressive Westminster School of Art, was appointed to the Professorship. 'Under his direction and that of the able assistants [and practising artists, Henry Tonks, 1862–1937 and Philip Wilson Steer, 1860–1942] a school of drawing was built up such as had never existed in this country, and a succession of brilliant students trained, beginning with Augustus John, William Orpen, and Ambrose McEvoy.'[26] His professorship also encompassed 'the emergence of a remarkable group of women artists, amongst whom may be mentioned Miss Ethel Walker, Mrs McEvoy (née Edwards), Miss Gwen John, Miss Beatrice Bland, Miss Anna Airy, Miss Pickard and Mrs Edna Clarke Hall (née Waugh)'.[27]

This talented and heady environment was to become Schwabe's spiritual home for the next five or so years – and later as Slade professor (1930–48). As one of the youngest students he was much in awe of Brown whom he described as a rather grim bespectacled figure with grey hair, moustache and chin-tuft. Sporting a black frock-coat, his jaw muscles prominent, Brown had the look of someone who would stand no nonsense. Nor

A display of life paintings in the Slade, *c.*1906
UCL ART MUSEUM, UNIVERSITY COLLEGE LONDON

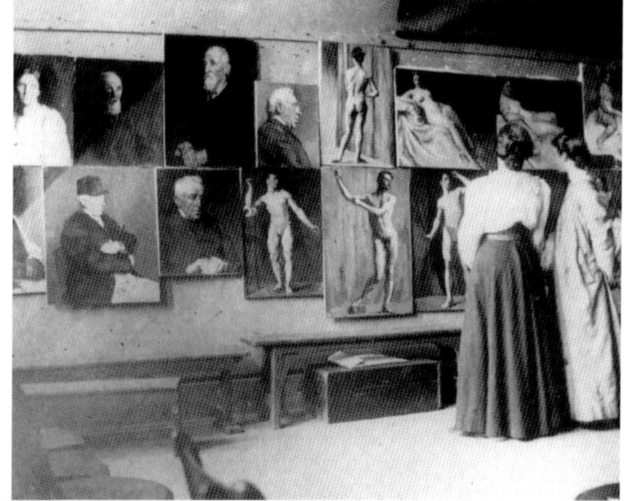

did he, Schwabe recollected; indeed he witnessed fellow student Wyndham Lewis (1882–1957) being 'seized, and hurled bodily through the double doors into the quadrangle beyond' for failing to fulfil the responsibilities and duties of his scholarship in the summer of 1901 and for having flagrantly 'lit a cigarette in the entrance hall… Smoking was prohibited in the corridors of the Slade.'[28]

As a new student Schwabe worked daily in the Antique Room, until he was adjudged sufficiently advanced to draw from Life.[29] The classes were open from 9.30 to 5, except on Saturday when the School closed at 1 p.m. Seats and easels were provided, but students had to provide other appliances and materials they might require, such as charcoal and sanguine. Schwabe recalled that Campion, the Beadle, 'ensconced in his little box inside the hall'[30] and resplendent in his 'maroon-coloured frock coat, with red facings and brass buttons, and a top hat with gold braid on it' oversaw the signing-in process[31] and would supply a penny-worth of bread, cut from a new loaf, for students who in general preferred not to use rubber. The vast cold Antique Room contained a large collection of Models and Casts of late Greek, Greco-Roman and Italian Renaissance sculpture, adapted for the purpose of instruction. Here Schwabe toiled on copying initially the Discobolus and then casts of the Dancing Faun or the Venus de Milo. Schwabe seldom spent more than a day on one drawing; Brown would inspect the result, addressing him as 'You, Mr What's-your name?' Clifford Bax (1886–1962), a fellow student, explained in his memoirs *Inland far: A book of thoughts and impressions* that if the work improved Tonks and Russell would scribble their initials on a corner of the Michelet paper. This meant that a day might be spent in the life-room.

Every subsequent scribble awarded another day until, in the end, one could say good-bye to the plaster images and devote the whole week to drawing from the nude. Nonetheless, even a novice could slip down to the Gentleman's life-room for the last hour of the day when the model held a series of short poses each lasting for 5–10 minutes. Ernest Blaikley (1885–1965), later Keeper of Pictures at the Imperial War Museum, explained the challenge of capturing the short poses:

> *There was no time for gradation: it was contours or nothing. Contours, hell! It was unmitigated outline. You were still trying to run it round a leg when the pose changed. I felt embarrassed by my lack of facility… It was a relief when the final pose came to an end, and the model retired to her box to dress.*[32]

Schwabe finished with the Antique and was rewarded with the unrestricted usage of Room 10, the big studio downstairs which rose through two storeys.[33] In the Life Classes a figure model posed every day and a draped model three days a week. Schwabe felt that the tone adopted by Brown with models was 'really impolite'. This was in marked contrast to Tonks who was deemed to be 'extraordinarily considerate'.[34] A Slade model wrote to Tonks' biographer, Joseph Horne, to explain how Tonks would never permit the model to sit in the nude when he entertained the slightest doubt about the warmth of the room; if he walked into a class during the set rest time and found the model still posing, he would sharply reprimand the students. During rest time lunch could be taken in the College Refectory where, according to Schwabe, excellent chops and steaks were prepared by the chef on its open grill; in the summer students congregated on the steps leading from the Slade rooms to the quadrangle bordered by other College buildings to chat and eat their sandwiches.[35] When they returned to work, the silence was broken only when the Professor issued short commands to the models to change their pose; conversing with models was strictly forbidden at least in the precincts of the School. Much had progressed 'from the days when Sir Edward Poynter could not be seen with students in the women's Life Room while a nude female was posing. They had to file out when he came in, and he wrote his criticisms, in their absence, around the margins of their drawing.'[36]

Beginners like Schwabe 'mixed' in the Life Class with more experienced artists, who had little to do with them, 'for the hierarchy was almost that of the public school.'[37] These 'old hands' had the middle places with the prime view of the nude model on the throne standing under a north top light, against a khaki-brown curtain. Newcomers had to find places at the side to position themselves astride their seats: four-legged wooden contraptions (known as 'donkeys') each with a wooden neck in front to place their regulation board against.[38] Finding a good vantage point from which to observe the model amongst the throng of donkeys required some courage from Schwabe.

Life drawing was at the core of the teaching at the Slade; Tonks, formerly 'a rising surgeon',[39] who in his spare time from the Royal Free Hospital had been taught by Brown at Westminster in the evenings, was an influential exponent of this. Tonks' theories and uncompromising approach owed much to Brown whom he joined at the Slade in 1893 and who had been the first man he had ever met who:

was able to make the principles of drawing clear: a lesson from him was a revelation, extremely practical, expressed in language

which was easy to understand, and illustrated by a few simple and masterly lines on the side of the paper, making clear what he had not explained in our drawings, laying particular stress, moreover, upon constructional points.[40]

Schwabe believed that Tonks' teaching of drawing was fundamentally sound, enforced by workmanlike charcoal diagrams and sketches on students' drawing paper. Tonks' mantra of 'Action, construction, proportion'[41] was impressed on all students, who viewed him with a mix of fear and adoration. Augustus John (1878–1961), who had left the Slade several years before Schwabe commenced his studies, but who was much talked about and to whom the students aspired, made impromptu visits; Schwabe recalled that visits by Tonks to the Life Room were looked forward to with excitement and some alarm.[42] Schwabe had lessons from Tonks almost from his first day and he too found himself on the receiving end of his penetrating, stern gaze and withering criticism. The tall, thin, authoritative Tonks in his loose, grey tweeds was not given to mincing his words; he once referred to the Slade as 'that crèche for the children of the middle classes'[43] and was known to reduce female students to tears, including Schwabe's friend Jean Inglis (1884–1959).[44] Tonks' sarcasms did not depress Schwabe unduly. Observing that other people bore up under them, he resolved to look upon them as all in a day's work. Besides, Schwabe reasoned, he had wit, and amused students and he spurred most of them on. However he was not oblivious to the fact that a few of his peers could not withstand Tonks' sometimes ruthless attacks and had gone elsewhere.

'To third and fourth year students [Tonks] spoke in a different strain, opening their eyes to the aesthetic values, and telling them that to look at a Michael Angelo drawing should be an almost unbearable experience: "Go and look at Tiepolo's," he might add, "but I don't know if I should tell you that." '[45] Schwabe responded to Tonks' direction and spent much time looking at works by the Old Masters and enjoyed his visits to the British Museum, to analyse amongst others the drawings of Leonardo da Vinci, Raphael, Dürer, Rubens, Rembrandt, Claude and Watteau. Tonks urged students to study one picture, make a sketch of its pattern and rhythm, buy a postcard reproduction and pin it up at home.[46] Schwabe also studied in the library at the Victoria and Albert Museum, in the National Gallery and, when he got the opportunity, in other permanent collections and museums.

Steer, Assistant Teacher of Painting, 'was regarded as the "doyen" of serious English landscape artists'[47] and weekly visits brought prestige to the Slade. In 1931 he accepted the award of the Order of Merit from the King. He was the opposite to his close friend Tonks, both in his kindly, sympathetic manner and in his patient approach to teaching, albeit he was no lover of theory. Schwabe, reflecting on his teachers at the Slade nearly four decades later in *The Burlington Magazine*, recalled that Steer was credited with saying his salary was 'the hardest guineas he had ever earned'. When teaching Steer would stand behind or slowly drag his painting stool from student to student, observing intensely (and sometimes falling asleep); he would say little if he could help it; his terse, quiet comment 'I should go on with that' was a mark of his approbation. 'In his judgments, spoken in a simple, almost commonplace way, [the students] recognise[d] rare wisdom.'[48] The painter, illustrator and writer

Adrian Daintrey (1902–88) who studied at the Slade from 1920–24 said that all the students liked Steer.

Although, as Schwabe recalled, Steer appeared outwardly uninterested in teaching, he remained at the Slade until 1930, retiring at the same time as Tonks. Significantly he brought to his teaching an insistence upon tone. Low-tones were in fashion at the Slade. While Schwabe was critical of Steer's painting he admitted that he did learn to appreciate his pictures – 'Of course he did not specialize in linear drawing – painting, including watercolour was his domain; yet he had a sense of form and his design is subtle.'[49]

The draughtsman and painter Walter Russell (1867–1949) was also an Assistant in the School, having been appointed by Brown in 1895. Like Tonks he had been ably taught by Brown at Westminster School of Art, and while he did not have the personal renown of Tonks, his dry sense of humour and his quiet approach were respected by the students. Russell joined a closely knit staff team who were central figures in the London art world and who exerted considerable influence on English painting. He remained at the Slade until 1927 when he was elected Keeper of the Royal Academy. Schwabe later acknowledged the valuable instruction he gained from Russell and acted as executor for him.

These men were the Slade during its greatest period. They gave it life and character. Together, they provided teaching of a range and quality unequalled at any other time in British art schools. Their teaching, their mannerisms, their views on art, became firmly imprinted upon succeeding generations of students, and in many instances remained with Slade graduates throughout their lives.[50]

This certainly was the case for Schwabe who learned his lessons well, winning several Slade prizes having gained his Drawing Certificate alongside 36 other students at the end of the session 1903–04, and the following year he was one of 28 students who received their Painting Certificate. The *Morning Post* reported on 16 April 1904 that he had gained one of the two much coveted Slade Scholarships [£35 per annum for two years], the other went to Ian Strang (1886–1952). The scholarship more than covered fees which had risen to £21 a year which must have been a great help to his somewhat impecunious family and his father's precarious financial affairs. The Scholarship competition was open to all students under twenty-one years of age; it consisted of submitting various works of drawing and painting, including composition as prescribed by Professor Brown. The prospectus listed the conditions attached to the holding of the Scholarship, namely as Senior Student the giving of assistance to the Slade Professor in the maintenance of order in the Schools, in superintending under his direction the younger students, and in taking charge of any Library and Collection of Works of Art formed for the use of the Fine-Art Schools. Brown had informed Schwabe previously saying, 'Of course it's much below the standard, but I don't see what we can do.'[51] Schwabe accepted Brown's judgment with some humility and crumbs of satisfaction recognising the 'recent vivid glories of John and Orpen'. Later Brown found Schwabe his first commissions, for replicas and decorative designs, and bought a drawing of his from a New English Art Club exhibition.[52]

The first prize Schwabe won was the highly competed for Summer Composition Prize in 1905 for his oil painting produced over the long summer holiday in response to the subject 'Suffer little children to come unto Me' (see p.10). He again shared the £25 award with Strang. Of all the prizes this was the most prestigious: it was seen as the final test of a student's accomplishment. The painter and draughtsman Hubert Wellington (1879–1967), in an essay on 'The Summer Compositions' since 1893, which he wrote shortly after he left the Slade, described the achievement thus:

> this direction marks the end of the first stage in the painter's education, the stage of pure studentship. In such a work a student may display all that he has learnt in the school, and elsewhere, of drawing and painting from life, of the setting of figures in space, of the design and construction of a picture. In addition to this he is afforded scope for original and imaginative creation.

Wellington commented 'The competition of 1905 is interesting as… It may be taken as evidence of a new tendency already in the air… Both these students took a view of the subject that might be called "conventional"; both aim chiefly at a decorative result, and owe largely to the Old Masters.' Of Schwabe's large-scale figure composition he wrote it was:

> carried out with great thoroughness and ability. It is the most academic of the paintings under notice, and in this case one feels that naturalness has been to some extent sacrificed to composition of line, which is, moreover, a little obvious. Nevertheless, it contains plenty of very good drawing of action and movement. It is curious that, contrary to the rest of the series, in both the works of this year the figures are practically all in one plane, parallel to the planes of the picture.[53]

Wellington concluded that once more the School had 'a group of clever students working with interest and vitality' and prize-winners like Schwabe were already 'producing work which confirms the choice made by the judges in their endeavour to distinguish real from superficial talent'. Of the judges, Steer's opinion was given great weight by Brown and Tonks and the success of previous winners such as Augustus John, William Orpen and Albert Rothenstein after leaving the Slade was testament to the veracity of his viewpoint.

Schwabe's studies also included attending some twenty lectures on anatomy from Professor Thane which were illustrated by demonstrations on the Living Model; lectures on Perspective delivered by G. Thomson and the History of Art by D.S. MacColl. Over the course of these studies Schwabe developed a number of close friendships. Nearly 50 years later Luigi Innes Meo, who came to the School about the same time as Schwabe, visited him at the Slade; they went down to the Life Room and discussed Tonks; they agreed as to his generosity (he sent Meo £5 when he was in difficulties at Oundle where he started his teaching career) and his occasional cruelty. They recalled working with Albert Rothenstein, Wyndham Lewis, Michael Carr, Wilfrid Walter, Cuthbert Hamilton etc – 'all brilliant in their ways'.[54] Schwabe recollected the poems and other things that Lewis used to write and that he had a reputation for not paying his models: this was unusual and considered rather 'low'. Rothenstein[55] became a lifelong friend and Schwabe used to go to his parties in Fitzrovia Street; they became colleagues during the Second World War when the Slade was evacuated to Oxford. He introduced Schwabe to his elder brother William, with whom Schwabe was to work at the Royal College of Art in the 1920s, and his circle of intimates. Schwabe also remembered J.D. Innes (1887–1914); in particular he called to mind Innes' special sense of colour and

being reproved by him 'for speaking disrespectfully of the purple heather which, till then, I had associated with chromo-lithographs of Highland cattle, and which, in my case, did not fit in with my proper, but narrow, youthful regard for Wilson and Crome.'[56] Another friend, Blaikley, reminded Schwabe whenever they met that he had helped to sit him in a basin of water in the little room where paintings were dried as punishment for behaving 'in a silly schoolboyish way that was not always appreciated', and that Bertram Nicholls (1883–1974) had looked on without attempting the rescue to which he felt he was entitled.[57]

Outside his studies Schwabe was an active member of the Slade's Sketch Club. The club 'issued a series of titles each term and students worked on compositions which were displayed and criticised at its meetings.'[58] At one of these public criticisms by Brown, Schwabe recalled that he:

> traced one of my efforts back to a Catena at Trafalgar Square. I knew the picture well and found myself guilty, though the plagiarism was, I believe, unconscious. I longed to tell him it was by Basaiti, not Catena. But I discovered that the labels had been changed. He was right according to the older attribution. Since then it has become Palma Vecchio, so we were both, apparently, wrong.

Schwabe's final year at the Slade, 1905–1906, was marked by some success when he shared the prize for the best Figure Painting from Life with Maribel Rough (1887–1970); they each received £4. She recalled that her drawing had earlier been seen by Tonks who commented 'Not bad'; it was the highest praise she had ever had from him.

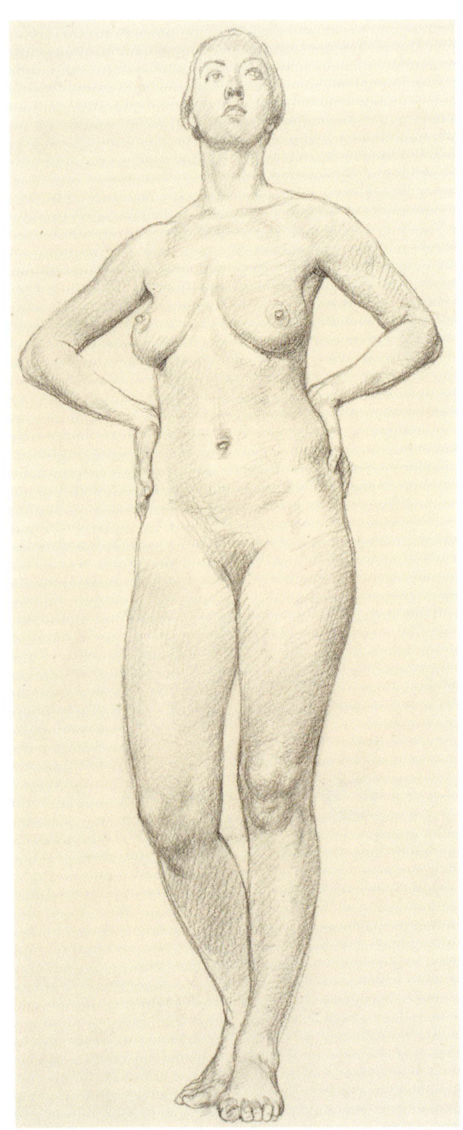

Figure Standing
pencil on paper | 34.6 x 15.3 cm
© UCL ART MUSEUM, UNIVERSITY COLLEGE LONDON

Schwabe left the Slade on the same day as fellow scholarship holder Strang and both followed in the footsteps of other British artists, crossing the Channel to further their studies in Paris, then a magnet for artists and intellectuals from France and Europe as well as America and Russia. His family had given him money to enable him to travel abroad for two years.[59]

PARIS AND THE ACADÉMIE JULIAN

Paris had much to offer aspiring artists with its académies and ateliers with their bohemian atmosphere together with its rich collection of galleries and museums. Yet,

> *Paris was as poor as it was rich, as sordid as it was sensual, and artists… reflected all of these aspects, just as they operated at every level from wooden shacks in Montmartre or from the magnificent studios in the Avenue de Villiers. In the process they reflected the splendour and the poverty, the action and the stillness, accidental fleeting effects as well as the established grandeur of the city's vitality and structure. Where they lived and worked reflected their role and standing in the city.[60]*

Schwabe lived first in the Hotel de L'Univers et du Portugal in the Rue Croix des Petits Champs which was a big, old hotel near the Louvre and Palais Royal. Importantly it was cheap; a factor also noted by Duncan Grant (1885–1978) who stayed there with friends from the Westminster School of Art, he recalled that the rooms ran out of one another, there was no passage.[61] Schwabe recalled that he had known Grant off and on since he was in Paris about 1907 and that he did not get on well with him. He thought Grant was often a very good painter, although he believed that later he gave way, rather weakly, to certain influences

La Conciergerie, Paris
1910 | etching | 20.8 × 25.2 cm
COLLECTION JANET AND DI BARNES

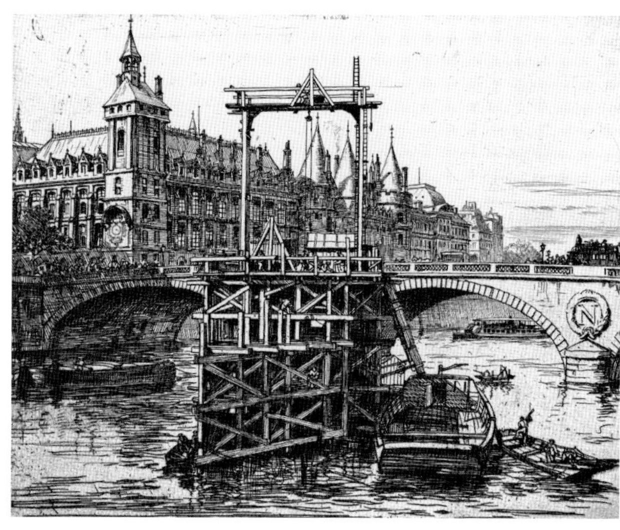

which had nothing really to do with his own personality.

Schwabe paid 30 francs for his room which he thought good value as Charles Ginner (1878–1952), studying painting at the Académie Vitti in Montparnasse, under Henri Martin, had paid 35 francs for a large room in the Rue de Vaugirard, facing the Luxembourg.[62] William Nicholson (1872–1949), the painter, poster designer and woodcutter, lived at the same hotel as Schwabe when he was a student; Schwabe felt Nicholson's description of the hotel, as recorded by Marguerite Steen in her biography, was grossly inaccurate. He wrote in his diary on 8 November 1943:

> *It is described, quite untruthfully in the light of my experience, as a 'small' (it isn't so small), 'incredibly dirty' (Benoit, the garcon, used to do my room beautifully every day), and 'shady' (why shady? – there was plenty of sun; or if its moral character is meant, it was quite respectable) little place that stank of bad drainage (not so) and unaired rooms (the windows were usually open).*

The popular and renowned Académie Julian was where Schwabe elected to study for about eight months under Jean Paul Laurens (1838–1921), one of the last great history painters of the late nineteenth century. Julian's was the foremost of the independent teaching académies and was established by Rodolphe Julian (1839–1907) the painter and draughtsman, in 1868, 'initially with the purpose of preparing students for entry to the École des Beaux-Arts. It soon became recognized as a rival to the latter... To keep his expenses low Julian rented ateliers [for men and women] which he could open and close as demand dictated.'[63] The admission policy was liberal and Schwabe signed on

in the ante room to the atelier, in the Rue du Dragon, off Boulevard St Germain on the Left Bank, paid his moderate fee and bought some charcoal and Ingres paper. As *un nouveau* his name was posted up in the atelier: he could have been banned had his fellow students disapproved. 'One purpose of this was to prevent a majority of English and Americans in the student body which virtually governed the atelier.'[64] The *massier* (head student) who was elected by ballot, dealt with the budget and discipline, and who posed the model, informed Schwabe that it was customary for *un nouveau* to buy the midday drinks at a nearby café. Following this Schwabe had to sing a song or make a short speech on the throne and undertake extra duties be it sweeping the studio first thing in the morning, lighting the smoky stove or cleaning the brushes.

The easy-going relaxed atmosphere of the crowded and hierarchical classes was in sharp contrast to the orderliness experienced by Schwabe at the Slade, where he had to arrive before 8 a.m. on a Monday to secure a good place amongst the densely packed easels. Nicholson remembered 'The stench was dreadful – human bodies, the palette scrapings that made a frieze up to the height of one's stretched-out arm, gave up their ancient reek of oil in the heat of the stove, caporal cigarettes – everybody smoked, either cigarette or pipe, and there were times when you could hardly see for the water running out of one's eyes.'[65]

Schwabe worked industriously and was careful with his money, well aware that, of those artists who had flocked to Paris and forged successful careers, one of the most noticeable things was the length of time they spent studying. The painter Henry Scott Tuke (1858–1929) who studied in Paris from 1881–83

William Strang
The Violinist
1910
PRIVATE COLLECTION

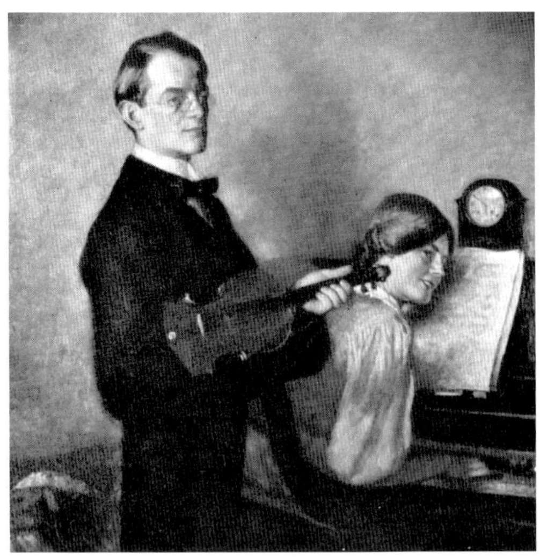

estimated that the time 'the big men study, [was]
8 or 9 years usually.'[66] Schwabe was on his way
to spending a similar time on his studies. One of
the great values of being in Paris was being able to
spend time in the afternoons, when it was too dark
in Julian's, to visit the Louvre. Schwabe found it a
great storehouse of spectacular paintings in colossal
galleries. Here, as at the British Museum, he could
study in-depth 'The control of effects in drawing,
tone, colour and composition… in the original largely
as their artists had left them.'[67] It was a stimulating
time to be in Paris and for Schwabe the 'tall buildings
along the quays, dove-grey, or sparkling white in the
sun, the trees leaning over the river, the bath houses,
the barges loading and unloading below the bridges'[68]
provided material for a number of paintings including
his drypoint of *Pont Neuf*, which had been the site of
paintings by Renoir and Monet in 1872. David Strang
(1887–1967), younger son of the renowned painter
and printmaker William Strang (1859–1921), printed
Pont Neuf, Schwabe's first drypoint. According to
Schwabe 'no professional printer could afterwards
get such a good result from the plate as he did.'[69]

Schwabe's teachers, well known painters, were much
liked and admired. Cora Gordon (1879–1950), a friend
of Schwabe's and fellow student at the Académie Julian,
wrote an article for *The Studio* in 1946 about Bernard
Meninsky (1891–1950) who was at Julian's in the
summer of 1911, a few years after Schwabe had left,
and described Jean Paul Laurens as the students' Pope.
Silence reigned when he or his colleagues were present
and completing their weekly inspection of students'
work and offering criticism. 'The harshest things they
said were honeyed compliments after the withering
comments of Tonks'.[70]

Working alongside Schwabe at Julian's during
1906–07 was the French painter and graphic artist
Segonzac (1884–1974), his old friend Cecil King
(1881–1942), and Ian Strang. Schwabe later posed as
a violinist for Ian's father William at the Strang family
home in Hamilton Terrace. Schwabe had many kindly
memories of Mrs William Strang. *The Violinist* was
exhibited at the Royal Academy in the summer
of 1910.[71]

Schwabe's studies overlapped with those of Maresco
Pearce (1874–1964) and George Kennedy (1882–1954),
both later painter/architects. Kennedy had been at the
Slade in 1904–06; his painting career was cut short
by an eye disorder. Their friendship continued after
Julian's and Schwabe holidayed with the Kennedys
in Ireland in Cashelnagore, Donegal. Schwabe thought
the mountain and lake scenery near Cashelnagore
probably the loveliest in the British Isles. When taking
a break from their studies, Schwabe and his artist
friends would spend time in cafés such as the Café du
Dome in Montparnasse, where they could eat cheaply
and watch the crowds. Well known as an intellectual
gathering place, 'that Arcadia' as Schwabe referred
to it, was frequented by the famous (and soon to be
famous) painters, sculptors, writers, poets, models,
art connoisseurs and dealers.[72]

Wilfrid Cave,[73] a friend from his Slade days, wrote
a belated letter to Schwabe in March 1907. Schwabe
by then had left the Hôtel de la Haute Loire, where
he was now living; the letter was forwarded to Rolph
House, Schwabe's home in Hemel Hempstead. It was
full of news of their contemporaries and a recent very
good show at Whitechapel. Cave thought Paris must
be too gorgeous for anything just now. Schwabe had

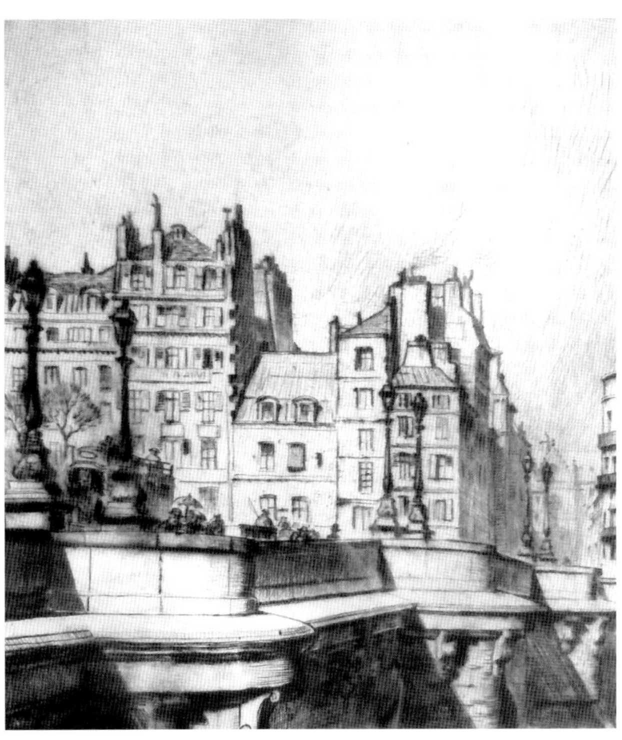

Pont Neuf
1909 | drypoint | 44 × 40 cm

previously described his visit to the Bal Bullier, the famous and fashionable dance-hall, which Cave thought sounded very gay. He asked Schwabe whether he had also adorned the Quatz' Arts, the notorious annual ball of the École des Beaux Arts, and how his work was going with Jean Paul Laurens. He also informed him that Robert Gregory (1881–1918) was going to Italy the following week and was talking of putting in a day or two in Paris and accordingly he might see him. Finally, he wondered if Schwabe would return for Easter. It seems probable that Schwabe did return to Hertfordshire around then as his mother died on 2 April 1907, aged 55. He recalled how non-complaining she was in the unhappinesses of her life, and how little a boy understands or sympathises with such things.[74]

Following the burial of his mother at Great Gaddesden, north of Hemel Hempstead, the location of which was deliberately chosen 'instead of a hideous modern cemetery', Schwabe returned for a short time to Paris. His diaries make reference to meeting a number of artist acquaintances, including the Russian Boris Anrep who did not arrive in Paris until 1908, having abandoned his law studies in St Petersburg University to study at the Académie Julian. At some stage Schwabe decided to leave Julian's and attend the Cercle International des Arts, 'a sort of Art School in the Bd. Raspail, run by a M. Bornet.'[75] Robert Gregory, whom Schwabe regarded as very gifted student, also worked there, as did A.E. Maude who recalled that Schwabe criticized his drawings.

Schwabe together with Gregory, Kennedy, Frederick Porter (1883–1944) and Henry Lamb (1883–1960) haunted Gertrude Stein's Saturday soirées in the

Rue de Fleurus in the sixth arrondissement, which began at nine and 'attracted a diverse crowd of artists, expatriates, and curious visitors'.[76] They were impressed by the rows of paintings of modern art on the walls of their flat acquired by Stein and her brother Leo – Matisse, Cézanne, Picasso and those on the walls of the adjoining studio by Maurice Denis, Honoré Daumier and many more.[77] Whether they were impressed by Leo Stein's posturing on modern art is another matter. Schwabe recollected that Gertrude Stein had first heard of Augustus John through Gregory, who showed her some photographs of John's work. She was rather contemptuous of them: 'Good stoodents work' (pronounced in the Bowery style) she said.[78] Schwabe met Picasso and Matisse but he was more excited by his discovery of Van Gogh. Although he thought if it came to a question of influence he was more influenced by John and Orpen who had just left the Slade before he commenced his studies there.[79]

One of the parties that Schwabe went to was particularly memorable. Present were Euphemia, Henry Lamb's wife, and an American man dressed as a woman, who had to shave his back to wear a woman's evening dress. Schwabe remembered the ultra-bohemianism of Lamb and Euphemia when he first knew them in Paris about 1907. He recalled how Lamb walked to Dijon with only ten francs in the world and Euphemia, very picturesque and beautiful, wearing a long cloak, sleeping on the floor of the studio of Charles Freegrove Winzer (1886–1940).

ITALY

In 1908 Schwabe left Paris and travelled to Italy for the first time with his friend Francis Unwin (1885–1925),

a draughtsman, etcher and lithographer of landscape and architectural subjects, with whom he had many tastes and associations in common. Unwin joined Schwabe at the Slade in 1902 having previously been a student at Winchester School of Art. Schwabe described himself as 'a sort of student-tourist' which he thought was the best thing to be in Italy.[80] Unwin had spent the winter in Egypt where he drew interiors of tombs for an archaeological expedition and American publication before travelling to Italy. He returned there in 1912 and 1913 and it is possible that Schwabe again accompanied him.

Schwabe worked for some time in Rome, and visited Florence and Venice and other Italian cities. He took great delight in seeing the paintings, sculptures and architecture, bringing back drawings and material for etchings and drypoints, including *The Basilica of Constantine* with the Coliseum in the distance and *Ponte Fabricio*, the oldest bridge in Rome. Both were exhibited at the New English Art Club, in 1911 and 1912 respectively, and owe much to Piranesi (1720–78). Schwabe had become well acquainted with Piranesi through the prints in Batsford's shop in Holborn. Unwin also bought some prints there, when he was living at 59 Great Ormond Street. Schwabe spent many days there as they worked together at the press Unwin had set up in his powdering-closet.[81] In Florence much time was spent at the Uffizi. 'This visit laid the foundation of a profound knowledge of Italian art and architecture which was to be of immense value to him afterwards.'[82]

In Venice what impressed Schwabe was the enormous importance of Tintoretto. He thought the average painter or critic did not do him justice. He wrote

Ponte Fabricio
1912 | etching
28.3 x 22.9 cm

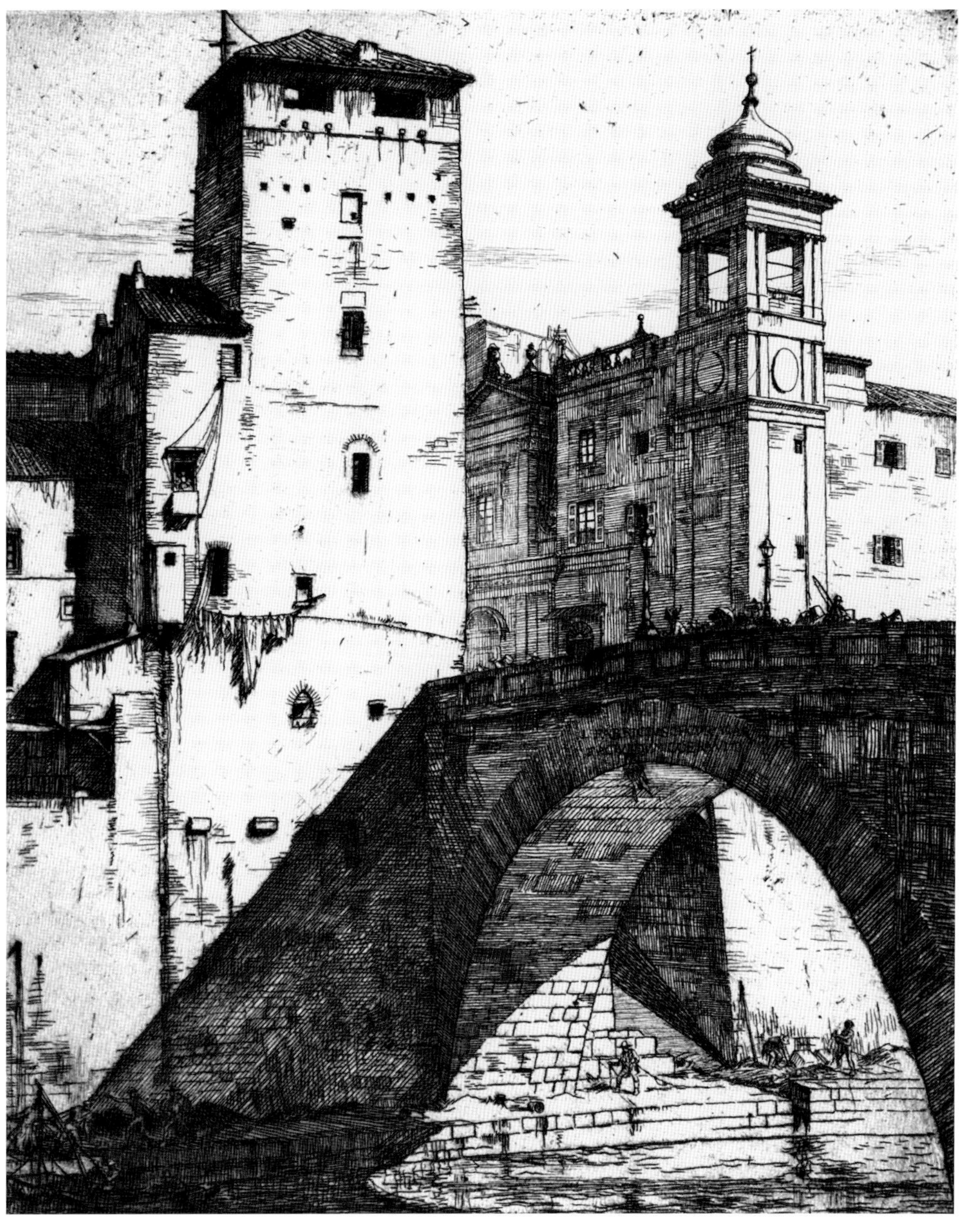

in his diary: 'a marvellously inventive composer, with the power of ten men: dignified and broad in portraiture, excellent in colour – and alive.'[83] Away from the galleries they sat in one of the frescoed rooms in the Caffé Florian on the Piazza San Marco. When Schwabe returned and took tea at Florian's in April 1935 the atmosphere was markedly different: not only was the tea very expensive like everything else, but there was a 'Review of Fascists in the Piazza. Every column plastered with placards – "Duce! Duce! Duce!"'[84]

Prior to 1935 Schwabe and Unwin had had work selected for the British Pavilion at the Venice Biennale. Unwin exhibited in 1922 in the Bianco e Nero section. Schwabe's work was exhibited on three occasions: a watercolour in 1924, a painting in 1926, and in 1928 in the Bianco e Nero section. That year he was also a member of the Artistic Committee which was presided over by Sir William Orpen; and included Charles H. Collins Baker, Gerald Brockhurst, Philip Connard, William Reid Dick, Jacob Epstein, Roger Fry and Augustus John.[85]

LONDON:
EXHIBITING, MARRIAGE AND FRIENDS

Schwabe returned from Italy and 'did nothing in particular – except work.' He had received a small income after his mother's death in 1907.[86] He went back to his rooms in 37, Howley Place, Maida Vale, London which at one stage he had let to Innes. Schwabe recalled that he was never paid and that his charwoman thought Innes 'was literally, the "devil", and she was undoubtedly terrified of him. To such as she there may have been something satanic in his

looks.'[87] Augustus John, with whom Innes painted in north Wales, said he 'cut an arresting figure: Quaker hat, a coloured silk scarf, and a long black overcoat, set off features of a slightly cadaverous cast, with glittering black eyes, a wide sardonic mouth, a prominent nose and a large bony forehead, invaded by streaks of black thin hair.'[88] While Innes was seen as handsome by many people, Schwabe recognised that others regarded him differently. His portrait of Innes was thought to be a good likeness. Schwabe had done it late one night after he had spent the evening with him, while he was still vividly impressed with his appearance – one of the few occasions on which he recalled doing a good likeness from memory. John appreciated it too.

During 1911–12 Schwabe revisited France, staying in Siouville, Normandy, for three weeks with Kate Syrett and Helen Maitland, who stayed in rooms in a cottage while he found accommodation in the inn. Maitland, a young music student in Paris in 1908, had had a brief affair with Lamb at the same time as Schwabe was in Paris. From 1911 she lived with Boris Anrep and after their second child Igor was born 'he put aside his prejudices and [they were] married.'[89] Syrett was a lifelong friend of Schwabe's; in December 1916 she designed some English toys (a British lion, two tanks and two rocking horses) for an exhibition of toys in the Pavilion Marsan (the Louvre's western wing) in Paris.

While in Siouville Schwabe drew the inn proprietor more or less from memory in what he described as an amateurish, Daumier-inspired sketch. The proprietor was a popular subject, for Augustus John had also painted him; this was reproduced in a book which Schwabe saw many years later in a shop window in

The Turl, Oxford. It was entitled 'Old Ledanois' – a study of a French peasant. Schwabe thought the proprietor was also painted by Lamb, when he, too, stayed in the same inn.

Back in England Schwabe was one of a little group of artists including Unwin and Gerald Summers (1886–1969) who had informal shows of their work on Saturday afternoons at a studio in Chelsea. This afforded opportunities for others to see their work as well as the possibility of attracting patrons. The latter were rare and Schwabe took the opportunity to exhibit firstly with the New English Art Club (NEAC).

The NEAC had been founded in 1886 in opposition to the conservatism of the Royal Academy by 'a new generation of young British artists who looked to France for their inspiration'[90] and who had even thought of calling themselves 'The Society of Anglo-French Painters'. The constitution which was based on 'restriction of privilege and the right of all exhibitors to vote in the election of juries and to serve on them if elected'[91] was drafted by Schwabe's professor at University College, Fred Brown, and it was no coincidence that the Slade became a 'chief source of talent for the Club'.[92] The Club contained 'almost every laudable painter in England, a period which might be roughly dated from 1889 to the Post-Impressionist exhibition of 1910'[93] organised by Roger Fry at the Grafton Galleries. Schwabe made his debut in 1909 showing a landscape drawing *Port St Michael, Paris*. He was a regular exhibitor for nearly four decades, and significantly the NEAC continued to organise exhibitions throughout the war although:

> *exhibits suggest that artists were slow to react to the war until the arrival of Francis Dodd's portraits of British generals and Muirhead Bone's drawings of the Western Front and the Grand Fleet, in the summer exhibition of 1917. Moreover, such painters as Attwood and Colin Gill elected not to show war works in the club exhibitions, reserving them exclusively for the new Imperial War Museum, London, and the big Academy 'War Pictures' exhibition of 1919, which New English exhibitors dominated.*[94]

Schwabe too exhibited some works relating to 'Women on the Land' that he had undertaken for the Ministry of Information at the 'War Pictures' exhibition.

Schwabe had become a member of the NEAC in 1917 and from the outset showed an interest in architectural subjects and the ability to work in more than one medium. He also exhibited watercolours and oil paintings. The *Westminster Gazette*, while critical of the younger generation of artists exhibiting in the winter exhibition of 1914, singling out Albert Rothenstein, Innes and Gertler, praised the genuine achievement of Schwabe: in particular, his appreciation of the value of shadow contrasts in the drawing *House in Cheyne Walk* and use of blue ink which was deemed to make the peculiar romantic atmosphere with which he invested the house yet more intense. Also mentioned was Schwabe's individuality as evinced by *The Confession*, and once more his sense of atmosphere and understanding of tragic contrast. The critics were not always so effusive: B.H. Dias writing in *The New Age*, a weekly review of politics, literature and art, admitted that there are naturally points where the critic's patience gives out – this was the case at the NEAC in January 1918, with Schwabe's lithograph *The Bath*, and his friend Francis Dodd's (1874–1948) portrait of *Gavin, the son of Muirhead Bone*. Dias conceded that *Stacking Turf* was one of Schwabe's better tries.

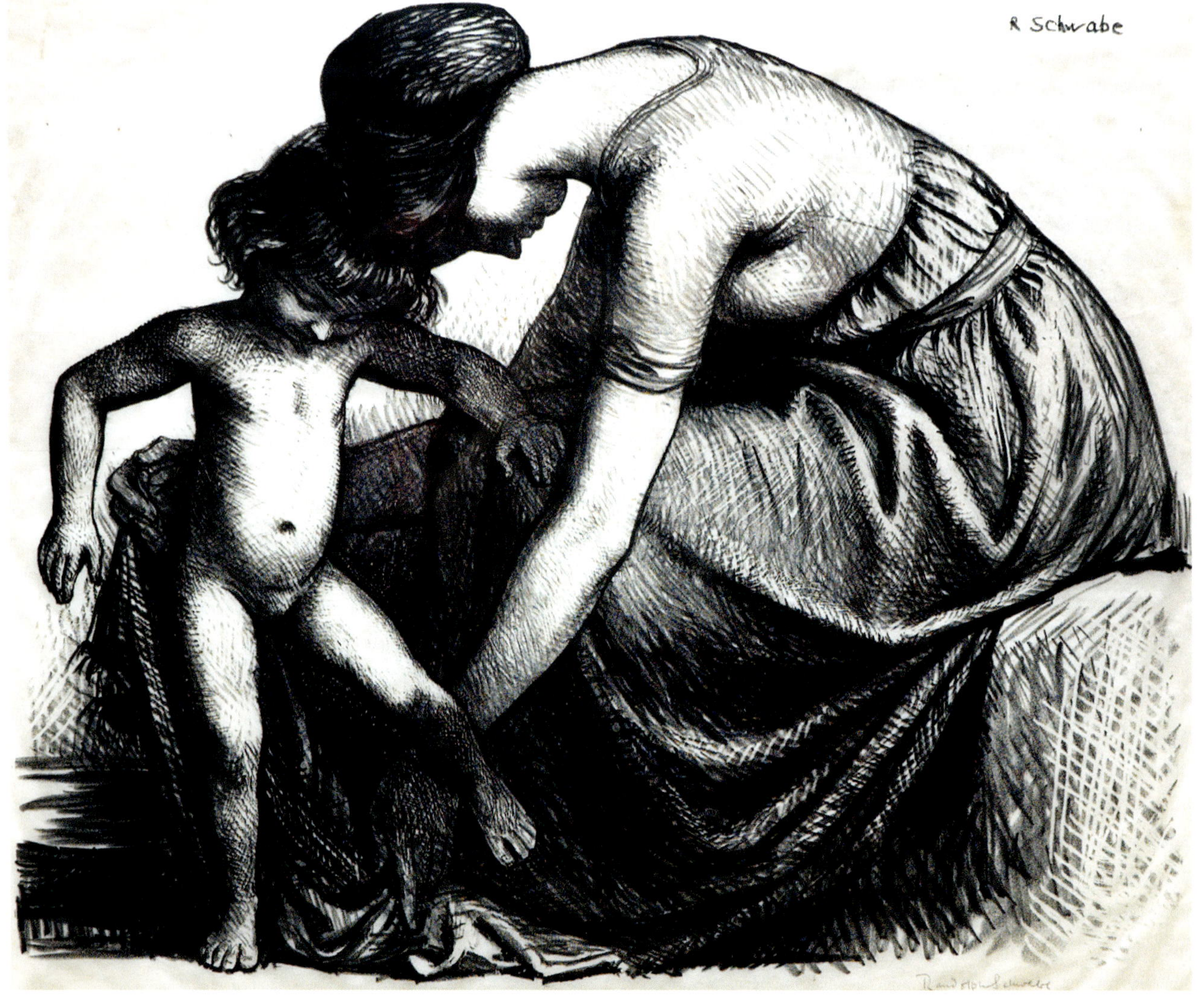

The Bath
1917 | lithograph | 36 × 44.5 cm

The Bath is an intimate portrayal of his young daughter
Alice born in March 1914 and Birdie his wife gently
drying her after she has stepped from the bath.
Schwabe married 'Birdie' Gwendolen Rosamund Jones
(1889–1978) on 19 April 1913 in Chelsea. The best man
was the painter Darsie Japp (1883–1973, Slade 1908–09),
who supplied Alice with her first cot; he was also a
good friend of Lamb and Stanley Spencer (1891–1959).
Japp later gave up painting professionally to farm and
breed race horses with some success. Schwabe and
Birdie had met at the Slade. She might have married
Maresco Pearce when she was there but he did not
pursue the matter, seeing that it was useless. Pearce
was looking for somebody to marry, but he was not
very attractive to some women, though rich, handsome
and likeable in many ways. Schwabe also gathered that
he was one of Euphemia Lamb's lovers.[95]

Birdie was the seventh and youngest child of Herbert
and Elizabeth Jones. Her father seems never to have
worked but spent his inheritance on buying books
until his funds ran out. He appears to have paid little
attention to the education of his children, except
for Birdie and her next older sister, Dora, who were
enrolled in the school run by the Sisters of the Holy
Child Jesus in Cavendish Square. It was they who
encouraged Birdie to enrol in the Slade in 1905. She
went there daily from her home in 5, Mandeville Place,
Manchester Square in a hansom cab. She was given
the nickname 'Birdie' by fellow students because
of her habit of perching on a shelf to eat her lunch
(half a chicken and half a bottle of Chablis) as she
was embarrassed that the family cook had packed
this. As a student she was much in demand to sit as
'she was so nice to draw.'[96] Albert Rothenstein drew
Birdie for *Girl's Head* in 1911. Birdie was painted by

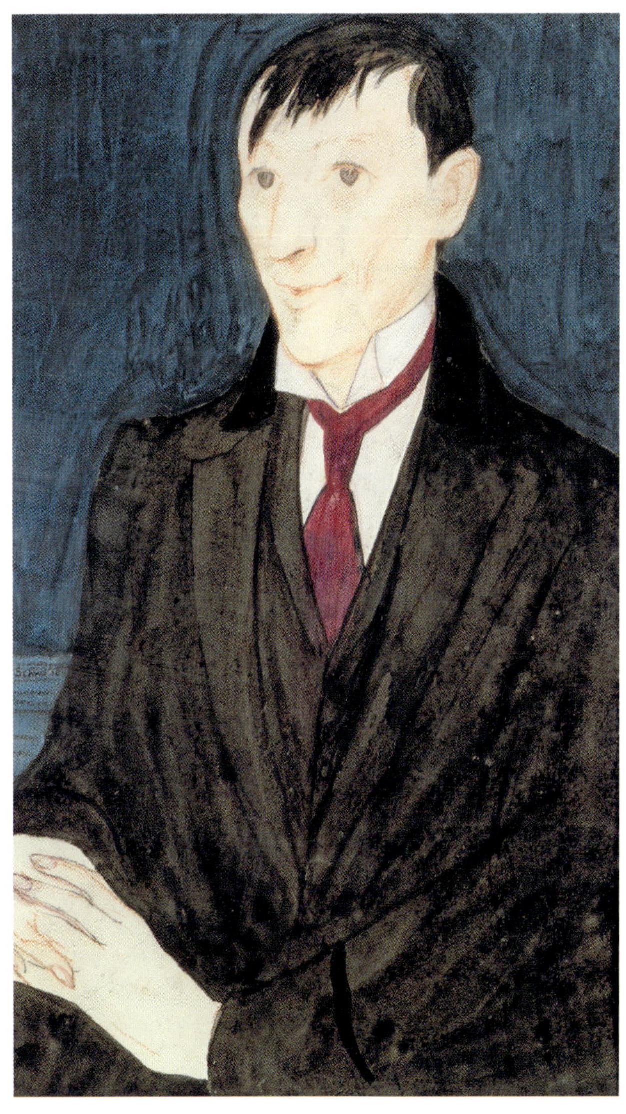

Portrait of J.D. Innes
c.1911/12 | watercolour and red crayon | 28.4 × 18 cm

Augustus John at Fryern Court and in 1915 in his studio in Chelsea:

> *where he insisted on her posing with her lips slightly apart and wearing a narrow red hat-band around her neck, both against her wishes. Originally known as 'Birdie: The Black Hat', it was followed by a full-length portrait which was acquired, unfinished, for the John Quinn collection...*[97]

Alice (1914–2010) recalled visiting Fryern Court and seeing Augustus John and all his children. Birdie reminded Schwabe of John's odd way of painting a head regardless of the background. When he painted the picture of her he did the head completely first on the bare canvas, and then said 'What sort of background shall we have? – bother the background.' The standing figure of Birdie was done with one of John's own paintings of a lakeside scene behind her. He made this look as if it was out of doors.[98] She once had a 'curious experience' with John when she went to Mallord Street at the time she was sitting for her portrait. John met her in a quite excited state, and dragged her in, saying 'Come – I've got something to show you.' Birdie was a little uneasy, knowing John's eccentricities; but when he flung open a door, the sight she was to see proved to be Dorelia, sitting by the fire-side with her hands on her knee in the attitude of the *Smiling Woman*, which seems to be unselfconscious and habitual with her; she had a pile of children's garments in her lap, having been airing them by the fire. Birdie thought she really looked very lovely, and that John's enthusiasm was not misplaced.[99]

After Birdie was married she was offered a job with *Vogue* magazine but she felt there should not be two artists in the family. She decided never to draw again.[100]

She was not alone in taking such a decision – her friend Ruth Lowinsky who had also studied at the Slade, on her marriage to fellow artist Thomas 'Tommy' Lowinsky (1892–1947) in 1919, did not pursue any artistic ambitions she may have entertained 'and contented herself with winning a considerable reputation as a magnificent cook and sparkling hostess'. The Schwabes often had 'excellent' dinners at the Lowinskys'. Birdie's own cooking would not have earned her a reputation; Alice recalled her cooking sausages on a pewter plate; but her 'scrubbing was, indeed, legendary: she would scrub for you whether you would or no, and the action would be either joyous or resentful according to mood.'[101] Birdie would take it upon herself to adopt struggling artists and friends.

The Schwabes spent their honeymoon in Whitby on the Yorkshire coast. Schwabe, always on the look out for material for his sketch book, found much to occupy him. *Whitby* was exhibited later that year at the NEAC show. They returned to the small flat (43A) they rented in a large rather dilapidated house in Cheyne Row, next to Terrey's greengrocers,[102] which was one of the oldest secular buildings in Chelsea and which James McNeill Whistler (1834–1903) had painted c.1885–6.[103] James (Jas) Wood (1889–1975), the painter, writer and aesthete in his semi-autobiographical work *New World Vistas* (1926) based his chapter 'Influenza' on a visit to Birdie. Schwabe felt it was 'largely a truthful description'. He recounted in his diary that:

> *There are a lot of circumstances that are very recognizable. When I read it before, years ago, the description of myself hardly sank in at all: I thought it much too important and exaggerated to be me. I had lost the book, and having told Wood this when I met him he sent me another copy.*[104]

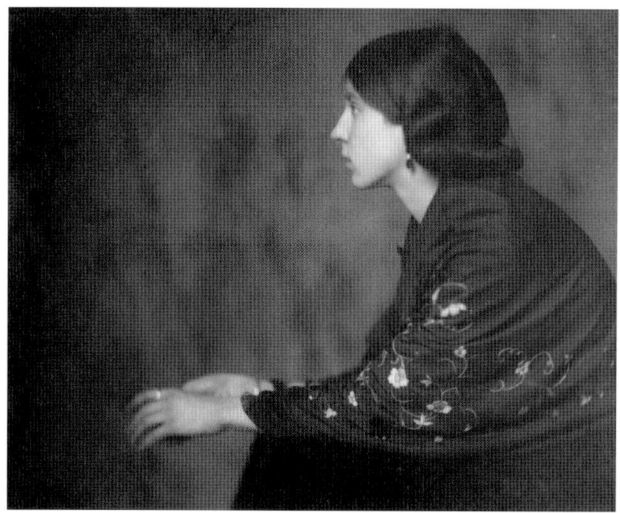

Fellow artist Allan Gwynne-Jones (1892–1982), god-father to Alice, lived above. The Schwabes introduced him to a number of their wide circle of artist friends including Augustus John, Innes and Albert Rutherston whose parties they frequented in Fitzroy Street where he and John Fothergill (1876–1957) lived. Fothergill, who was editing *The Slade*, kept whippets which John used to draw.[105]

Schwabe and Birdie used to attend salons at the house of Lady Ottoline Morrell, the literary hostess and patron of the arts, in Bedford Square. Schwabe recalled that they were fortunate in their relations with her when they were young, finding her of a genuinely kindly nature. He recorded in his diary around the time she died in April 1938 that:

> *Many of the people she took up, artists and writers, were ungrateful, and poked fun at her behind her back, or wrote satires on her. Birdie was taken to one of Lady Ottoline's parties in Bedford Square by Boris Anrep, who, after making a great fuss of her (Birdie), abandoned her for someone more important, and left her to get her own taxi and go home alone. Ottoline was considerate and concerned about this, being always an excellent hostess.*

Schwabe and Birdie also joined in the fun at the Chelsea Arts Club Ball with fellow artists and art students and paid their guinea for tickets to attend the Ball on New Year's Eve 1910. 'The *Illustrated London News* described it as the "greatest fancy-dress ball ever held in London, four thousand dancers on the floor of the Albert Hall".'[106] The balls ceased on the outbreak of war.

Of their close friends, Charles Rennie Mackintosh (1868–1928) and his wife Margaret Macdonald (1865–1933) were particularly important to them

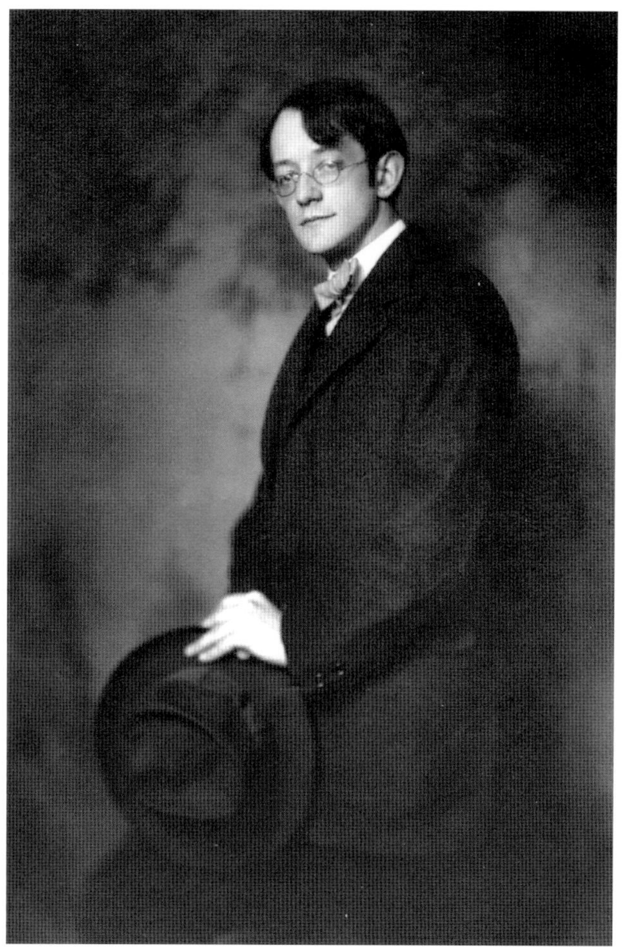

'Birdie' Gwendolen Rosamund Jones
and
Randolph Schwabe

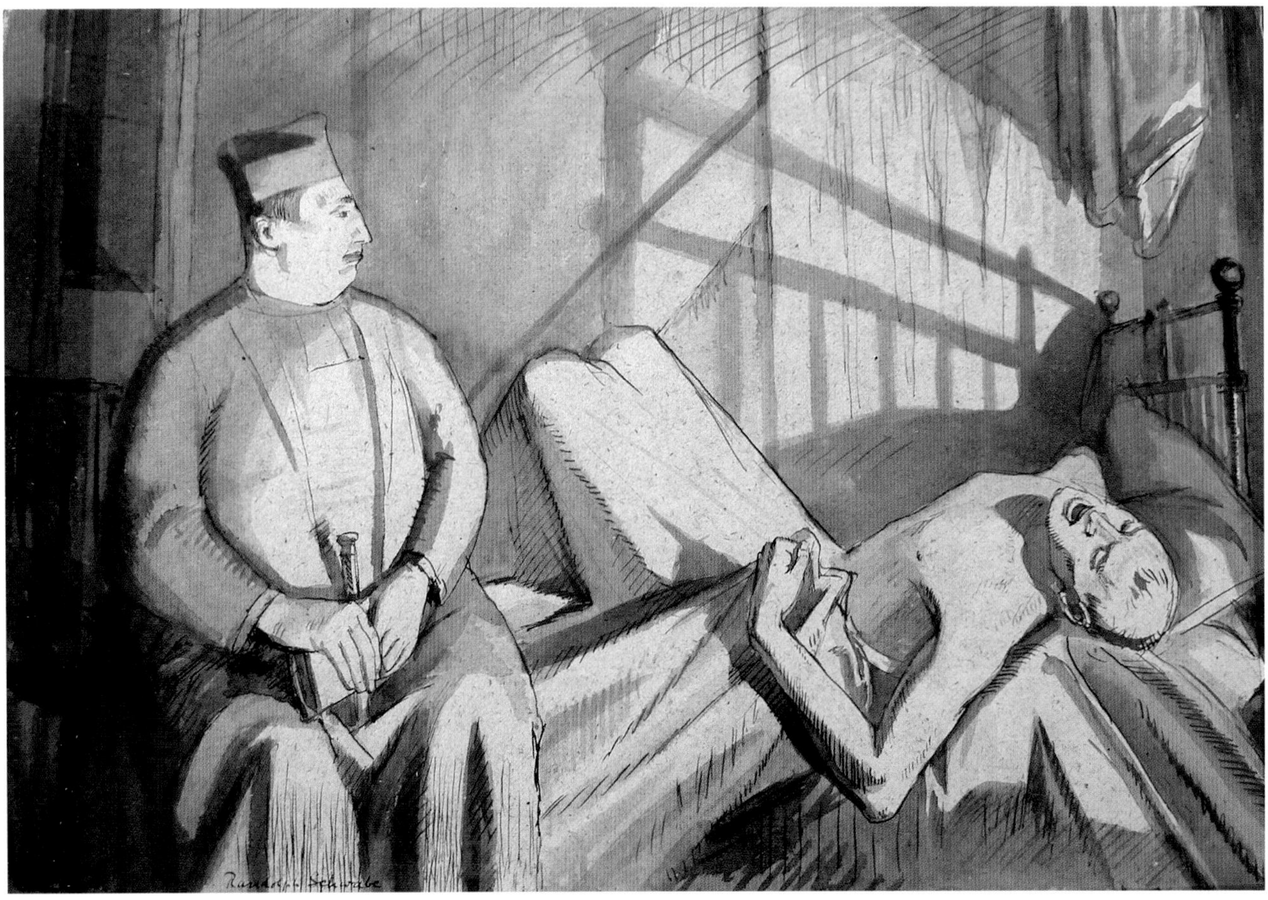

The Confession
1914 | watercolour wash and black ink | 38.5 x 56.3 cm

during the years the Mackintoshes lived in Chelsea (1915–23) – the young Alice was a favourite of theirs and Margaret would later refer to them as the 'beloved famille Schwabe'. Often they would all eat together at The Blue Cockatoo, 35 Cheyne Walk, Chelsea, a noted artists' rendezvous on the Embankment where they were served by the infamous waitress Hettie Swaisland who Alice recalled used to do or say outrageous things.[107]

Another meeting place for Schwabe was the Friday Club which had been founded by Vanessa Bell in 1905 and 'became one of the liveliest exhibiting groups before the first War.'[108] Schwabe, an early member, was at one time the Honorary Secretary, Fred Winter, the sculptor, was the paid secretary. He valued the very good annual shows that the Club held of what were then ultra-modern pictures.[109] Given that members were not only painters, Schwabe's academic interests were met through opportunities for discussion and lectures by the likes of Clive Bell (1881–1964), art critic and philosopher of art, and Roger Fry (1866–1934). Schwabe exhibited with the Club in the New Year of 1913 at the Alpine Gallery, Mill Street. The critic for the *Athenaeum* in a review of the exhibition wrote, 'It is still a record, though of an impression rather than a fact, that we confess to seeing more promise in work which, if less fluent, shows more definitely the constructive and inventive instinctive such as Mr Randolph Schwabe's "Exotic Dance".'[110] Schwabe's work was noticed the following year by the critic from the *Observer* who found his visit 'distinctly pleasant and exhilarating'. He recorded that 'Arresting work is shown by Mr A. Rothenstein, Mr C.R.W. Nevinson, Mr Hamilton Way, Mr Randolph Schwabe and Miss Vera Waddington.' Schwabe exhibited with the Club throughout the war years; in 1916 his *Grave*

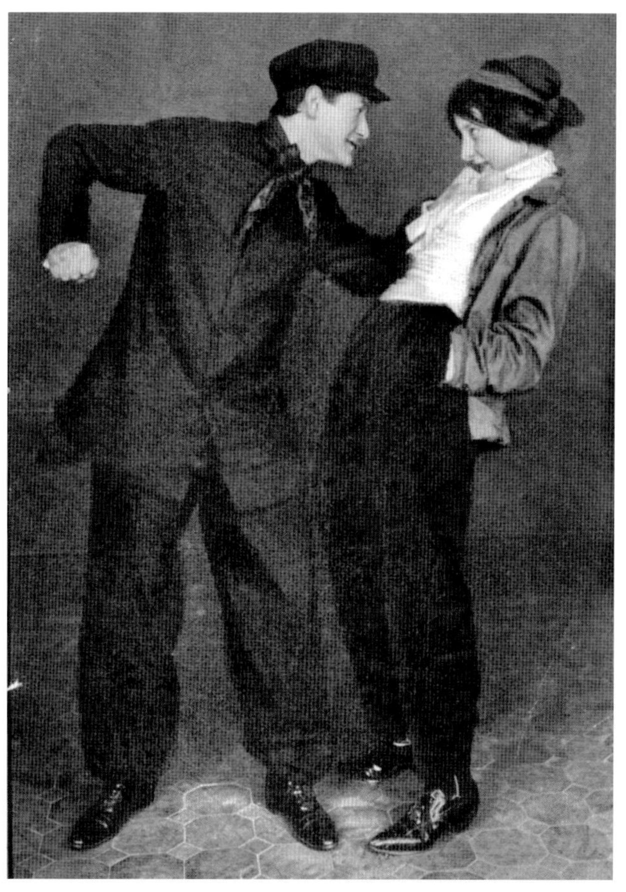

Randolph and 'Birdie' at the Chelsea Arts Club Ball, Albert Hall *c.*1910

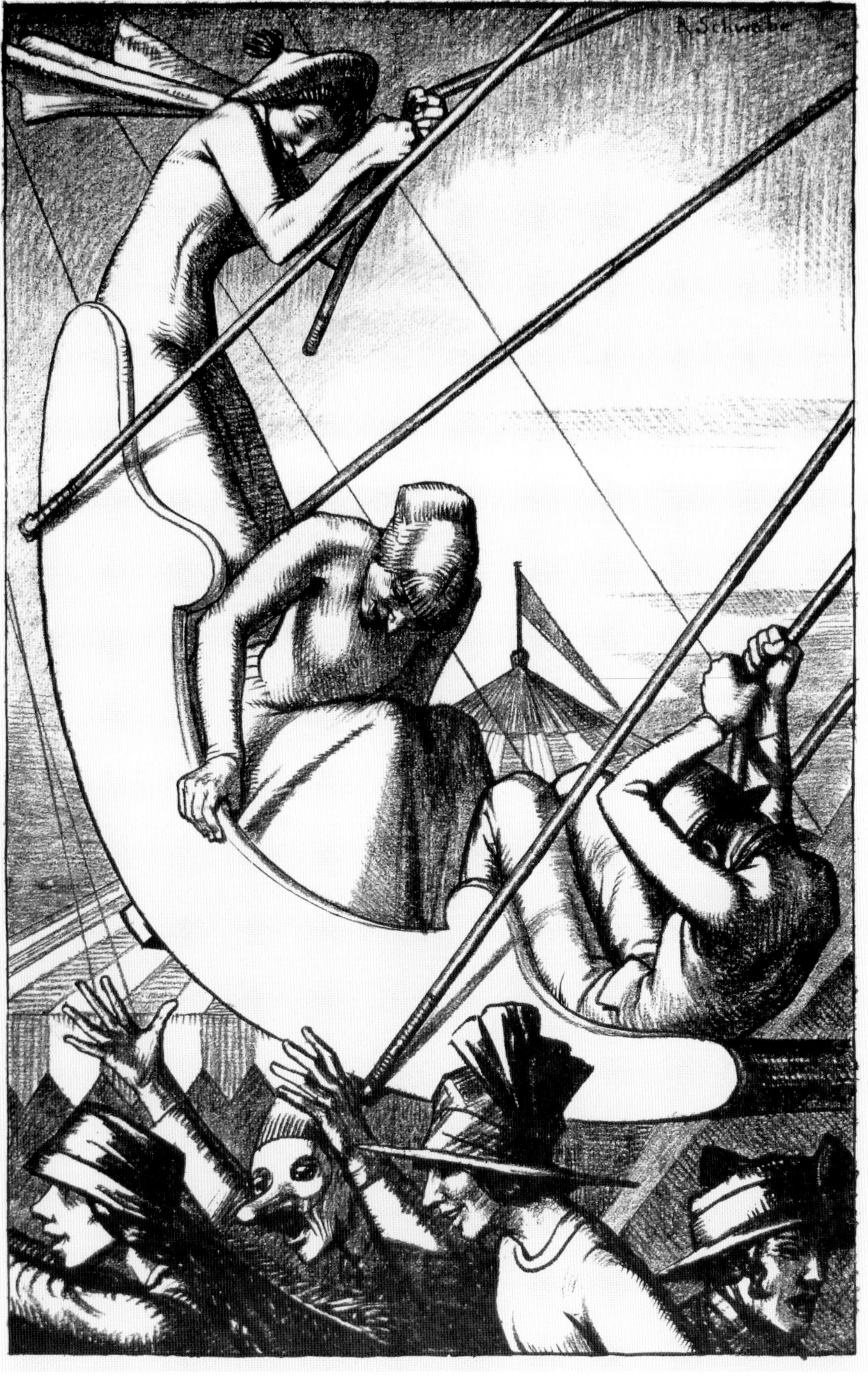

Bank Holiday – The Swings
c.1915 | lithograph | 37 × 24 cm
COLLECTION JANET AND DI BARNES

Diggers attracted attention for its simple forms and massive volume, it being reproduced in the art magazine, *Colour*. In 1918, unusually, he was joined by Birdie who exhibited *Rotten Row*.

It was a mark of Schwabe's growing reputation that in April 1915 he had his first exhibition of drawings and etchings at the Carfax Gallery, Bury Street. The Gallery, started by the enterprising Fothergill, with William Rothenstein as his art adviser, had previously staged solo shows for a diverse range of artists including Max Beerbohm (1872–1956), Walter Sickert (1860–1942), Augustus John, Gwen John (1876–1939) and Albert Rothenstein. Schwabe shared the gallery space with his friend Francis Unwin. Sir Claude Phillips, the eminent critic and formerly keeper of the Wallace Collection, reviewed the 'modest and attractive' little show for the *Daily Telegraph*:

> If the true personality of Mr Unwin is a little difficult to disentangle at this stage of his well-grounded and promising art, to find that of his companion in the exhibition, Mr Randolph Schwabe, is a much harder task. He possesses considerable power as an executant, and gives that power full scope in styles so many and various that which, if any, is to be deemed his own is not easy to guess.

> There is no direct copying of any definite work by a precursor or contemporary, but there is a very marked — and indeed, undisguised — imitation of many. The nearest approach to originality is to be found in two highly coloured, yet gaunt and dreary land-scapes, 'The Mausoleum' and 'From Finavara'. Here a certain power, not of execution alone, but of vision, makes itself felt. In 'Bank Holiday' we are suddenly confronted with an attempt to Cubism: 'In Bed' — a study of some young girl reclining, which must rank among the most successful of

> the imitations or assimilations — irresistibly recalls Mr Augustus John in his most mannered phase. In 'The Basilica of Constantine' there is open, and here not inappropriate, imitation of Piranesi. 'No. 14, Regent-street' the simple, powerful rendering of prosaic motive technically resembles the work of the great Anglo-French etcher, Méryon. 'Woman in a Long Coat' owes much to the example of William Strang. 'The Quadrant' is an admirably firm and accurate piece of representation, impersonal, but satisfying in its completeness, and so far as we are aware, attributable to the inspiration of no other artist. In 'The Confession' we have a weird death-bed scene, genuinely dramatic. In it the figure of a truculent and unsympathetic ecclesiastic, who looks on unmoved at the death agony of him whom he is called upon to console, is rendered with much power.

The artist and teacher Walter Bayes (1869–1956) who himself had had a show at the Carfax Gallery in 1913, writing in the *Athenaeum*, was also critical although he recognised in Schwabe's etching *The Quadrant* that the difficult problem of balancing a design which had for the subject one side only of a street was cleverly resolved, yet somewhat at the expense of belief in the freedom of the roadway. Bayes felt that the etching of *Piccadilly Circus* looked as if it had been inspired by some eighteenth-century model, but that the too conscious intention of historic record had defeated itself. Like Phillips, Bayes thought Schwabe's drawing *The Confession*, dramatic, and for him it was in this work and *Bank Holiday* that Schwabe revealed his best talent — which was inventive and tersely expressive of character. He wished for more work of the same kind as he was less interest in his painted landscapes.

The rebuff from the critics was somewhat alleviated for Schwabe by the kindly encouragement he received from his friends. Albert Rothenstein wrote:

I must offer you a word of congratulations on your show at Carfax & I hope you won't mind my saying how admirable I think many of your things there are — certainly your work gives me a very high degree of pleasure & many other folks must share this feeling. Your big water colour of the Mausoleum is quite extraordinary & I wish that I could be the possessor of it. This is the first time I have seen water colours by you, exposed in their frailty & they came to me as an astonishing surprise. Your 'Bank Holiday' is fated to live with me in the future & very glad I am to be lucky enough to have secured it.

In November 1915 Schwabe exhibited for the first time with the London Group and was elected a member, as was Mark Gertler (1891–1939); he was to be a prolific exhibitor with the Group showing over 70 artworks over the course of two decades; from 1917–19 he served on the hanging committee and later on the executive committee. The London Group owed 'its origin to the amalgamation of several small groups of painters [the Fitzroy Street Group and the Camden Town Group] who were dissatisfied with conditions prevailing towards the end of the first decade of the present century.'[111] The Group held its inaugural exhibition at the Goupil Gallery, Regent Street in March 1914. At his first exhibition with them Schwabe showed *Head of an Old Woman; Mrs Randolph Schwabe; Portrait* and *Landscape in Devonshire*. Writing in *The Queen, The Lady's Newspaper and Court Chronicle* on 11 December 1915, the art critic and collector Randall Davies (1866–1946), whose portrait Schwabe painted in 1939, saw it as a vast improvement on the previous show. Schwabe's *Landscape in Devonshire* was hung next to Sylvia Gosse's (1881–1968) large Sussex landscape on which Davies lavished much praise, concluding 'it is so natural and true without any fuss about it, and one can feel the sun all the time.' Of Schwabe's landscape he commented:

This is a more detailed account of a more detailed scene — a village in a hollow — and there is no sun. The truth, accordingly, is colder and more precise, and one would be glad of a little more glow and colour, such as we may have seen in Mr Schwabe's water-colours, or as we may now see in the fine 'Portrait' in the next room. But Mr Schwabe is not like a Zeppelin, that has to wait for the weather to display his talents, and his flight is sure and strong.

To develop his talents Schwabe in June 1917 took lessons from Nevinson on lithography, in which he was joined by Gertler. Following the lessons they all went back to Gertler's studio where interesting discussions on art ensued.[112] Schwabe also learnt much from Unwin as an etcher and remained in close contact with him till his fatal illness was far advanced; tuberculosis was diagnosed in 1916. They continued to travel at home together and in the summer of 1917 Schwabe took a working holiday with Unwin who was convalescing at Verdley Farm, on the ridge between Haslemere and Midhurst in West Sussex. They had worked together for a summer at Barden in Yorkshire and had joined forces again at Hawsker in 1913.[113]

The ninth exhibition of the London Group was held at the Mansard Gallery – Heal & Son, 196 Tottenham Court Road from 1–29 November, 1918. Serving alongside Schwabe on the hanging committee were Harold Gilman (President of the Group), Robert Bevan (Treasurer), D. Fox-Pitt, Nina Hamnett, S. de Karlowska and E. McKnight Kauffer who also designed the post-card advertising the exhibition. Schwabe had first met McKnight Kauffer in Chelsea about 1914 when he and his wife were driven away from Paris by war conditions; at that time he was painting in the manner of Van Gogh. Schwabe exhibited an oil painting of *Leghorns*. By the time the exhibition closed World War I had ended.

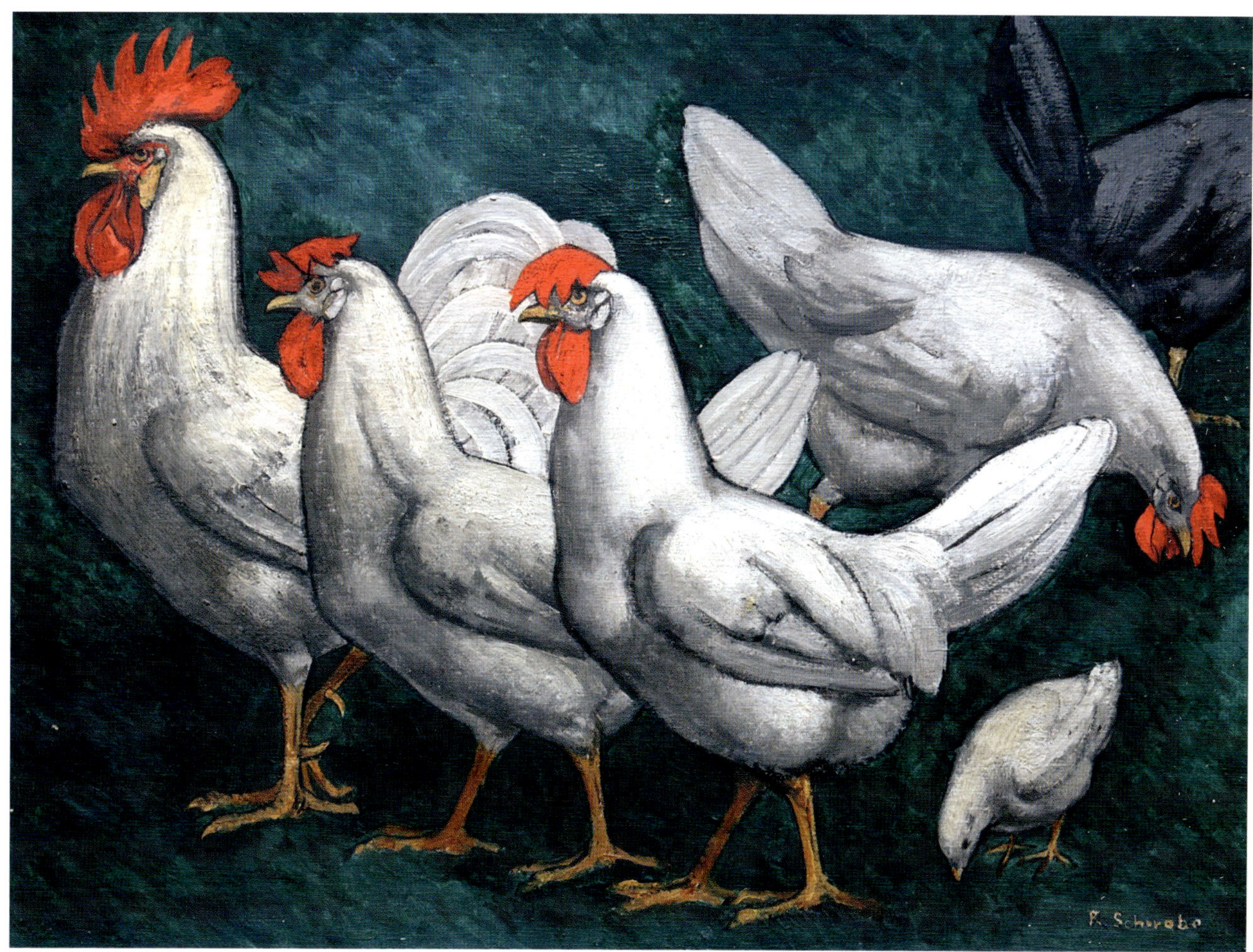

Leghorns
1918 | oil on board | 44 x 59 cm

1   The Times, 14/5/1931, p.12.

2   'The business became subsequently "Ermen & Roby", and was finally absorbed, long after my grandfather's death, in the 1880s, by the English Sewing Cotton Company.' See Schwabe's diary 1948.

3   Schwabe diary 1933. His father died in Buckhurst Hill, Essex.

4   Schwabe had twenty-six uncles and aunts. See Oxford Mail 27/5/1943.

5   Schwabe diary 1938.

6   Barnes, J. (2012) The family of Randolph Schwabe, unpublished paper.

7   The 1901 census lists the family as living at 40, The Marlowes. They likely moved there in 1895.

8   Kelly's Directory 1882.

9   Schwabe letter to Saunders c.1899. Private collection.

10 See the online article on Heath Brow School, The Gazette, Wed. 7 July; published by Dacorum Heritage.

11 The College of Preceptors was founded in 1846, by a group of private schoolmasters from Brighton who were concerned about standards within their profession. It pioneered a system for the formal examination and qualification of secondary school teachers and many acquired the qualifications of the College: ACP (Associate), LCP (Licentiate) and FCP (Fellow). It was also one of the first bodies to examine and provide certificates for secondary school pupils of both sexes, from England and Wales, at different levels, in a variety of subjects. http://www.ioe.ac.uk/services/957. html accessed 24/1/2012.

12 I am grateful to the late Alice, Lady Barnes and Janet Barnes for sharing their memories of their father and grandfather and for lending me Randolph Schwabe's books of newspaper cuttings.

13 Schwabe letter to Saunders, 31/12/1898. Private collection.

14 Schwabe diary 1935.

15 Schwabe's diaries contain a number of references to his school days.

16 A musket shot from the French ship Redoubtable mortally wounded Nelson at the Battle of Trafalgar.

17 Boxmoor Baths were pits which had provided clay for lining the canal; there was a public bath and a private one, with keys available for a small fee. The baths were unheated, weedy and open to fish and were closed in 1937. I am grateful to Aubrey Lawrence for this information.

18 Schwabe letter to Saunders, 12/1/1900. Private collection.

19 Schwabe, R. (1943b) 'Three teachers: Brown, Tonks and Steer', Burlington, June, p.141.

20 Schwabe (1943b) Ibid., p.141.

21 Schwabe (1943b) Ibid., p.141.

22 Schwabe diary 1942.

23 Harte, N. & North, J. (2004) The world of UCL 1828-2004, p.98.

24 Inglis, A. (2004) 'Poynter, Sir Edward John', Oxford Dictionary of National Biography.

25 Wright, H.L. (1931) The etchings, drypoints and lithographs of Alphonse Legros 1837–1911, p.12.

26 The Times, 10/1/1941, p.7.

27 Aitken, C. (1926) 'The Slade School of Fine Arts', Apollo, p.2.

28 O'Keeffe, P. (2000) Some sort of genius: A life of Wyndham Lewis, pp.37–38.

29 Fees for the session October-June 1901 were payable in advance, these amounted to £18 18s – no mean sum for Schwabe's frequently cash-strapped father to find.

30 Janet, Sister (1972) Mother Maribel of Wantage, p.13.

31 Daintrey, A. (1963) I must say, p.54.

32 Blaikley cited in M. Reynolds (1971) The Slade. The story of an art school, 1871–1971, p.277.

33 O'Keeffe (2000) Op. cit., p.30.

34 Horne, J. (1939) The life of Henry Tonks, p.173.

35 Ruck, B. (1959) A smile for the past, p.62.

36 Schwabe (1943b) Op. cit., p.142.

37 Holroyd, M. (1974) Augustus John, Volume 1: The years of innocence, p.42.

38 See Daintrey (1963) Op. cit., p.55.

39 Schwabe (1943b) Op. cit., p.142.

40 Tonks, H. (1929) Notes from 'Wander-Years', Artwork, p.230.

41 Schwabe (1943b) Op. cit., p.142.

42 John, A. (1962) Chiaroscuro: Fragments of autobiography, p.37.

43 Ruck (1959) Op. cit., p.62.

44 Inglis later won several Slade prizes and received an Honorable Mention at the Paris Salon (1928).

45 Horne (1939) Op. cit., p.77.

46 Everett, K. (1951) Bricks and flowers, p.74.

47 Aitken, C. (1926) Op. cit., p.8. Steer was awarded the Order of Merit in recognition of his eminent position in the world of art, both as painter and teacher.

48 Rothenstein, J. (1929/1970) A pot of paint. The artists of the 1890s, p.140.

49 Schwabe (1943b) Op. cit., p.146.

50 Arnold, B. (1981) Orpen: Mirror to an age, p.44.

51 Schwabe (1943b) Op cit., p.142.

52 Schwabe (1943b) Op cit., p.142.

53 Wellington, H.L. (1907) The Slade School summer compositions in J. Fothergill (Ed.) The Slade. A collection of drawings and some pictures done by past and present students of the London Slade School of Art, pp.27–30. Schwabe in his final year at the Slade contributed the title-page.

54 Schwabe diary 1948.

55 Albert Rothenstein and his brother Charles changed their surname to Rutherston on 13 April 1916.

56 Schwabe, R. (1943a) 'Reminiscences of fellow students', Burlington, January, p.6.

57 Reynolds (1971) Op cit., p.154 and Schwabe diary entry 1939.

58 Chambers, E. (2004) Student stars at the Slade 1894–1899 Augustus John and William Orpen, p.23.

59 Oxford Mail, 27/5/1943.

60 Milner, J. (1988) *The studios of Paris. The capital of art in the late nineteenth century*, p.27.
61 Duncan Grant, interview with Tate Archivist Sarah Whitfield, 1970.
62 Schwabe diary 1935.
63 Fehrer, C. (1994) 'Women at the Académie Julian in Paris', *The Burlington*, p.752.
64 Macdonald, S. (2004) *The history and philosophy of art education*, p.284.
65 Steen, M. (1943) *William Nicholson*, p.47.
66 Cited in Macdonald (2004) Op. cit., p.289
67 Milner (1988) Op. cit., p.6.
68 Rothenstein, W. (1931) *Men and Memories: Recollections of William Rothenstein 1872–1900*, p.38.
69 See Schwabe's (1930) review of Strang's book *The printing of etchings and engravings* in Artwork, 24, winter, p.viii.
70 Ruck (1959) Op. cit., p.70. She studied at Julian's in 1904–05.
71 The painting was caricatured in *Punch* 11 May 1910 along with other paintings and retitled *Accompanying under Difficulties*. Schwabe's wife always thought it a good likeness done not long after his student days in Paris.
72 http://en.wikipedia.org/wiki/Le_D%C3%B4me_Caf%C3%A9 accessed 6/7/2011.
73 Slade 1901–03.
74 Schwabe diary 1941.
75 Schwabe diary 1934.
76 Beplate, J. (2011) 'Friends and Fauves', *Times Literary Supplement*, December 23 & 30, p.22.
77 Hobhouse, J. (1989) Op. cit., p.48.
78 Schwabe diary 1934.
79 *Oxford Mail* 27/5/1943.
80 Ibid.
81 See Schwabe, R. (1926) 'Francis Dodd', *Print Collector's Quarterly*, 13, 3.
82 Tennyson, C. (1951) Introduction, *Randolph Schwabe Memorial Exhibition*, The Arts Council of Great Britain, p.3.
83 Schwabe diary 1934.
84 Schwabe diary 1935.
85 Schwabe was listed in the Watercolours, Bianco e Nero section in 1930.
86 *Oxford Mail*, 27/5/1943.
87 Schwabe (1943a) Op cit., p.6.
88 John, A. (1962) Op cit., p.177.
89 Clements (1985) Op. cit., p.77. From 1925 she lived with Roger Fry until his death.
90 Robins, A. (1986) *The New English centenary exhibition*, Christie's, unpaginated.
91 Brown, F. (1930) 'Recollections (II) The early years of the New English Art Club', *Artwork*, p.276.
92 Thornton, A. (1935) *Fifty years of the New English Art Club*, p.10.
93 Bertram, A. (1951) *A century of British painting 1851–1951*, p.64.
94 McConkey, K. (2006) *The New English. A history of the New English Art Club*, p.133.
95 Schwabe diary 1935 & 1938.
96 Letter from Maribel Rough (*Mother Maribel of Wantage*) to Schwabe 19/10/45. Private collection.
97 Jenkins, D.F. & Stephens, C. (Eds) (2004) *Gwen John and Augustus John*, p.186.
98 Schwabe diary 1937.
99 Schwabe diary 1939.
100 Correspondence from Margaret de Villiers (née Cobbe, Schwabe's niece) to the author, January 2012 and see Schwabe's diary 1933 re Bob (Robert) Wellington (founder of the Zwemmer Gallery) talking about the depressing prospects of our younger painters busy with the business of living and domestic chores, pushing perambulators and cleaning studios.
101 Tennyson, H. (1984) *The haunted mind*, p.132.
102 Both now demolished.
103 *Manchester Guardian Weekly* 18 November 1932.
104 Schwabe diary 1935.
105 Schwabe diary 1943: 'Albert says that the drawing by Aug. John, of a whippet, bought by the National Art Collections Fund in 1933, dates from [that] period'.
106 Cross, T. (1992) *Artists and Bohemians: 100 years with the Chelsea Arts Club*, p.59.
107 Hettie wrote to Mr Schwabe when she heard that he had become Professor of the Slade. She said she was 'very pleased. I wish you all were coming in again. I hope Mrs Schwabe is quite well and Miss Alice and also Mrs Gwynne Jones… I do hope you wont think me rude but I felt I must write.' Private collection.
108 Shone, R. (1975) 'The Friday Club', *The Burlington*, pp.279–84.
109 Schwabe (1943a) Op. cit., p.9.
110 Location unknown. I am grateful to Richard Lowndes for bringing this review to my attention having located it in the papers of the artist Camilla Doyle, a friend of the Schwabes.
111 See Thornton (1928) *London Group Retrospective Exhibition 1914–1928* catalogue.
112 See Carrington, N. (Ed.) (1965) *Mark Gertler. Selected letters*, p.147.
113 See Schwabe (1934) 'Francis Sydney Unwin, etcher and lithographer', *Print Collector's Quarterly*, p.59 & p.66.

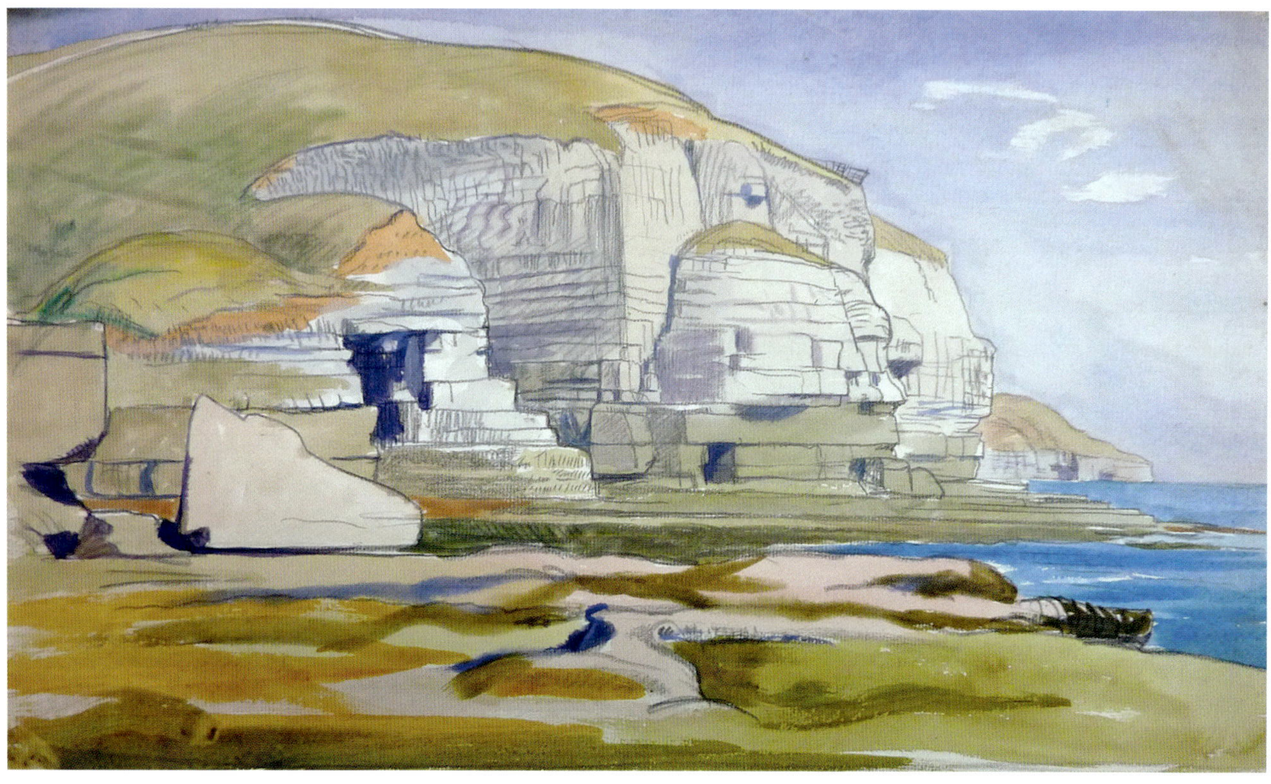

Near Matravers

*c.*1920 | pencil and watercolour | 32.3 x 47.5 cm

TEACHER AND SLADE PROFESSOR

After the war Schwabe with a wife and young daughter to support turned his attention to the business of making a career. He supplemented his income from the sale of paintings shown at the Friday Club, London Group and the New English Art Club by teaching drawing at the Camberwell and Westminster Schools of Art and at the Royal College of Art, South Kensington.

CAMBERWELL SCHOOL OF ARTS AND CRAFTS

Camberwell School of Arts and Crafts was opened in January 1898 in premises adjoining the South London Art Gallery on the Peckham Road. It was, Gilbert Spencer (1891–1959) remembered, a comparatively new building, splendidly solid, the entrance supported by two Herculean figures.[1] The School aimed 'to give the best artistic and technical education to all classes in the district', 'supplement knowledge gained by craftsmen in workshops' and 'help the craftsman become the designer of his own work'.[2] It was Walter Bayes, who had been critical of Schwabe's first exhibition, who got him his first part-time teaching job at Camberwell as art master in 1919. Bayes had changed his opinion about Schwabe's work, having been struck by a decoration he did for an Arts and Crafts Society show at Burlington House in 1916.[3] One of the few practising artists employed at Camberwell, Schwabe worked briefly under William Dalton (b.1863), a sculptor and ceramic decorator who had been the Principal from 1899, and from 1920 under Stanley Thorogood (1873–1953), a notable potter and teacher of pottery. Under Thorogood's direction the study of drawing and painting, commercial art, and crafts such as pottery, dressmaking and embroidery

was extended. The school had 30 workrooms and offered day and evening classes from its foundation.

When teaching drawing at Camberwell in the evenings, Schwabe used to stick photographs of acclaimed artists' work on the wall for his students to study: on one occasion using portraits he bought from the National Gallery by the Italian painter Giovanni Antonio Boltraffio (c.1467–1516) who was Leonardo's principal pupil in Milan. The number of students in his mixed classes varied from 9–20, many of whom were in full-time work in their trades during the day. The wood engraver, painter, designer and illustrator Lynton Lamb (1907–77) was one such, working in an estate office while studying life drawing in the evenings.

Schwabe would often go to The Windsor Castle with Bayes for supper and a drink. On one occasion he met Professor Brown who asked him about 'his doings', and he explained that he was teaching drawing in the LCC (London County Council) Art School. An unexpected gleam came across Brown's face. 'I'm glad to hear it', he remarked. 'We're winning all along the line now.'[4]

Schwabe left Camberwell in 1930 for the Slade. When Thorogood consulted him about his possible successor, he mentioned Ian Strang, William (Willie) Clause (1887–1946) and Frank Medworth (1892–1947) who had studied at Camberwell from 1912–14, stressing them in that order.[5] Clause showed Schwabe a portfolio of his drawings. They were pretty good evidence, Schwabe thought, and, when selected, there were some excellent drawings among them.[6]

The applicants for Schwabe's job included Margaret Barker (b.1907) but Schwabe knew the appointments panel would not consider 'a young girl'. Schwabe admired her work when she had been at the RCA and had persuaded her to show her canvas *Any Morning* at the NEAC in 1929. It was purchased for the Tate through the Chantrey Bequest. Albert Houthuesen (1903–79) and Raymond Coxon (1896–1997), who with Henry Moore (1898–1986) and Leon Underwood (1890–1975) founded the short-lived British Independent Society in 1927, were also interested in the job. Schwabe thought Clause would be a better candidate.

Other artists to show interest included Edgar Ainsworth (1905–75), later art editor of *Picture Post*.[7] Morris Kestelman (1905–98), who had studied at the RCA from 1926–29 and who had developed a particular interest in theatrical design, asked Schwabe if it was any use his applying for the Camberwell job. Schwabe considered him a decent, shy fellow and a promising artist but thought he would not fit in with Thorogood's idea of someone with a reputation.[8] Donald Towner (1903–85) also came to talk about the Camberwell job. Schwabe described the position, laying stress on the already large numbers of applicants and the fact that a specialist in figure drawing was demanded. Towner decided not to apply.[9]

Clause feared he had made a bad impression with Thorogood. It was a mark of Schwabe's loyalty that he tried to find out if this was the case and to put it right if possible.[10]

Schwabe's farewell function to celebrate over a decade of teaching at Camberwell was held on 3 July at The Cheshire Cheese at Wine Office Court off Fleet Street where a dozen or so colleagues enjoyed a dinner of Ye Famous Pie, Ye Pancake and Ye Toasted Cheese.

Thorogood, presenting Schwabe with two pots made in the school, made a complimentary speech and there was 'Much roaring of songs ("Community singing"), George Holland at the piano. Pleasant and amusing.'[11] Notable by his absence was Charles Vyse (1882–1971), the studio potter who had just left Camberwell after five years' service. He had had a major row with Thorogood. Schwabe noted in his diary:

> Thorogood is the old fashioned type of art master who is not interested in art, but merely in running the school, and is, as Vyse says 'sitting on a cushion and waiting for a pension'. Vyse has the loyal support of his few students, and is one of the keenest, most valuable and disinterested teachers the place has had.[12]

WESTMINSTER SCHOOL OF ART

Bayes was also instrumental in Schwabe's obtaining work at the Westminster School of Art in Vincent Square where he was Principal, having succeeded the painter Mouat Loudan (d.1925) in 1918. He had been Brown's pupil at Westminster from 1900–02. Brown before taking up the reins of the Slade had 'from the smallest beginnings… made… [Westminster] the most important school in England, exclusively for figure drawing and painting.'[13] The atmosphere at Westminster was, according to Alfred Thornton (1863–1939), a former student and assistant, different from that of the Slade and most of the students had to make a living from their work.[14]

Schwabe was a sympathetic teacher and well suited to the atmosphere. He was now concentrating more on drawing with pen, his brown ink specially made by Stephens, and with pencil and water-colour, often using antique paper. On a visit to Dedham in September 1930 he bought from the antique shop some albums of old paper which had belonged about 1830 to an artist called Glennie. He wrote in his diary 'History will repeat itself in some junk shop in 2030 A.D.' Westminster had a particular system of drawing from the mirror, and drawing everything together, figures and surroundings, which Bayes had inherited from Sickert. Bayes, Schwabe noticed, was always encouraging the students to do it – and there was a long mirror for the purpose which could be adjusted anywhere and to any angle. It was, Schwabe believed, an aftermath of the Camden Town Group, of which Bayes had been a founder member.[15]

Some of the artists Schwabe taught and who went on to forge successful careers included David Jones (1895–1974) and the designer and graphic artist James Gardner (1907–95). In 1930 when Schwabe was editor of *Artwork* he chose, with Jones, some of his work for reproduction in an article he had commissioned by Eric Gill.[16] Gardner recalled how Schwabe 'would stroll over, gently pin a fresh sheet of paper over my tentative effort, and commencing with her left foot would slowly work up the figure to produce a drawing as precise as silverpoint – like a conjuring trick'.[17]

Later at Westminster, Schwabe recommended his friend Clause to Bayes as a possible successor to himself, but Bayes wanted Wyndham Lewis. Schwabe appreciated his point, recognising that Lewis would be a good draw. Bayes also wanted to keep Schwabe's post open for a bit, so that Bernard Meninsky, who had replaced Sickert as teacher of life drawing in 1920, might temporarily have some extra work.

At The Windsor Castle, Schwabe spoke briefly with Bayes who, he thought, had been overworking lately with lectures, journalism, painting and teaching. Schwabe perceived that this healthy energetic man had a hard life and a cynical good temper and noted that, at 61, Bayes ran up the stairs of the tall Westminster building at a pace he hoped he might equal at that age.[18]

THE ROYAL COLLEGE OF ART

Schwabe was appointed to the Royal College of Art (RCA) by the Principal William Rothenstein in 1921 as a part-time assistant on a salary of £240 for teaching two days a week. The College at that time comprised four principal Schools – Design, Architecture, Sculpture and Painting, presided over respectively by Robert Anning Bell (1863–1933), Beresford Pite (1861–1934), Francis Derwent Wood (1871–1926) and Gerald Moira (1867–1951). Engraving under Sir Francis (Frank) Short (1857–1945)[19] later became a full-time school. Rothenstein over the course of his 15 years at the College sought to change it 'from being in large part a training school for teachers to an active school for practical designers and artists.'[20] Schwabe was one of his carefully chosen and highly skilled assistants, for Rothenstein 'had a conviction that students would and could learn only from teachers whose own achievements they respected.' As John Piper (1903–92), a student from 1928–29, noted Rothenstein 'transformed the "climate" of the Royal College, and made a total change from the high, stiff-collared teaching of earlier days.'[21] He employed part-time practising artists and designers – an innovation at that time – many of whom were former RCA students. Such changes attracted a rich intake of highly talented students including Henry Moore in 1921; a colleague of Schwabe's from 1924.

Eric Ravilious (1903–42) and Donald Towner, both from Eastbourne School of Art, took the entrance test together and spent the day at South Kensington drawing from a nude model. Edward Burra (1905–76) joined them; while the pair each completed a drawing of the figure which occupied virtually the whole sheet of cartridge paper Burra drew exquisitely a small eye in the centre of the paper.[22] They all passed and worked alongside distinguished fellow students such as Edward Bawden (1903–89), Percy Horton (1897–1970), Douglas Percy Bliss (1900–84) and Vivian Pitchforth (1895–1982). Burra recalled that Schwabe and Coxon, an ex-RCA student, were his principal drawing tutors and in particular that Schwabe was interested in theatre-design.[23] Towner, a friend and neighbour of Schwabe when he moved in 1928 to 20 Church Row in Hampstead, was well taught by Schwabe of an evening. The move came about as a result of Enid Morse, the landscape painter, to whom the Schwabes had let the top studio in Cheyne Walk, setting fire to it.[24] Towner's work for the College Sketch Club was praised by *The Times*' critic, although he stressed that 'Mr Towner has not yet got over the difficulty of bringing sky and solid objects into the same convention, but his work impresses by the variety he gets into his colour without losing its constructive function.'[25] Another of Schwabe's students who had favourable memories of his teaching was the 'precocious and conscientious' illustrator, painter and print maker Stanley Badmin (1906–89) who had won a scholarship to the College in 1924; he described him as 'a fantastic draughtsman and a wonderful illustrator, especially in the figure drawing'.[26] They were to remain close friends and Schwabe later tried to encourage Hugh Dent (1874–1938), son of the publisher and editor of the Everyman's Library series and whose portrait

he had undertaken, to buy one of Badmin's drawings which was 'a very pleasant view of Burford Street.'[27] Edward Pullée (1907–2002), another scholarship holder, was strongly influenced by Schwabe and went on to be the youngest college principal in the country in 1934 when he was appointed to the Gloucester School of Art.[28]

Helen Binyon (1904–79) who entered the Design School on the same day in September 1922 as Ravilious recalled that all new students:

> *found that for their first term they were all to work in the School of Architecture for an introductory course under Professor Beresford Pite. That was to be for four days a week, from half-past nine in the morning to half-past three in the afternoon, and then drawing classes from four to six in the evening.*[29]

The intention was not to produce architects but to 'bring home the importance of planning in every branch of visual creation and to emphasize the special relation between the other arts and architecture itself.'[30] Schwabe assisted in the drawing classes, alongside Allan Gwynne-Jones and (Walter) Thomas Monnington (1902–76, RCA 1928–29). Rothenstein had by then taken over running the School of Drawing and Painting. Gwynne-Jones took over as Professor in 1929. As a distinguished artist Rothenstein provided inspiration and criticism, for not only would he advise but he would also drop into classes and demonstrate. It was through Schwabe and his other trusted assistants such as Leon Underwood that Rothenstein 'kept his fingers on the pulse of the College, even though he might be working in his studio and his fingers be otherwise engaged'.[31]

Schwabe enjoyed the company of his fellow colleagues, often lunching at The Clan with sculptor Alan Durst (1883–1970) who taught woodcarving, Hubert Wellington registrar and lecturer in art, Harding instructor in the School of Architecture, his new Professor W.G. Newton, Moore and Gwynne-Jones. After lunch he would go for the usual glass of sherry with Moore and Durst. Tea was frequently taken with Charlie Mahoney (1903–68)[32] and Horton, who in January 1930 was painting Ishbel MacDonald, daughter of Prime Minister, Ramsay MacDonald. Horton had given up his teaching at Bishop's Stortford on starting at the RCA. Towner took on the two days' work as he needed 'extra money, having little, and selling less'.[33] The economic slump of c.1924–34 which accompanied 'the changing social and political pressures of the Depression forced a crisis in the economic and cultural consumption of Modern Art which was primarily registered in a collapse in the London art market'[34] and was starting to impact on practising artists such as Towner. On another occasion Schwabe, Mahoney and Horton were joined by Rothenstein who 'brought in Gilbert Spencer, whom he was showing round as a prospective addition to the Staff, in place of Alston, who retires at the end of the summer';[35] Schwabe had heard that Bawden was coming on the Staff of the Design School too. He was pleased when Mahoney and Horton, after their holiday in Paris and Chartres, brought him some photographs of drawings by Ingres.

Schwabe was also an assistant in the School of Design under Ernest William Tristram (1882–1952) who had replaced Anning Bell on his retirement. Schwabe took the opportunity to speak to him about the students' lack of principle and structural knowledge in pattern designing. Tristram used to put students through a couple of questions about geometric bases, and he agreed it was time that some such thing was revived.[36]

Schwabe was frequently called upon for testimonials. He wrote one for Stanley Lewis (1905–2009) who in 1930 was runner-up for the prestigious Rome Scholarship: 'Mr Lewis is an able draughtsman and has undertaken large and ambitious figure paintings with much interest in the composition of them. His work is entirely sincere and straightforward…'.[37] He also wrote a testimonial for Henry Bird (1909–2000) who had been awarded the Travelling Scholarship in June 1930: 'He has done some remarkable drawings, but his sense of colour is beastly.'[38]

EXHIBITIONS AND PORTRAIT COMMISSIONS

Despite his teaching commitments, Schwabe exhibited widely during the 1920s and 30s. He was a member of the Council and the Artists' Committee of the Arts League of Service (ALS), serving alongside J.D. Fergusson, E. McKnight Kauffer and Edward Wadsworth. The ALS 'was at the cutting edge of cultural life in Britain from the time it was founded in 1919' by Miss Ana Berry who had come over from South America to Europe to study art and 'who became the driving force behind the Art Section of the League.'[39] The ALS sought to 'bring the public into closer touch with the artists – particularly the younger ones'.[40] Schwabe along with more than a hundred painters, sculptors, writers and their friends attended the first – and last – public meeting of the ALS in spring 1919 at the Margaret Morris Theatre where Wyndham Lewis outlined a policy of decentralisation.[41] Through its

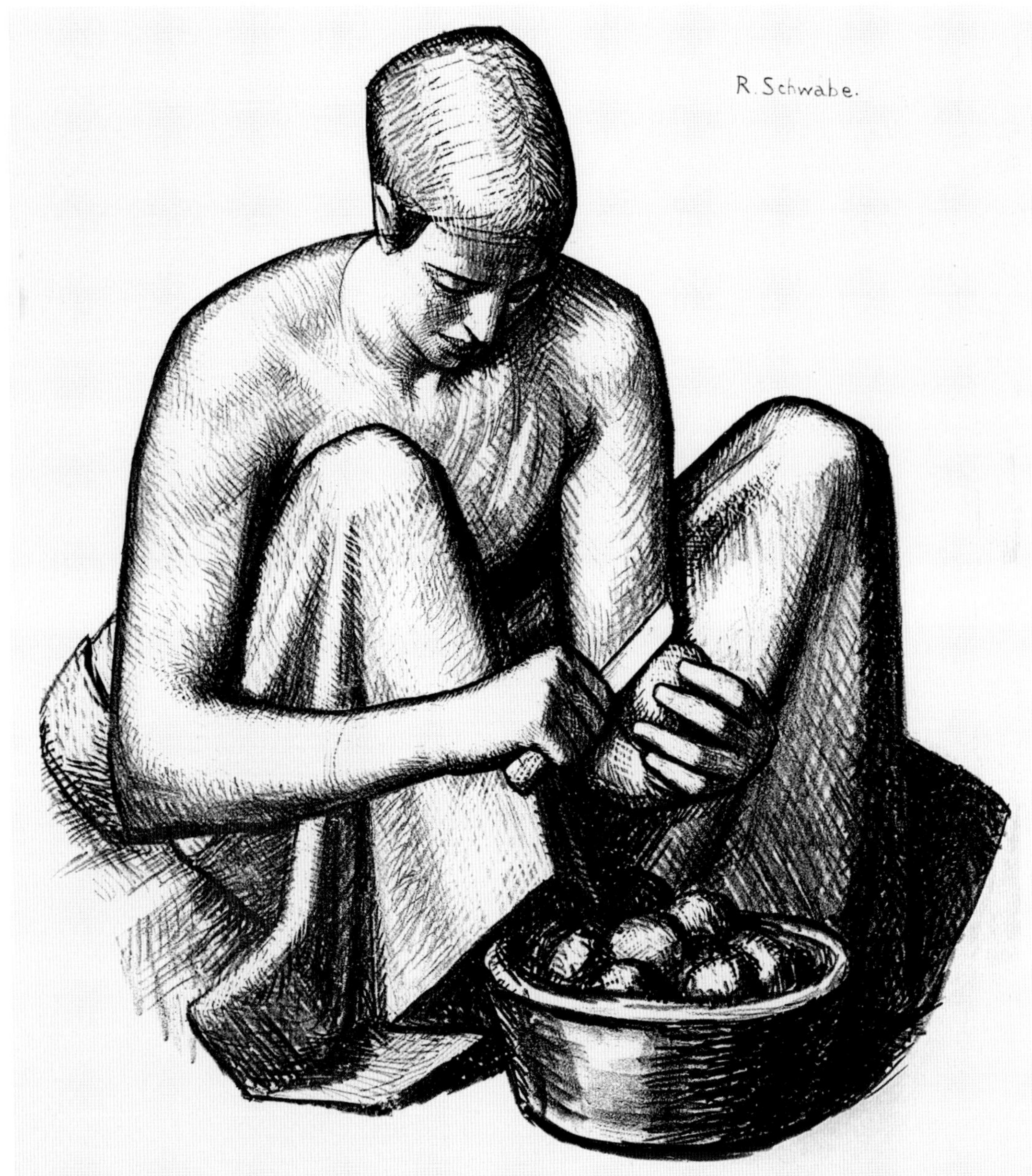

Peeling Potatoes
1917 | lithograph | 43 × 38 cm
COLLECTION JANET AND DI BARNES

Travelling Portfolios of Pictures scheme, water-colours, drawings, wood-cuts, lithographs and engravings by well-known contemporary artists were sent all over the country and could be kept by applicants for one week, the price of pictures ranged from one to fifteen guineas.[42] Eleanor Elder pioneered a Travelling Theatre section which provided entertainment in country districts; in addition lectures were given on subjects bearing on art. In the landmark 1919 exhibition at the Twenty-One Gallery of articles of everyday use designed by artists, Schwabe contributed an ebony and a painted inkstand; Birdie contributed two illuminated manuscripts with Allan Gwynne-Jones who did the lettering for her miniatures. The Art Section had its heyday in the 1920s; in December 1924 one portfolio contained drawings and engravings by established artists including Duncan Grant, Charles Ginner, Schwabe and Paul and John Nash. It closed when Berry returned to South America and no one emerged to take her place.[43] The League itself continued to 1937.

Schwabe became involved with the South London Group (SLG) which was formed in 1920, 'primarily with the object of bringing before the public the works of artists associated in the past with the Camberwell School of Arts and Crafts.'[44] Schwabe served as President of the Selection Committee in 1931. Dalton was President and Thorogood Vice-President.

A notable event in October 1923 was the fuss created by Schwabe's oil painting *The Girl and the Lamb* which had been purchased by the Contemporary Art Society (CAS) whose aim:

> was to encourage by purchase and exhibition the more remarkable examples of painters who in any other country would enjoy a

> certain official patronage... The Committee... believes that with the exercise of discrimination pictures by contemporary artists should be purchased in ordered to supply what may seem to posterity an inexcusable gap in our public museums and galleries...[45]

The painting of a nude girl holding a lamb in her arms was offered by the CAS to the Oldham Gallery but the chairman of the Art Gallery Committee, Mr Alderman Brierley, declined the offer. The *Manchester Guardian* reported Schwabe's surprise that 'such an early insignificant little work should have created such a big stir.' 'If the picture had been offered to Manchester or one of the big cities I doubt whether anything would have been heard of the matter.' *The Girl and the Lamb* languished in the cellars of the Tate Gallery for some time before it was accepted by Bradford Museums and Galleries in August 1927.

Schwabe held his second one-man show, in Old Bond Street at the Redfern Gallery, from 26 February–18 March 1924. Entitled *Drawings* it was an opportunity to generate further public interest in his work and for potential buyers, patrons and of course critics to assess how the work was developing. William Rothenstein wrote the catalogue entry and said that Schwabe:

> uses drawing as a language. He has wise and interesting things to tell us and he conveys his meaning in straightforward lines and forms... [his] drawings have a quiet strength and authority which entitle them to particular respect. His etchings of London, while preserving topographical accuracy, have a dramatic quality which to-day, by reason of the destruction of the buildings represented, gives them an added value. Their artistic distinction comes as a natural accompaniment to his concentration on the subject before him.

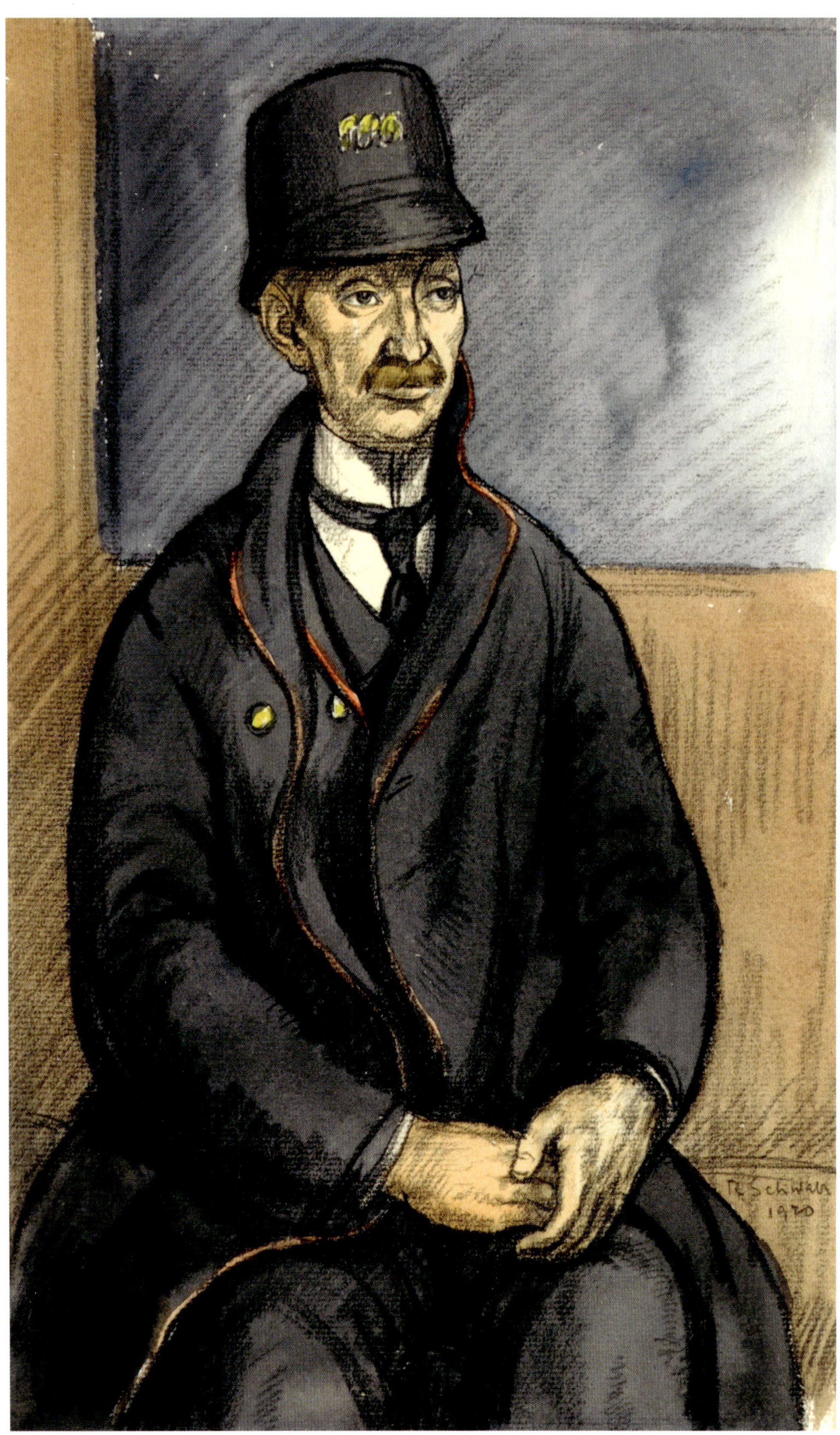

The Postman
1920 | pencil and watercolour | 32.5 × 20 cm

Such was Schwabe's total concentration when working that he would be unaware of his surroundings. Once, when he set up his easel on the island in Piccadilly Circus, Birdie got a lift down to Piccadilly Circus to deliver his lunch. They went round and round the island three or four times shouting before he noticed them.[46]

Fortunately Schwabe was noticed positively by the critics, who wielded much influence; *The Times'* critic pointed that, although during the past 12 months they had been disappointed by the drawing in Schwabe's water-colours where bits of what looked like laborious fumbling spoilt ambitious designs, there was nothing of that sort in his show of drawings and etchings:

> *the impression one gets is that, looking very closely at an actual subject–figure-study, portrait, landscape — he is so delighted with its contours and masses that the lines draw themselves, swinging along in glad ease… This succinctness and liveliness of statement, with no show of force or forcing, are very refreshing. Such simple delight in the object, and such direct desire to record and fix by making a new thing are rare.*

In a newspaper cutting from Schwabe's scrapbook about his *Drawings* exhibition the unnamed reviewer praised his drawings: they were the sort of thing one would like to live with on a rainy day while the landscapes in monochrome gave 'great delight'. The elements in *The Mill, Heyshott; Cocking Mill-Pond, Cottages, Dunford-Front View; West Mersea Regatta* and *Cottages, Dunford-Back View* were 'concerted into harmonies of light and happiness'. Schwabe's keen eye for character was also highlighted and specifically the expression of *Mrs Sargant Florence* (1857–1954, herself an artist who lived close to Schwabe in Cheyne Row), *The Postman*

and *The Unprepossessing Child*. It is not known whether sales were good but all were priced between 8–10 guineas. Another cutting said:

> *While adhering to the best traditions of the Slade School, Mr Schwabe is a draughtsman of sobriety and strength, whose work is certainly not lacking in personal force. He has in him the makings of a distinguished portrait-painter, for his portrait drawings and figure studies are the most impressive of his exhibits… we feel that the artist's real strength is in actuality… and that his future lies in the direction of portraiture and the portrayal of 'things seen'.*

The following month Schwabe exhibited with the short-lived Modern English Watercolour Society;[47] his *Near Matravers*, a study of sandy cliffs in Dorset, was lauded by *The Times'* critic for the way he had got 'into landscape the grasp of structure which he displays in the figure.'[48] The Schwabe family had holidayed with Charles Rennie Mackintosh and his wife Margaret Macdonald in Worth Matravers in July 1920. Mackintosh made sketches and watercolours and it is likely that Schwabe undertook this drawing at the same time.[49] Alice recalled that they all visited the Newberys in Corfe Castle.[50] Francis (Fra) Newbery (1855–1946) had moved there after he retired as Headmaster and Director of Glasgow School of Art with his wife the artist and embroiderer Jessie Newbery (1864–1948) who had established the Embroidery Department at Glasgow School of Art in 1894.

Schwabe contributed several lithographs to the first exhibition of the Society of Print-makers, held at St George's Gallery, 32A, George Street in May 1924. His fellow exhibitors – John Nash, Maresco Pearce, Charles Ginner, Robert Bevan, Lucien Pissarro,

Edward Wadsworth and Ethelbert White – were all members of the Modern English Watercolour Society. *The Times'* critic wrote 'All are good draughtsmen, most have something original to say, and they say it idiomatically.'[51] The works were hung in groups and Schwabe and Unwin were deemed to have produced the most massive effect, the former with *Standing Figure* and *Peeling Potatoes* and the latter with *The Wetterhorn*, also a lithograph.

Later that year Schwabe's reputation was further consolidated with the publication by Ernest Benn of *Draughtsmen*, one of a series on Contemporary British Artists under the general editorship of his old friend Albert Rutherston. The 28-page monograph was priced at 8s. 6d. and contained 36 plates, the author R.H.W. (Reginald Howard Wilenski) focused also on Henry Rushbury, Leon Underwood and Edna Clarke Hall. The art critic for the *Manchester Guardian* on 9 September 1924 commented on the power of the draughtsmanship:

> These artists are alike only in that each of them has a sense
> of style and that each uses drawing not for mere display of
> skill but to give definite form to a personal vision of the world.
> All the drawings are worth examining. Mr. Schwabe is, in
> a good sense, the most academic of the artists represented; Mr.
> Rushbury's fine landscape drawings are well known; Mrs. Clarke
> Hall's draughtsmanship has a refinement and individuality that
> deserves wider recognition; Mr. Underwood's gift is perhaps
> rather perverse, but his drawings have an undeniable power.

Schwabe continued to exhibit prolifically with the NEAC over the next decade. In 1925 he showed in the summer and winter shows and had five watercolours or drawings accepted in each. On 11 April he received a charming letter from Fred Brown:

> I am very pleased to be the possessor of your admirable drawing
> of ballet dancers at the NEAC – it is well drawn, witty &
> xcellently [sic] composed – & in sentiment irreproachable –
> It is I feel, too much undervalued, so I propose to offer it again
> for sale at a much higher figure to any one who might be anxious
> to possess it, & needless to say, if successful the xtra [sic] money
> would go to you & I might have some little sketch or drawing
> as compensation for my giving up a drawing I should be/or am
> proud to possess – with kind regards to your wife and yourself.

Mixed reviews accompanied Schwabe's exhibition at St George's Gallery in Hanover Square in February 1926 which he shared with fellow draughtsman Charles Ginner. Herbert Furst writing in *Apollo* acknowledged that:

> There are a few things by Mr Randolph Schwabe… which
> are decidedly worth noticing, such as the old, but pleasant,
> design 'Musidora', an etching, and several others such as the
> Méryonesque[52] 'Piccadilly Circus'. Also a very few competent
> drawings, for example 'Petersfield, the Square'. His water-colours
> are less distinguished. But Mr Schwabe's genius is commencing
> to become puzzling: for years now he has held out the promise
> of great things: he still does, but are we never to see fulfilment?

The Times' critic while echoing some of Furst's sentiments noted that 'There is a certain sympathy between them [Schwabe and Ginner] in their unflinching honesty and thoroughness, but they differ considerably in aims and methods: Mr. Schwabe being more varied, more stylish, and more obviously concerned with aesthetic require-ments.' He singled out an important part of Schwabe's work – etching – and described *The Quadrant, Regent Street* as 'a remarkably fine performance.' He hoped that the British Museum had a proof of it: the Contemporary Art Society gave it to the British Museum in 1930.

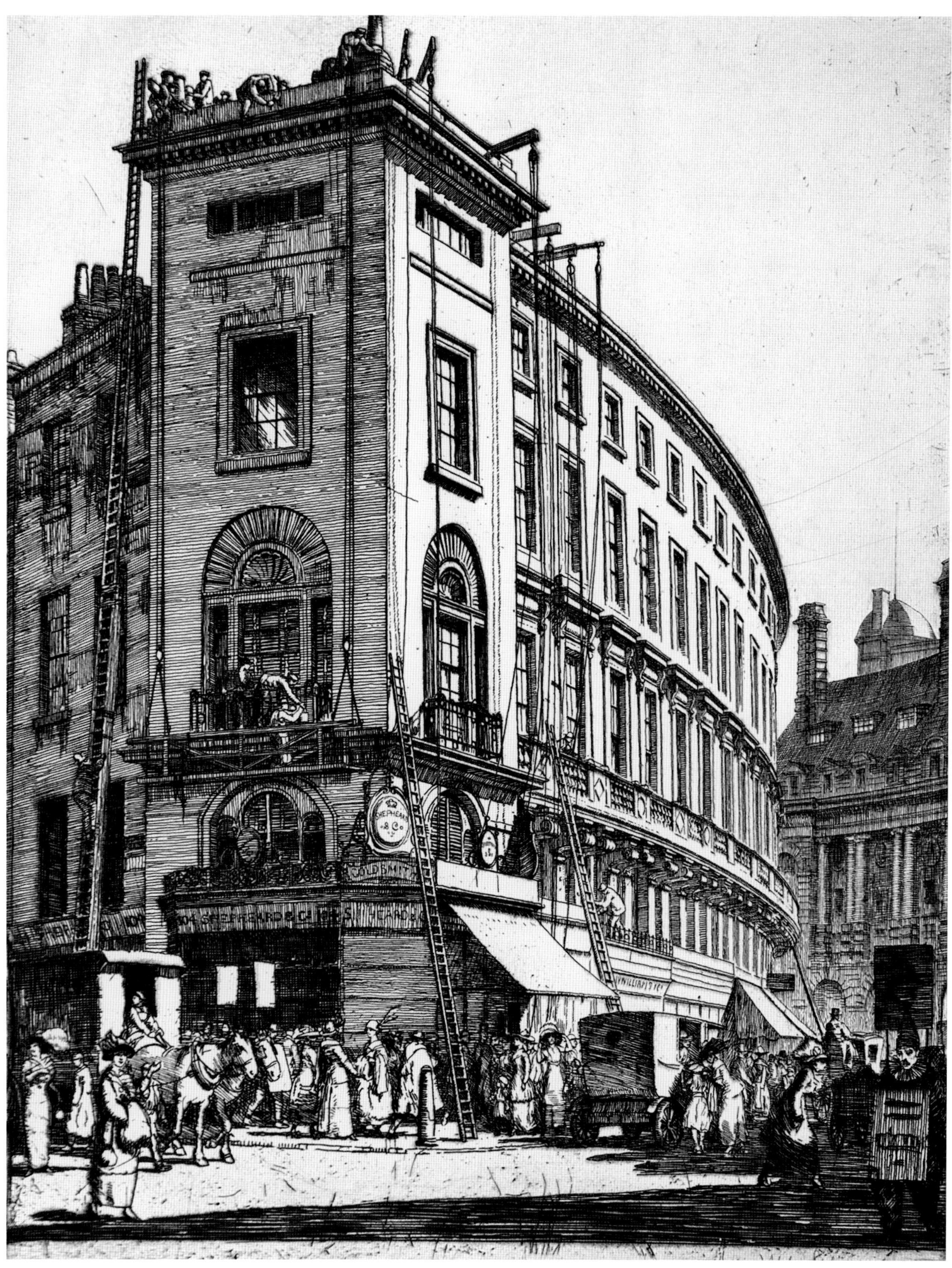

The Quadrant, Regent Street
1912 | etching | 33.3 × 25.8 cm

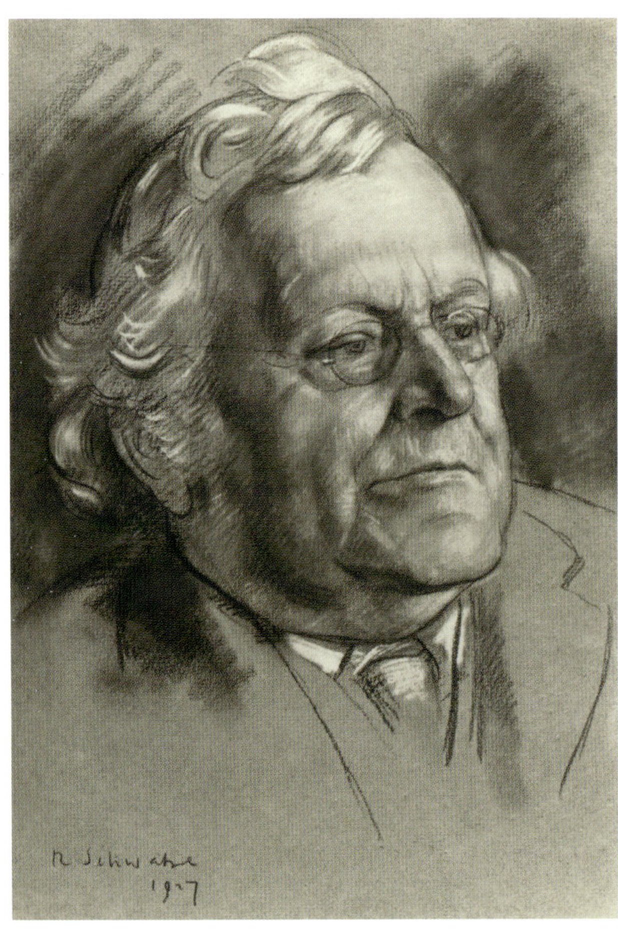

Augustine Birrell
1927 | coloured chalk | 45.7 x 63.5 cm
COLLECTION JANET AND DI BARNES

Schwabe was involved in helping lesser-known British artists through a series of exhibitions organised by Sir Joseph Duveen. He served on the selection committee alongside Orpen (Chairman), John, Epstein, Connard and Tonks. The first exhibition was held at Leeds Art Gallery in April 1927. Some 1,400 pictures were submitted and 325 were selected, with a price limit of £50. By June four exhibitions had been held across the country. It was something of a bad month for Schwabe as he was run over by a car. In a letter to the publisher Cyril Beaumont on the day that it happened he said '[I] feel as if I had been knocked out by a heavy weight and kicked in a football scrum... I know nothing whatever about it − was completely gaga for a quarter of an hour.'

The London Group held a 10-year Retrospective Exhibition in April–May 1928 at the New Burlington Galleries. Schwabe was a member of the Executive Committee together with Allinson, Bayes, Fry, Meninsky, Thornton, Walton and Wolfe. Roger Fry wrote in the catalogue, 'we may say that the London Group has done for Post-Impressionism in England what the New English Art Club did, in a previous generation, for Impressionism.' Schwabe exhibited in the Oil Paintings section *Braunton, Devon*, which he had painted in 1915 (priced £35), in the Drawings and Watercolours section *Pastoral* 1925 (£15 guineas) and he loaned the lithograph *The Bath* (1917).

The year closed with great sadness with the death of his close friend Charles Rennie Mackintosh from cancer of the tongue on 10 December 1928. Schwabe, together with Jessie Newbery and Margaret Morris, had 'tried to help him learn again how to speak'.[53] Schwabe recorded in his diary that:

When Birdie saw Margaret Mackintosh after Toshie died, Margaret told her not to take his loss hardly — she herself thought it a relief: 'Fancy — Toshie free from pain!' But it broke Margaret. The constant attention and strain were too much for her.

Schwabe always regretted that he had never drawn Mackintosh.

Schwabe undertook a number of portrait commissions to supplement his income, including two for Trinity College, Cambridge which in 1926 had inaugurated a series of portrait drawings of distinguished Fellows and Honorary Fellows. The architect and designer Edward Maufe (1883–1974) had suggested him. The artists already represented included Clausen, Rothenstein, Dodd, Kennington, Lamb and Eric Gill.

In 1929 Arthur Mayger Hind, Slade Professor at Oxford 1921–27, writing a review in *Artwork* of the recent portrait drawings thought the soundest in style and best balanced in design were the two by Schwabe of Dr Walter Leaf (1852–1927, Chairman of the National Westminster Bank) and Sir Ernest Rutherford (1871–1937, Nobel Prize winner for Chemistry in 1908). Hind praised Schwabe's broad and thoroughly considered touch. The Marquis of Hartington was also complimentary about Schwabe's Trinity drawings and visited him at the Royal College of Art on 17 March 1930 to see if he would be interested in undertaking portrait drawings for Grillion's Club, of which he was the secretary. Hartington was apologetic about the price offered – 15 guineas. Although Trinity paid £20, Schwabe was willing to accept the commission. He was apprehensive about maintaining a sequence of portraits of members of the club as so many of

them were put off by the works of Sir Frank Dicksee (1853–1928), who had lately been 'artist-in-ordinary' and had not give much satisfaction. Earlier drawings had been done by Joseph Slater, George Richmond and Henry Tanworth Wells. Schwabe showed Hartington a photograph of his drawing of the author and politician Augustine Birrell (1850–1933), whom Hartington knew.

Grillion's Club originated in 1812 in London as a dining club and meeting place for political members. It took its name from the Grillion's Hotel where members met from 1813. A resolution passed in 1826 established the tradition of commissioning an engraved portrait of each member.[54] As the Club was hesitant, Schwabe sent Hartington some photographs of portrait drawings, at his request, to impress members. Two weeks later Schwabe heard that he had been accepted as 'artist–in–ordinary'. Hartington wrote to members reminding them of the rule about portraits and informing them that they might choose their own artist, but that Schwabe had agreed to draw any member at 15 guineas, considerably less than his normal fee. Schwabe was familiar with the series of drawings, and his work would harmonise with any portraits already in existence. Members wasted no time and by 1 May Schwabe had his 'first victim a gentleman called Warren Hastings'. Schwabe thought he would be a good head to draw. Hartington also sent him letters from Lord Cromer, Lady Lyttelton (about her husband); and another from Lord Newton. Schwabe visited the Grillion Clubroom at Grosvenor House Hotel and observed 'one rather poor thing by Legros and a lot of Dicksees'. Not all his portraits were successful. Lord Fiztalan told Schwabe that he should not have recognised himself in the drawing and more-

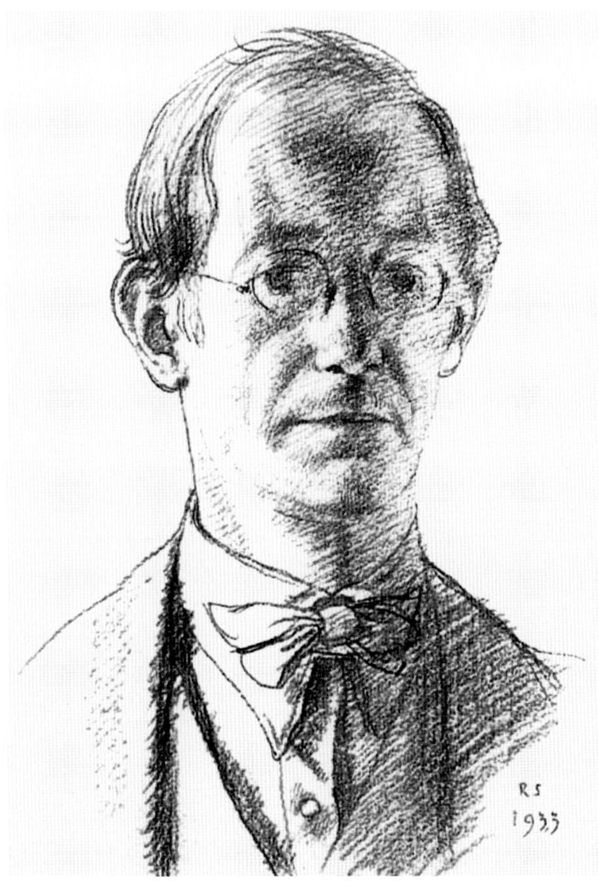

Self Portrait
1933 | sanguine | 20.5 x 17.5 cm

over when Lady Fitzalan visited she said in no uncertain terms that she thought both drawings horrible. Fortunately she thought the new drawing Schwabe was doing was distinctly better.

In April 1930 the Goupil Gallery was the location of Schwabe's last exhibition in England before he took up the Slade Professorship. He was sharing the exhibition with Neville Lewis (1895–1972), whose paintings he considered shallow and sometimes vulgar. MacColl came in, unexpectedly, to offer condolences about John Yockney, the manager of the Goupil who had worked with Goupil and Co. since 1891 and who had died suddenly of heart failure the previous Wednesday. Schwabe thought it almost painless, and a good way of dying. He was rather perturbed as MacColl looked hastily at a few of his drawings but did not say much. He was sure he did not like the elaborate ones. Eddie Marsh (1872–1973), civil servant and patron of the arts, came in too. Schwabe remembered disagreeing with Marsh over an Ingres, which Marsh thought laboured and 'studentish'. Marsh, he recollected, had theories about the 'tempo' of good drawings, and preferred the more spontaneous. But in Schwabe's view if it was in one's nature to be 'dull' (in his own case, he meant) it was better to be dull than to try for something not in one's nature.

The private view at the Goupil on 3 April was well attended, Schwabe having sent out over 100 invitations, but the only sale was a drawing of *Chelsea Old Church* at £21. It reminded Schwabe of J.D. Fergusson's show in Glasgow, which Fergusson told him was 'a terrific <u>success</u>': Schwabe asked if it had sold well? Fergusson replied 'Oh no, I didn't sell anything, but it was a <u>terrific</u> success.'

The exhibition generated considerable, but mixed, press interest. The influential critic Frank Rutter writing in the *Sunday Times* observed:

Like his predecessor, Mr Tonks, in the Chair of Art at the Slade, Mr Randolph Schwabe has spent so much of his time in helping other artists to improve their practice, that his own output of works is severely restricted. It is one of the misfortunes of our time that artists of genuine talent produce comparatively little, while painters of no talent at all are able, and even encouraged to produce much. The small collection of Professor Schwabe's water-colours and drawings, now being exhibited at the Goupil gallery enables us to see how well qualified he is to teach others, and we feel that in his hands the great tradition of the Slade School for good draughtsmanship will be ably maintained. His classical sense of form can be seen in such accomplished figure drawings as his 'Standing Nude' in sanguine, and 'The Armchair'. His 'Dover, Alexandra House' displays not only the probity of his architectural draughtsmanship, but also his ability to organise brilliant colour into a vivacious synthesis of sparkling sunlight. Another water-colour 'Chelsea Old Church', in lower tones, combines tenderness of colouring with severity of draughtsmanship. Professor Schwabe in the main adheres to the ideals of the early English water-colourists, as we see, for example, in his scholarly monochrome of 'Chelsea Backs'; but one remembers having seen on rare occasions strong, individual paintings from his brush, so there is room for hope that this modest collection of his drawings may be the prelude to some future exhibition of his work in oils.

The *Observer's* critic Paul G. Konody commented on the 'absolute artistic integrity' of Schwabe's water-colours and drawings of landscape, architectural, and figure subjects. These he contended showed the artist's admirable fitness for his new post as professor at the Slade School. It had:

been the tradition of the Slade for many years to concentrate on the development of the student's efficiency in draughtsmanship – perhaps even at the expense of their training as painters. Mr Schwabe may be relied upon to uphold this time-honoured tradition. His exhibition proves him to be a draughtsman who combines a keen sense of form with meticulous accuracy in the rendering of tactfully selected details. And they have real style – which is a very different thing from a deliberate striving for stylishness.

Walter Bayes informed Schwabe that he been critical about one of his drawings in the *Week-End Review*, but he was reassured that there was a good notice in *The Times*. Bayes asked his readers:

to judge for themselves whether there is not 'something about' this old fashion of taking trouble in drawing a scene… The Slade School has dominated British Art now for so long… Its particular vice is that of perpetual contour drawing from the posed model, with an attention to suavity of curvature which tends to lull the axial sense. Mr Schwabe sins less in this respect than most men who have come out of the Slade, but I think that in so accomplished a drawing as 'The Empire Chair,' he had forgotten by the time he came to the foot and ankle of the girl's crossed legs which foot he was drawing… I take this as indicating that Mr. Schwabe has done for the moment as much drawing from the model as is good for him. The remark comes ill from me, perhaps, who was in the first instance responsible for luring him into the teaching profession, of which he is now so accepted as an ornament.

In May 1935 Schwabe had an exhibition of drawings and prints in the Print Room at the Museo Nacional de Arte Moderno, Madrid. The catalogue explained that:

True to its intention to alternate the national with the foreign, today the turn has been accorded to an English artist, who is a master in his field… it is art which deserves to be known and studied attentively for its undeniable strength, for its precision and love of the stark truth, at times dry and hard, even sour, which enlighten you.

Professor Randolph Schwabe is the perfect English islander, and his drawings and prints have been born in his island as typical products of England. They have been executed conscientiously, with strict thoroughness and with a skilled hand, which to Spaniards, restless and brutal, appears perhaps a little cold. Nevertheless, the artist as a good Englishman, does not lack sentimentality in any of his works.

Look at his landscapes. Schwabe loves the meadows of his country, permanently green and damp, shaded by thick trees, undulating and limitless, he loves their melancholy, their quiet grandeur, their peaceful, noble spaciousness.

Sometimes his landscapes derive from the classical Dutch, but it is not just in the method of drawing, but in feeling that they are typically English.

The English urban landscapes by Professor Schwabe also give an honest interpretation. Whoever sees these landscapes with their provincial houses, and their weighty monuments, can say he has seen and knows something of England.

As a draughtsman, Randolph Schwabe follows the great tradition of English drawing, rigorously precise, constructive, bold and steady.[55]

SLADE PROFESSOR

The turning point in Schwabe's career occurred in late February 1930 with his appointment as Professor and Principal of the Slade School, succeeding Tonks from 1 August for seven years in the first instance at an annual salary of £1,200. One of his sponsors was William Rothenstein who made the point that, 'Drawing is the tradition of the Slade School and Schwabe is a dignified and scholarly draughtsman.

He also has a wide and impartial outlook on the arts, and a generous sympathy for gallant experimentation as for disciplined achievement.'[56]

Tonks' retirement had been reported in the *Manchester Guardian* on 9 October 1929 as was the rumour that 'Mr Randolph Schwabe, of the Royal College of Art, is likely to be his successor.' Rothenstein told Schwabe that Wellington was competing for the Professorship and that [Eric] Maclagan, [Sir Charles John] Holmes and MacColl were on the Advisory Board. Albert Rutherston later wrote Schwabe a 'very decent frank letter' to tell him that his name was also on the list for the Slade. Albert, as he was known to friends, did not consider that he had the smallest chance of being appointed but he wanted Schwabe to know, for among all his old friends there was not one he esteemed more highly or felt greater warmth of affection for. He also said that nobody would be happier than he to see Schwabe succeed Tonks. Birdie and Schwabe still thought Albert was a strong competitor. Philip Connard (1875–1958) was supposed to be another candidate. Bayes, over a drink at The Windsor Castle, wished Schwabe luck and said he would not object to Connard getting it as he believed there was more to him than to Wellington[57] or Rutherston.

The interviews with the Advisory Board for the Slade Chair were held on the afternoon of Monday 27 January 1930. Schwabe worked in the morning and lunched with Rainforth Armitage Walker, Assistant Editor of the *Print Collector's Quarterly*, at the Swiss Restaurant, Old Compton Street, and arrived at the University 20 minutes too early. He was allowed to smoke in the waiting room and to pass the time he read Stevenson's *Charles of Orleans* but, as he noted in his diary, mostly inattentively. Rodney Burn (1899–1984) to Schwabe's surprise arrived at 2.55 in a state of high nervous tension – they were the only interviewees. Schwabe was also on edge but not so marked as Burn who went in first. Schwabe kicked his heels for half an hour, practising little steps on the carpet, and when at length he was summoned, put a good face on it. He recognised only Gregory Foster (Vice-Chancellor, formerly Provost until the end of 1929), Maclagan, Holmes and MacColl. They asked Schwabe various questions:

> Had I ever had to deal with cases of insubordination? (Gregory Foster – 'certainly not, never had any') Had I a good constitution? Told them about my weak heart, discharge from Army, and total disbelief in cardiac affection. By the way missed a good chance of reply to Gregory Foster, on insubordination. Might have reminded him that he threatened to expel me from the Slade on that score years ago – breaking windows was the last offence. 'Difference between art teaching at the RCA and Slade'? – reply 'considering that the RCA staff was half ex-Slade men, there couldn't be much'; but commented on weak charm of the lesser sort of Slade drawing, and urged that Design side should be strengthened. Thought I saw approval from Holmes. 'Where was I educated?' – 'At a small private school in Hertfordshire' (Burn in Harrow). Other questions as to literary work and lectures. Said I <u>had</u> given three lectures at RCA (Design School – on Costume) but that it was not my métier.[58]

Afterwards, being told not to wait, he went to see the RCA Sketch Club and thence to Camberwell School. The following day at the RCA Rothenstein had heard that the Board had decided unanimously but that their decision would not be announced for some time. Evelyn Shaw, Honorary General Secretary to the British School at Rome, telephoned Schwabe to go over at once to Lowther Gardens. Schwabe found Monnington there, and both very solemn. Shaw asked him earnestly and in confidence whether he would like to have Monnington at the Slade should he get the job. Schwabe made it clear that he would like to ask him but did not know how far his hands might be tied. Monnington had had a caller early that morning who had asked whether he would work with Burn if he was appointed.

> After a short interview with Anonymous Important Person M. said 'yes'; but reflected afterwards that he didn't want to – or at least not so much as he wanted to work there with me; because he thinks B. has no experience and would be incapable of the work (this he said deliberately as a friend of Burn's, and knowing him better than I) so that M. would have to do the job of Professor himself and supply B.'s want of experience. This he does not wish… The Anonymous Important Person told him that it would make the greatest difference to Burn's chances of being appointed if it were known that Monnington and Burn would work together. Therefore as Shaw and Monnington both say they want me to be at the Slade, they put it to me that it was of the utmost importance to my chances if it could be known that M. would work with me. Then followed a more remarkable revelation. Shaw this morning has also been visited by an Anon. Imp. Person (whether the same or not I don't know) who had said that 'if Schwabe goes to the Slade, he will take Gwynne-Jones with him, and he (G.J.) will clear out half his students from the School!: and that this must not be allowed. Followed some instances of G.J.'s tactlessness and indiscretion, from Shaw and Monnington and they ended by asking me if I would undertake not to press for G.J.'s appointment. I replied that I could not go back on what I had said. It had been my intention to ask G.J. to teach painting, as I honestly thought that he taught it very well, as was evident at the RCA and I thought that the assumed ill effects of his being appointed were very much exaggerated. 'Very well', said Shaw. 'You destroy your

*own chances': and continued to explain that there was an
impression that G.J. would run the Slade through me. I held my
ground: and it then occurred to me that, after all, appointments
suggested by the Slade Professor have to be ratified by the Senate,
or who ever it is, and there would be plenty of opportunity for
Anonymous Important Persons to make their objections felt, and
quash unwelcome aspirants, when such suggestions had been put
forward in a formal way. 'Would you resign if Gwynne-Jones
were not appointed?' asked Shaw: and I replied 'certainly not'.
So it was settled that Shaw was to explain the position to the
person concerned, on those lines. I thought it extremely friendly
of Shaw and Monnington (and said so to them) that they should
give me their support: but it occurred to me on the door-step that
Shaw has an axe to grind, charming and friendly though he is in
many genuine ways. Tommy has nothing, personally, to make out
of it. He hates intrigue as much as I do. But Shaw is in a difficult
position with the School at Rome now that Lord Esher is dead.
His Committee, except Esher, never was very interested in the Arts,
and would cheerfully give up much that Shaw has been working
for. Shaw wants the support of the artists, and feels that the Slade,
if well run and sympathetic, would give him strong backing.
Having worked with me on the Imperial Gallery, he finds, I
gather from Monnington that my interests, in sculpture, painting
and architecture combined, are wide enough for his purposes.*[59]

The day after this intrigue MacColl told Schwabe that
he had 'impressed the Committee very favourably'.
Schwabe found this admission 'Pleasant to hear, as
one never knows what impression one makes on other
people. They might have thought me a dammed fool.'[60]
Schwabe received a letter from his old friend Dodd
congratulating him on the Slade Professorship. He
did not look upon this as anything but rumour. Later
Birdie told him that Randall Davies, an old Chelsea
friend, had telephoned and Rushbury telegraphed
to the same effect: but both could be traced to Dodd.

Schwabe telephoned Dodd thanking him and also
asked for his sources of information. The source
was Professor Adshead who was on the Senate of the
University. Schwabe resolved not to spread the news
before the official announcement. Coming home from
Camberwell on the evening of Wednesday 26 February
1930, Schwabe was met inside the door of no. 20 by
Gwynne-Jones with congratulations. Birdie, waiting
upstairs with the news (as it was on the radio), was
furious at Gwynne-Jones' tactlessness in not waiting
for her to get it in first. Mrs Gwynne-Jones apologised
for her son, who himself later did the same.[61]

A plethora of congratulations followed. Anna Airy
(1882–1964) wrote 'I'm so glad one of Brown's men
has it!' Clause and Schwabe's close friends Charles and
Ivy Tennyson wired telegrams of congratulation. When
he arrived at the College Rothenstein congratulated him
warmly and affectionately; Schwabe said Gwynne-Jones
might want to go to the Slade with him, a prospect
that Rothenstein took well. When Schwabe went into
'Q. Room', the students clapped and 40 of the girls
from downstairs were ushered into the Staff Room
and cheered. Schwabe found it all embarrassing
but gratifying. He was particularly pleased to get a
congratulatory letter from Tonks. Tonks later advised
Schwabe on no account to allow himself to be seduced
into too much organising work but on the other hand
never to consent to the appointment of someone else
as 'manager'. Tonks told Schwabe to:

*remain, as Brown and he always were, teachers in the school and
practising artists outside it: [and] be on good terms with the
carpenters and odd job men, and a sort of clerk of the works
named Voysey. He spoke well of his staff and said 'they were very
good to teach the beginners', which is after all not saying much.*

When I asked him about them, especially Gerrard [Head of Sculpture], whom he describes as a good fellow, who will take on any work he is wanted to do, and not think of extra pay: said that Steer has definitely resigned. I thereupon said something about G.J. taking on the work that Steer did, and mentioned my desire to have Monnington. Tonks was silent about G.J.: but said that Steer only got £200 a year (for about one day's teaching); and as to the question of appointments it was my duty to see the provost at once. He describes the Slade as run in a 'ramshackle' old-fashioned way, and would not have it otherwise: not a typewriter in the place, and bad accommodation for the staff.[62]

Schwabe met with the Provost (Allen Mawer) of University College and debated the question of Gwynne-Jones and Monnington and salaries. The Provost dissuaded him from immediately dismissing any of the present staff: he would know better after he had worked with them. Schwabe told him that he wanted Gwynne-Jones two days and Monnington one day a week. Schwabe went to see Charles Koe Child (1868–1935), Tonks' senior assistant and friend from Westminster. Koe Child agreed that the present staff were not very efficient and saying that he had advised Tonks to get rid of some. He suggested cutting down the number of days they worked, so that there might be money for Monnington and Gwynne-Jones. Porter, the lecturer on Perspective on a salary of £125, was aged over 70 and about to retire. Schwabe thought he could be replaced by Bayes, who would come for less. Tonks had no private room whatsoever, and 'the boys' as Koe Child called the junior staff were 'on top of him and each other at all times in what [was] known as "the Professor's room".'[63] Koe Child had been making enquiries as to what other accommodation could be provided for the staff. Schwabe expressed a strong desire for a relative privacy.

He later told Gwynne-Jones about the financial position at the Slade and that there was at most £200 for extra staff. Gwynne-Jones told him that he would apply for his job at Camberwell but Schwabe did not consider he would be much good as a teacher of drawing. He met the Provost again in May:

'An important person' (who?) has told Mawer his opinion that Gwynne-Jones will seriously hamper the running of the Slade, and that from the nature of his temperament he is thoroughly undesirable. I said I knew he was indiscreet, but that his indiscretions were controllable, and not of a nature to do the harm anticipated: that in any case he was a good teacher of painting of a kind that Monnington was not so much a master of. Mawer had mentioned Monnington as more desirable and of more prestige than G.J. I repeated that I wanted T.M. on the staff but that he was underestimating G.J. as an artist.[64]

Schwabe recognised that there was considerable opposition but he was prepared to put up a strong case to the Advisory Sub-Committee. He wrote to Mawer suggesting that it should be possible to appoint both. However he had heard that Gwynne-Jones had succeeded in spreading an impression that he would run the Slade through Schwabe. Frustrated by all the shenanigans, Schwabe wrote in his diary, 'Damn all this indirect work.' He had what he described as a 'Painful interview with Gwynne. Told him that his appointment had been strongly opposed.' He thanked Schwabe for backing him, but he did not appear to be conscious of his tactical and diplomatic errors. Schwabe was upset to get a note from Monnington refusing to come to the Slade.

Schwabe continued at the RCA until Friday 17 July. He was present for the College photograph which as usual was taken in the Fountain Court of the Victoria and Albert Museum. In the evening he went to the College Social in order to make valedictory speeches to Rothenstein but left early after the play.

Schwabe's tenure at the Slade did not start well. Before the new term he conducted interviews with Slade candidates and examined specimens of their work and turned a good many down. On Friday 3 October he wrote to Sir George Clausen, RA (1852–1944) inviting him to criticize the Summer Composition Paintings. This was 'against all tradition, and Tonks' known views.'[65] Clausen replied by return accepting the invitation and thanking him for 'his generosity in offering a fee – quite an unusual thing!' He feared that his 'old-fashioned ideas might not be altogether acceptable to your bright young people!' The result was, Schwabe noted, 'rather a fiasco, as he was long, – perhaps over conscientious – and owing to bad organization of the room… partly inaudible.'[66] The students were enraged about his address and comments on their individual paintings and his rather contemptuous remarks about Far Eastern art, and by his warning against the pernicious influence of Cézanne and Van Gogh. William Townsend (1909–73), who had been a student at the Slade since 1926, recalled that by the time Clausen had finished half the room was empty and part way through he was appointed door-keeper by Peter Brooker, lecturer in Drawing, to prevent anyone else from leaving the room.[67]

Clausen wrote to Schwabe seemingly oblivious of the furore:

> *I am very glad to have been of any service, and hope perhaps*
> *to have given a little! But it was really very difficult, and you*

> *have a difficult task – one that can't be got over in half and*
> *hour's talk! For what struck me, as a whole in the work was*
> *a cultivation of mannerisms!*
>
> *There must always be some, but I don't think it can have*
> *been so wide-spread as in your time – But then these pioneers*
> *had not been exploited for the market! And there is unconsciously*
> *a tendency to be attracted by and imitate what is in favour at*
> *the moment.*

Such was the students' wrath that a stinging open letter to Clausen was posted at the main entrance. The art critic of the *Daily Mail* reported that 'The letter also implies a censure of the good judgement of Professor Schwabe, in choosing Sir George to criticise the students' work.' Clausen was subsequently telephoned by the *Daily Mail* inviting a reply; he wrote to Schwabe informing him that he was sending this reply:

> *Sir, I have read your Art Critic's article a propos of my criticism*
> *of the Slade School paintings. May I say with regard to the 'open*
> *letter', that I did not make contemptuous remarks about Far Eastern*
> *art, nor did I warn students against Van Gogh and Cézanne.*
>
> *I'm afraid I cannot have made myself very clear if that is the*
> *impression: on the other hand, is it quite the thing to run round*
> *to the newspaper and complain?*

Schwabe apologised for the 'ill advised young man at the Slade [who had] taken upon himself to insult you by what he is pleased to call an "open letter"'. He had instructed him to withdraw the letter;[68] but in the meanwhile to his annoyance it had slipped into the *Daily Mail*. It was, he said, in very bad taste and naturally hurt him that Clausen should be made a victim of a little press stunt. One of the senior students contacted Schwabe to tell him that he and others were taking steps to make it clear, by collecting signatures,

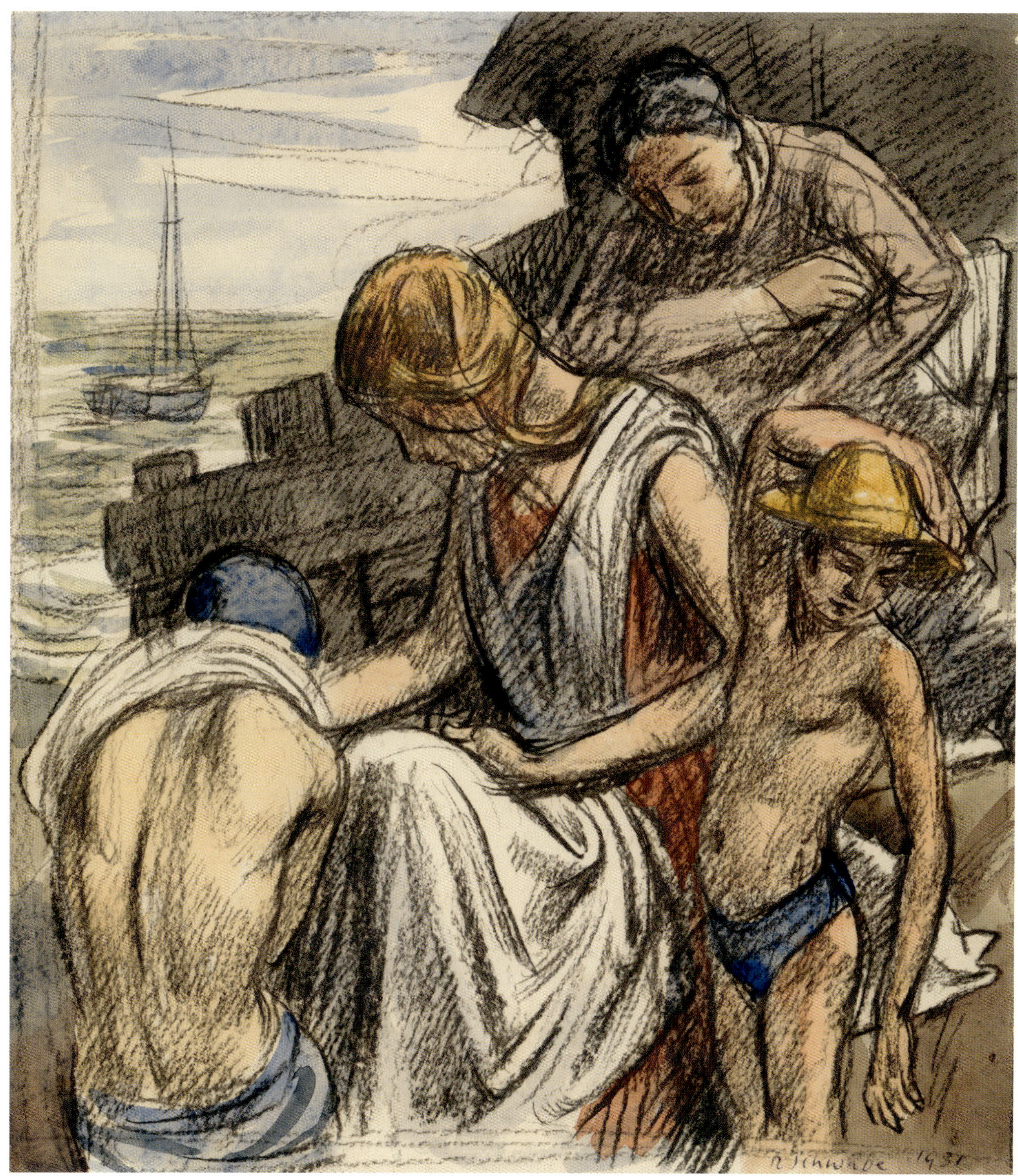

A Beach Scene
1931 | watercolour and pen and ink | 56 x 40 cm
UCL ART MUSEUM, UNIVERSITY COLLEGE LONDON

that they had no share in the manifesto. Several days later the *Daily Mail* reported that the majority of the students had disassociated themselves from the insults to their guest and quoted from Sir George's denial.[69] Clausen was grateful:

As to my original 'cause of offence' — well, you will realise that in the circumstances it was not possible to do more than make a hasty summary & without pretence of infallibility — I was trying to find the principles that the works were done on. And naturally one cannot expect agreement in all things!… Damn their press stunts!

Of course I know your school teaching is sound — What is difficult at the present time for the student, is to find the application of it — crude realism is no good — your prize man had realism <u>and</u> <u>vision</u> — The Polunin students were frankly and logically conventional. Between these it seemed to me there were all varieties & influences of course one expects this; I was only trying to make a rough analysis of the different points of view.

Well again, I'm sorry to have caused you all this bother especially at the start of your professorial career!

The following October the Summer Compositions were judged internally and not by an external adviser.

Schwabe wrote in his diary 'A bad beginning. Wish I was a more able speaker myself.' Because of his stammering, public speaking caused Schwabe much anxiety, a concern he shared with Koe Child. The latter did not think this inability a ground for resigning.

The Slade Dinner on Friday 27 March 1931 kept Schwabe in a state of extreme apprehension all day. He managed to control his nerves with the help of burgundy and to lose his self-consciousness enough to say a few things without disaster. The affair seemed sufficiently uproarious to indicate that people, including Schwabe's guests Bayes and Rothenstein, were enjoying themselves. Schwabe fared better at the Prize-giving at the end of the summer term when scholarships were awarded to Olga Lehmann (1912–2001), Neil Cook and Roger Hilton (1911–75). He managed to offer a few platitudes. He gave a nominal five minutes each to speak on the work of their departments to George Charlton, lecturer in Drawing since 1919, Frank Ormrod, assistant in Ornamental Design, Gwynne-Jones, and George Havard Thomas who had taken over direction of the work in Sculpture in 1921 on the death of his father, Professor Havard Thomas. The speeches were followed by the customary strawberry tea.

Schwabe continued as a practising artist. He found the time over a weekend in February 1931 to convert a study of a model into a water-colour of a beach scene. He recorded in his diary that 'Clause came in, and likes it. Promised to go and see his new picture tomorrow.'

Schwabe held his first exhibition of drawings and watercolours since his appointment in May 1931 at the Batsford Gallery in North Audley Street. He attended the private view after working at the Slade but was disappointed that no-one was there at 2.30. Later Fairlie Harmar, R.A. Walker, Edward (Eddie) Marsh, Mrs Copley (Ethel Gabain 1883–1950) and her son in a tall hat and tail-coat from Westminster School, the Clauses, Charlton, Franklin White and a few others came. Walker bought a small drawing of a nude; Rothenstein purchased a drawing and wanted to carry more than one away from his 'lovely show, full of tender and beautiful things'.[70]

Charles Marriott of *The Times*, although regarding Schwabe's work as individual, felt that he 'seems to belong in style to the tradition of Legros. He draws both the figure and the landscape, and what one observes in the present exhibition is an increasing command of atmospheric effects and a relaxation of manner without loss of probity.' He went on to praise *Dover: the Basin from Above* in smoky light, and *The Lake on the Plateau, Donegal* with its 'basking' effect of rounded hills under a tender sky, as demonstrating a new addition of temperamental qualities to 'brains' (he too thought Schwabe a scholarly artist). For Marriott there was much greater variety in the exhibition than he had been prepared for; he compared *Dedham Churchyard* with its smouldering colour with the deliberate slightness of *The Stour at Dedham*. Gwendolen Raverat, art critic for *Time and Tide*, who had trained at the Slade shortly after Schwabe, preferred his figure drawings and, above all, the figure compositions, to the landscape and architecture work. The later she thought solid but not inspired by real affection; whereas she found the figure drawings such as the *Study of a Child* or *Sewing* as having great charm. She concluded that 'It is an exhibition worthy of the reputation of the new Head of the Slade School.'[71]

As Head of the Slade much of Schwabe's time was spent serving on selection juries and committees,[72] panels of experts and examination committees.[73] He also found time to assist Bayes raise a subscription for Meninsky, who was suffering from a nervous breakdown in Liverpool, caused partly by worry of diagnosis of cancer of the tongue. With Bayes and Gertler also on board, by early February 1932 the fund stood at £95-16-0 which Schwabe thought was not bad for about 10 days actual effort. Vanessa Bell's response

was typical of those artists who contributed to the fund for Meninsky, 'I hope you will get enough to help over this difficult time – I'm afraid most artists are finding times very hard now & cannot give as much as they would like to'. Money and commissions were scarce, but Schwabe, Bayes and Gertler decided to send £30 a month to Meninsky. Having been examined by a specialist, Meninsky was to be sent to the Cassel Hospital for Functional Nervous Disorders at Swaylands, Penhurst, Kent.

Although Schwabe had been an active member of the London Group for many years he was beginning to feel 'out of it' altogether when he attended as a member of the selecting jury on 1 October 1932. He took his picture *Danbury* with a glass over it and found this was 'not done'; moreover a lot of people did not know him, nor he them. Schwabe saw Kenneth Morrison, Frederick Porter, Keith Baynes, Noel Adeney, John Farleigh, Rupert Lee, Diana Brinton, Adrian Allinson, Richard Carline, Horace Brodsky, Henry Moore, E.M. O'Rourke Dickey – these were all that he recognised out of 18. Vera Cunningham, Elliott Seabrooke and Robert Bevan were not there. Schwabe found it very instructive to see what the jury liked and didn't like. Ithell Colquhoun was rejected; Rodrigo Moynihan and Elinor Bellingham-Smith provisionally accepted. Nina Hamnett was nearly rejected, but was given a D (doubtful).

The following month Schwabe served on the NEAC jury with Holmes, MacColl, W. Rothenstein, Albert R., Gwynne-Jones, Cundall, Connard, Jowett, Clause, Cheston, Ethel Walker and Manson. Holmes confided to him after lunch at the Bristol that years previously when he was clerk he took offence at Rothenstein's manner to him and threatened to punch his head in public: the only occasion when he was driven to use threats of violence. The jury in Schwabe's view made the usual errors: they rejected Gilbert Spencer and then reinstated him. Towner's pictures were well received, as were Karl Hagedorn's, while Grimmond was accepted without difficulty. Ethel Copley had her two (which Schwabe had chosen for her) accepted. The previous week she had written him a rather touching note, about always being rejected by the NEAC. Schwabe later bumped into Ethelbert White, annoyed at having one of his pictures thrown out. Schwabe sympathised, as he was sure that it would not have been rejected had it been properly and carefully considered by the Jury. He wrote to Ethelbert, taking one twelfth of the blame on himself.

Hopes for sales at the New English were not high. Connard had sold only one picture in the last two years, which was why he was teaching at Westminster. The hanging did not start well the following day as Gwynne-Jones knocked a hole in Gilbert Spencer's picture and broke a glass in an attempt to re-organise Schwabe's hanging of the drawings. Schwabe was very disappointed with the look of his big picture (*Fructidor*, a composition of three groups of nude or lightly draped figures among three apple trees, brackish in colour), feeling that it might have looked better hung low, but he had no cause for complaint – it would take up too much room on the line. Ethel Walker told Schwabe the figures were over-modelled, but she was enthusiastic about Schwabe's 43A *Cheyne Walk* (painted in March 1927) she had bought some years ago. Later Rothenstein[74] said nice things about *Fructidor* but Schwabe did not feel that people liked it and, compared with a Steer below it, he thought it looked terribly crude. However, he was phlegmatic, believing that pictures usually get

some recognition if they deserve it; he expected exhibitions to be trying; and from experience he knew that pictures seldom look their best in more or less accidental company. The critics did give Schwabe some positive recognition. J.B. writing in the *Manchester Guardian* thought *Fructidor* the 'most ambitious and scholarly effort of the show' and, while agreeing with Schwabe's assessment that it suffered 'by its proximity to the beautiful Wilson Steer', judged that 'in the rhythmic interweaving of the figures and the branches of the trees and the fine balance of the whole design it is an unusual achievement in these times, although Walter Crane, whom it recalls, might have done it on a smaller scale with the grace it lacks.'[75]

Schwabe was also busy with arrangements at Barbizon House in Cavendish Square for his private view of 23 recent water-colour drawings of scenes in Cornwall, Kent, and Holland which he had done during holiday times. Marsh came first, followed by Marriott, *The Times'* critic, who Schwabe found very friendly; and Hanslip Fletcher, and some others, before lunch. Schwabe went off to have lunch with Walker to discuss the possibility of writing a book on English Illustration: the suggestion appealed to Schwabe, although he had just refused a suggestion from a publisher that he should do a book on 'Art in my Time' – 50,000 words for £150. He 'preferred to spend his time making pictures'. But Walker's proposition could be tackled at his own time over years. Early sales were encouraging: one drawing was sold before Schwabe came in and three more in the afternoon. The architect Sir Andrew Taylor (1850–1937) bought one.

Marriot's review in *The Times* on 15 November 1932 was positive:

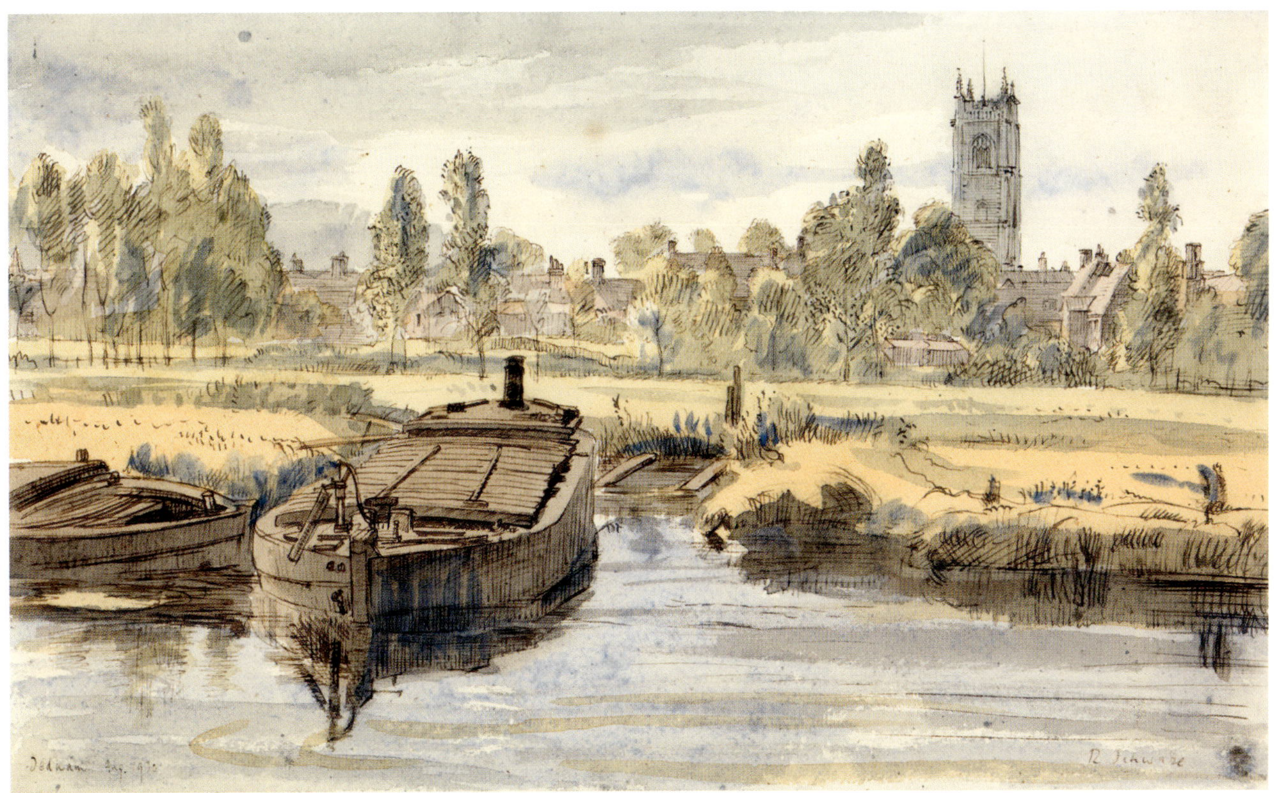

The Stour at Dedham
1930 | watercolour and pen and ink | 40 x 56 cm
UCL ART MUSEUM, UNIVERSITY COLLEGE LONDON

*Those who like deliberation, precision, economy, and good order
in their art would do well to visit Barbizon House… Though
most… are coloured they are quite definitely drawings, and upon
two things in particular is Professor Schwabe to be congratulated:
for keeping his colour down to the convention he has adopted, and
for finding his material in odd corners, – mostly in the neighbourhood of Polperro, Cornwall. One of the very best of the drawings,
certainly in composition, both as regards line and tone, is a study
of some rather ramshackle 'Farm Buildings, Pont'. It has the
qualities of an old French aquatint… the work of Professor
Schwabe is not in the least laboured – the labour has been done
beforehand – and the drawings have the advantage of being well
adapted to the modern interior. 'Mill, Penpol', 'Interior-Lanteglos
Church' and 'Lanteglos Church' are three especially good examples.*

While staying in or near Lanteglos Schwabe also
recorded in great detail the busy scene as farm workers
were *Sheep Dipping*. The critic for the *Morning Post* also
praised the Cornish scenes including *Farm Carts,
Lanteglos* which was later bought for six guineas by
the Contemporary Art Society for the British Museum
collection. He claimed that Schwabe 'does not make
farms and churches and harbours too picturesque:
that is, stagey. His drawings are just homely, in
hodden-grey and low-toned green and yellow, devoid
of frippery and fumbling, and all the more delightful
because of their simplicity.'[76] Frank Rutter writing
in the *Sunday Times* drew attention to Schwabe's:

*noble sense of composition [which] takes us into a serene
upper air in which controversies are forgotten and all is peace.
Mr Schwabe has his own magistral personality, and while his
respect for tradition is openly acknowledged, he succeeds in giving
his own personal touch to his interpretations, whether they be
architectural subjects, as 'St James's Square' or more rural themes,
such as 'Hall Farm, Bodinnick.'[77]*

The *Sketch* review unusually made reference to
Schwabe's wife as 'dark and handsome' and pointed
out that she had 'frequently been drawn and painted
by her husband' and while a former Slade student
'her artistic abilities are now only expressed in her
Hampstead house, which is furnished and decorated
with remarkable taste.' Birdie spent lavishly on
20 Church Row to redecorate to the period and
was assisted by Hardinge-Papillon, an antique
dealer and decorator.[78]

It was a busy week for Schwabe as on Saturday
12 November he went to Camberwell to hang the
South London Group with Medworth, Millen and
Russell Reeve. He recorded in his diary 'Some good
things by Francis Dodd, and prints very remarkable
technically by Washington, whom I have not
noticed before.' That evening he went to a party
at the Avenue Studios, Fulham Road. Rushbury was
there and again told him that he ought to resign from
the Executive and Hanging Committee of the NEAC
in favour of younger people. Schwabe was aware that
there was dissatisfaction with the NEAC. Rushbury,
Connard and Manson, Director of the Tate, had
threatened to resign. One of the reasons given which
Schwabe had heard before was that the Club was
run by a lot of 'Art Masters'. He found this somewhat
ironic as Connard was teaching at Westminster and
he knew that Rushbury would have been glad to
get a teaching job a short time ago, and further
he did not see that Gallery officials were superior
to artists who taught. He had no personal axe to
grind in the NEAC and resolved not to serve on
the Hanging Committee if re-elected. In the event
he was automatically cut off by the imposition
of a new rule.[79]

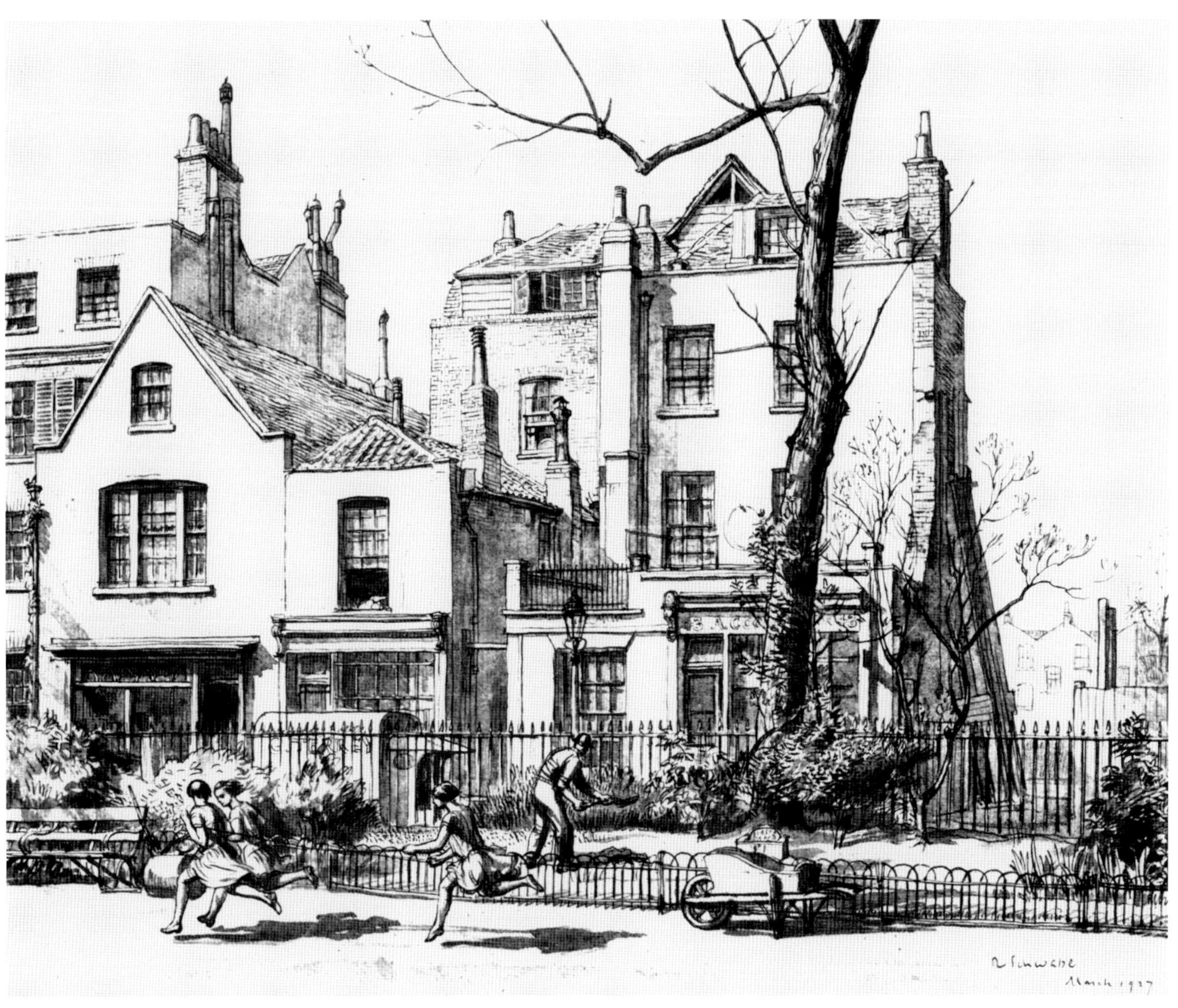

43A Cheyne Walk
1927 | pen and ink

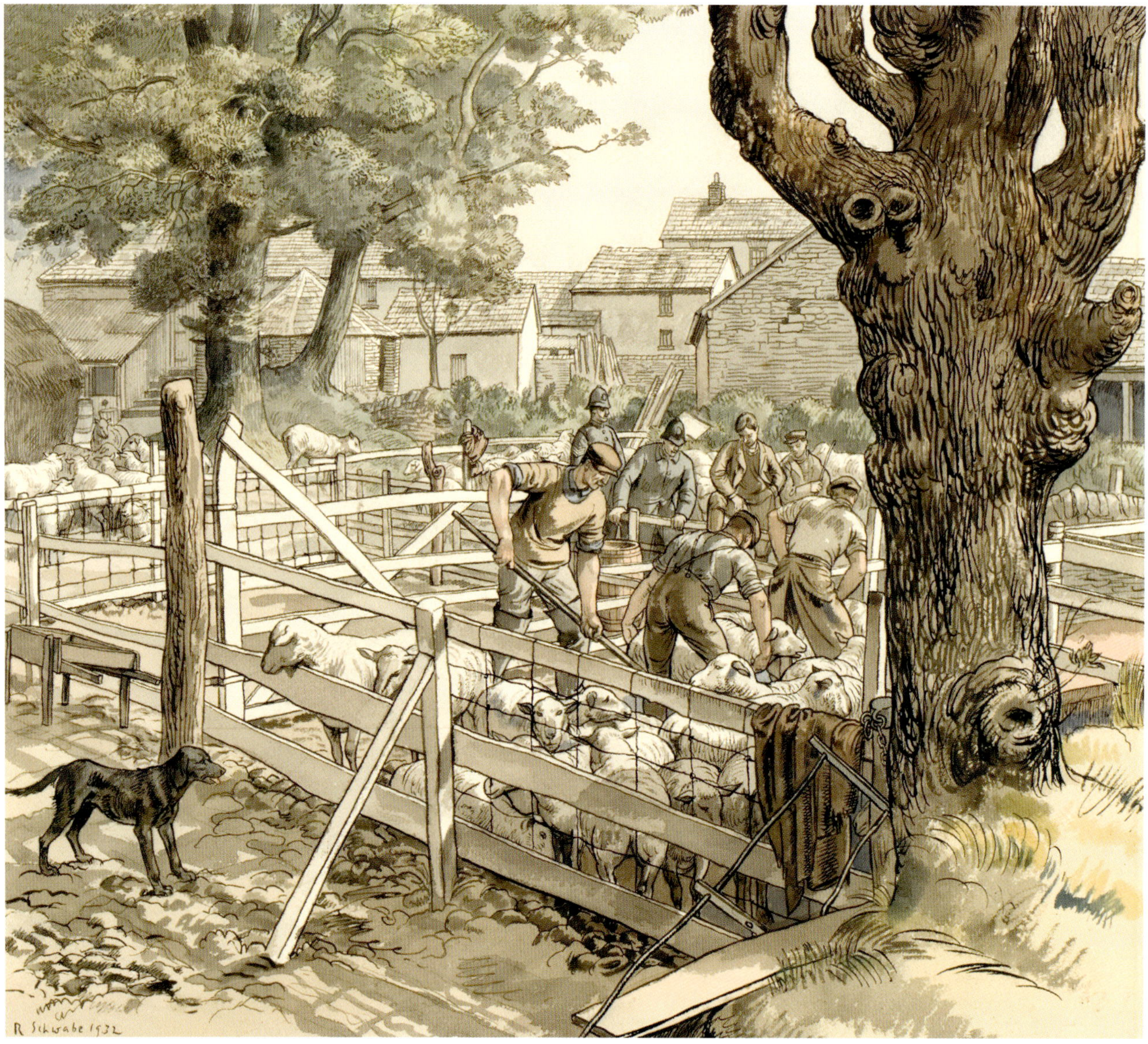

Sheep Dipping
1932 | ink, pencil and watercolour | 48.3 x 43.7 cm

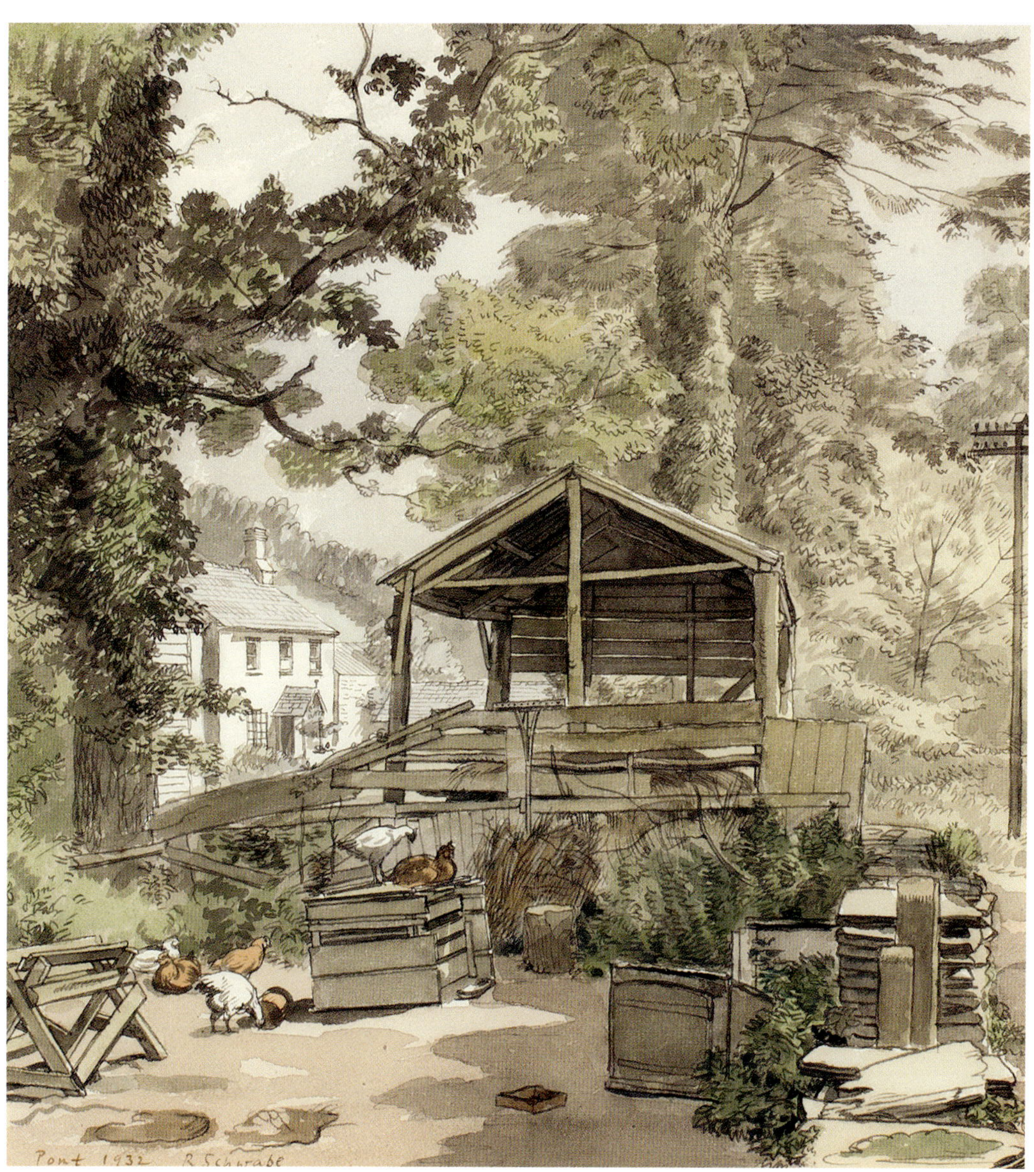

Farm Buildings, Pont
1932 | watercolour | 30.5 x 28 cm
COLLECTION ABBOTT & HOLDER LIMITED

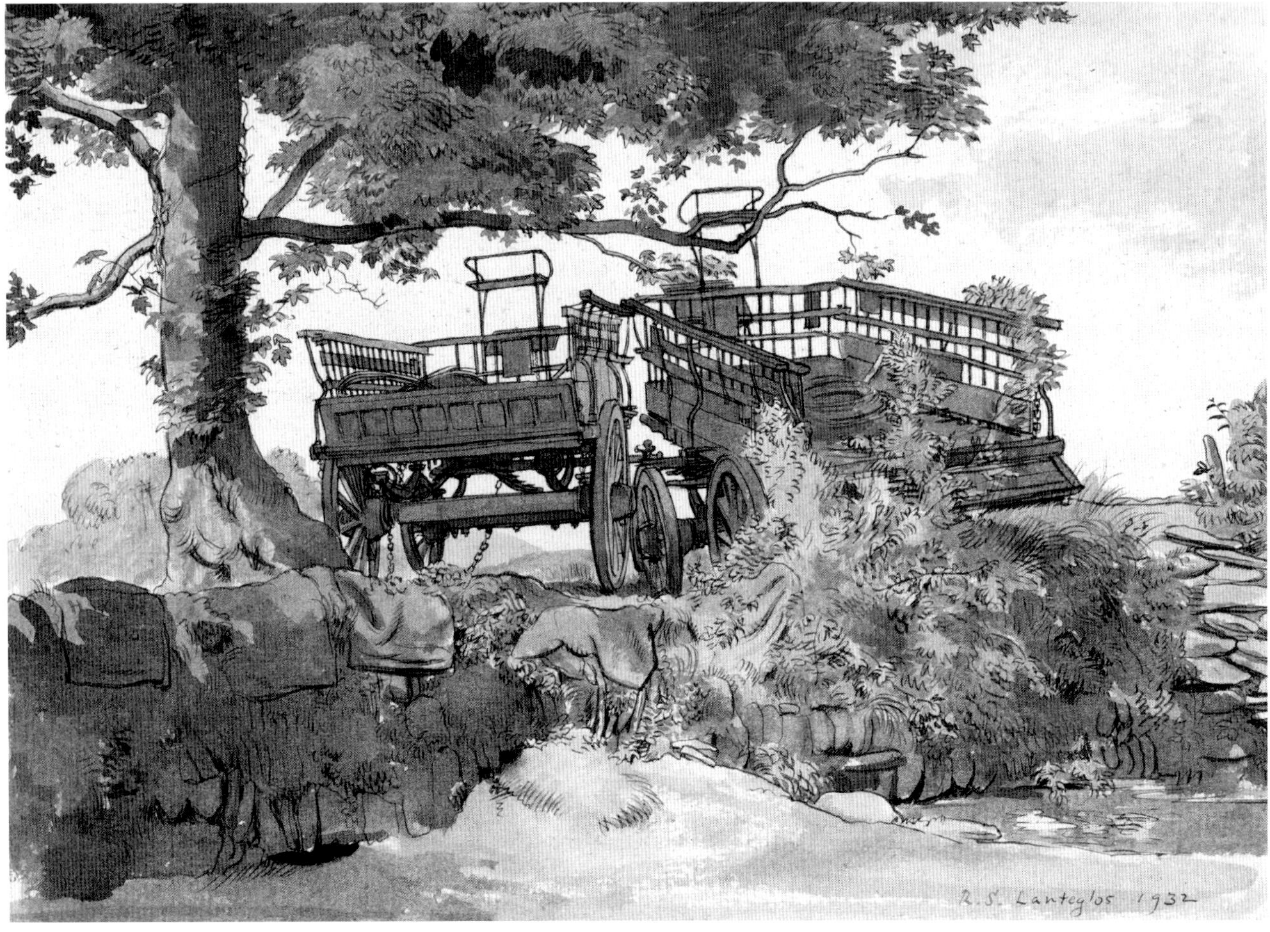

Farm Carts, Lanteglos

1932 | pen and grey ink, with grey wash and watercolour | 26.5 × 37.4 cm

The Schwabes spent Christmas with the Tennysons in Aldeburgh; prior to leaving London, Schwabe went to see Margaret Mackintosh at 10, Chelsea Manor Studios in Flood Street, who was faced with the problems of living in a studio which was practically one room. Her heart condition meant that she was hardly able to get up and yet she hated the presence of the servant she had to employ. Schwabe was aware of her attitude towards the 'lower classes': being kind but not bearing to be intimate with them.[80] On 7 January 1933 he learned that Margaret Mackintosh was seriously ill in a nursing home. The Schwabes were leaving Cambridge Terrace, Dover, where they had been staying with Birdie's sister Dora and husband Tom Cobbe; although they went straight to Chelsea, they were told that Margaret had died that morning. She was, Schwabe thought, heroic all along, not wanting to cause any trouble. He went with Birdie to the cremation service at Golders Green. A cousin Joseph Tilly Hardeman had travelled from Liverpool and a woman unknown to the Schwabes was there; her brothers were too ill. The modest ceremony was dignified and they watched the coffin slide noiselessly on its bronze slab through the door in the side wall of the chapel.

Schwabe met with her lawyers to go through papers and drawings belonging to both Mackintoshes. This gloomy business reminded him of what it was like when Tonks took him to Sargent's studios in Fulham Road. It was a dirty business too: the lawyer's man and Schwabe stayed till late in Glebe Place. Schwabe thought it better to destroy most of one's work as Brown had done. In her will Margaret Mackintosh left Schwabe her three Catalan elephants and her old French oil and vinegar cruet in white; to Birdie she bequeathed her crystal lamp and any china, pottery, linen, pillows and cushions; to Alice she left her Catalan crocheted shawl with yellow fringe.

Jessie Newbery contacted Birdie from Corfe Castle. She had seen the notice of Margaret's death in *The Times* and wrote:

> *As Margaret – in her last cheerful letter to us, written only a few weeks ago, said 'The Schwabes are my best friends' and told us that you and your husband often came to see her, I write to you to tell me what happened… Margaret and her sister; McNair & Mackintosh, have been our friends for forty years – with never a rift between us.*
>
> *Our lives, until 1914 were closely & affectionately interwoven… Margaret's gifts were a great asset to Toshie – as advisor, appreciator collaborateur…*
>
> *We are very grateful that she had you & Professor Schwabe to care & sympathise with her.*

Shortly after the funeral Schwabe was interviewed for the *Glasgow Evening News* about Charles Rennie Mackintosh who had died a little over three years ago:

> *My own view is that Mackintosh was the father of the modern school of architecture… It has been said that throughout his career Mackintosh's aims and achievements were better understood and appreciated abroad than at home. All the more reason then why Glasgow in particular, and Scotland in general, should take steps to honour and revive his name… The present, too, would be a most opportune time, for only a few days ago his wife, Margaret Macdonald who was his partner in a great deal of the work he did, died.*[81]

The work of Charles Rennie Mackintosh and Margaret Macdonald Mackintosh which had been much neglected in their lifetime was showcased in a joint Memorial Exhibition in May 1933 at the McLellan Galleries in Glasgow. Jessie Newbery wrote an appreciative foreword to the catalogue.

When not at the Slade teaching and attending to administrative matters Schwabe spent time – as in his student days – researching in the Reading-Room at the British Museum. Hind, who had succeeded Laurence Binyon as Keeper of the Department of Prints and Drawings, saw Schwabe there one Thursday in March 1934 and told him that he had been elected to the Athenaeum, and also that he would like him to give some drawings to the Print Room. Albert Rutherston and Professor Coker from UCL had supported Schwabe's candidature for admission to the Athenaeum when it was up for balloting by the Members.[82] Schwabe was worried about the expense, and whether it was wise to spend 15 guineas a year and 30 guineas entrance. He made his first appearance as a member with Rutherston on Saturday 24 March 1934, after spending the morning at the Slade writing letters and drawing a model. While there he met Hind and Augustus Daniel (1866–1950), who had retired in December from the National Gallery where he had been Director since January 1929. Afterwards they went to the RWS together and from there to Gilbert Spencer's show. Schwabe was again struck by one or two of the land-scapes but unfavourably impressed by the large figure composition of some people carrying fruit and flowers down a village street – a harvest festival, he supposed. Spencer some two years later was asked by the Slade Society, which had been formed in 1935, to criticise the Sketch Club. He went round the work very conscientiously, advising the students in a grandfatherly way to stick to drawing – and told them very much

what Schwabe and his staff always told them about the advantage of the academic background.[83]

Over the next 14 years Schwabe was to make much use of the Athenaeum which had been founded in 1824 as a social club for leading artistic, literary and scientific men and for patrons of the arts and services. In 1938 he became a member of the Art Committee serving alongside Rothenstein, Hind, Charlton, Bradshaw, St John Hornby and one or two others.[84] He enjoyed the extensive library, the series of exhibitions and the social opportunities. Schwabe later presented to the club a number of portraits of members including his etching of his long-time friend, the artist and etcher Francis Dodd, completed in 1916; his pencil drawings of the physicists and Nobel prize winners Lord Rutherford of Nelson, OM, FRS completed in 1928 and Sir William Henry Bragg, KBE, OM completed in August 1932; and Reginald Morier Yorke Gleadowe, Slade Professor, Oxford completed in 1944. He also presented his lithograph of Campbell Dodgson, Keeper of Prints and Drawings, drawn in 1932 on the occasion of his retirement from the British Museum.

While Schwabe may not have been a great innovator at the Slade and 'the work produced in the School remained academic with perhaps rather less awareness of the artworld outside than previously'[85] it was a period of much stability. He listened to the advice of his staff. One such occasion was over the matter of the teaching of painting in the School. Charlton came to see him in February 1935 about giving more time to it. The students had been agitating about it. They were not dissatisfied with Gwynne-Jones but wanted more lessons than he and Schwabe gave. Charlton pointed out that there was more teaching of painting in his time when McEvoy,

Tonks, Russell and Steer all contributed. In Schwabe's
time, Brown and Steer alone taught painting.[86] Charlton
later informed Schwabe that the Slade students were
getting too slack and idle and that he must do something about it. Schwabe agreed.[87] Some progress must
have been made as Schwabe was pleased to find that
the highest marked life-painting in the Board of
Education Examinations in June 1938 turned out
to be by a Slade man, Roebuck.

However, prior to this progress, Paul Feiler (b.1918),
a student since 1936, was brought before Charlton.
According to Feiler, Charlton said:

> *'I want you to see the Professor with your drawings.' So, being*
> *a dutiful student I attended... I was ushered into the room, stood*
> *to attention and there was the Professor behind the desk smoking*
> *his usual cigarette and Charlton said, 'Feiler's been here two years*
> *and he hasn't done a great deal of work.' So I said, 'excuse me, sir,*
> *I've only been here one year.' Schwabe looked up and said, 'Oh.'*
> *So he looked through my drawings, turning the pages very slowly*
> *and he smoked the cigarette at which, with the ash coming off*
> *all the time because he had a terrible stammer and that was his*
> *way of being able to speak rather than stammering... he stopped*
> *at one drawing and he got hold of his pencil and he sharpened it*
> *very, very carefully and it's the only time anyone ever taught me*
> *how to sharpen a pencil and I've done it ever since. And he said,*
> *'this doesn't look like an eye,' and proceeded to draw. Charlton's*
> *standing behind, he standing to attention and after about a silence*
> *of five minutes he looked up and he said, 'this doesn't either.'*
> *And Charlton took me off.*[88]

That was to be Feiler's only encounter with the Professor
during his London days although he recalled Schwabe
peering down into the Life Room from the balcony
of his room to see what was going on.

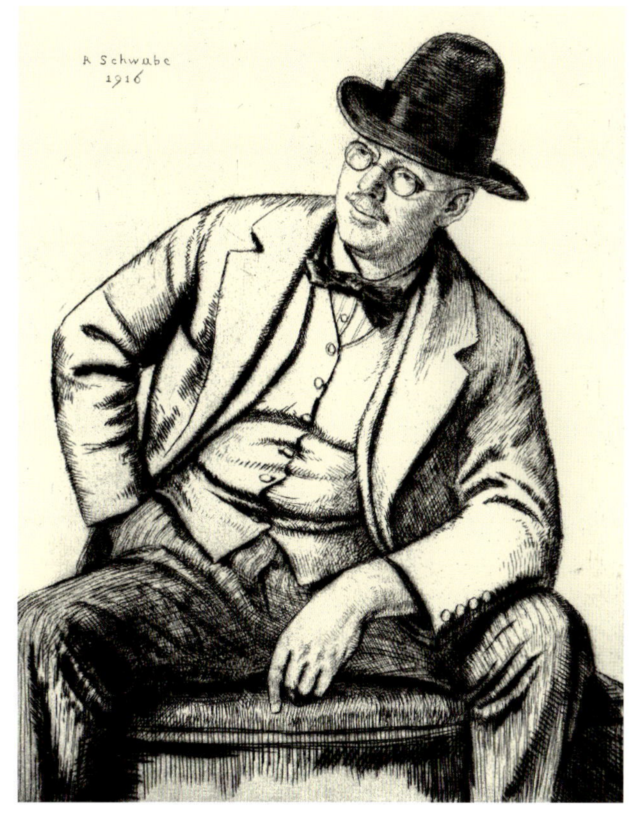

Francis Dodd
1916 | etching | 33 x 25 cm

Margaret Thomas (b.1916), a contemporary of Feiler, was not enamoured of the Slade nor her encounters with Schwabe. Awarded a scholarship, she was bitterly disappointed by the whole experience, believing that 'For girls it was really like… a finishing school because all the fathers could afford the University College high fees.' Thomas, who won several prizes at the Slade, including sharing with Rhoda Glass the first prize for Painting the Head in 1936–37, disliked intensely Schwabe's:

> way of standing behind one if one was sitting on one's donkey drawing and that I couldn't bear so I usually got up and offered him my seat. And then he spent a couple of minutes at least sharpening an H pencil to a half inch of lead and then drawing a very hard single line onto one's work. I don't remember him making much in the way of comment but he mucked the drawing up and went on to the next student. So I was very unhappy.[89]

She transferred to the Royal Academy Schools.

Schwabe inaugurated a new scheme of painting models at the Slade with a background of furniture arranged to look like an ordinary room. A screen was covered with wall-paper (the design was by Edward Bawden) and pictures hung on it. The model posed on a sofa of Victorian lodging–house pattern, which Peter Brooker bought for 5/- and which was covered at some expense. The students liked this and, according to Schwabe they 'evidently take much thought for the composition of their pictures'.[90] He also installed a new model throne which he hoped would help him (and the students) in drawing portrait heads, as they could now stand up and be on a level with the model's head, when the model sat in a chair. Schwabe used Henry Moore as an illustration of the fact that a

backing of academic study, of drawing particularly, did no harm to a modern artist.

Writing in *The Studio*, James Laver (1899–1975), Assistant Keeper in the Department of Engraving, Illustration and Design at the Victoria and Albert Museum, praised the excellent teaching of drawing at the Slade and the support that Schwabe and the authorities had given to encourage scene-painting under Vladimir Polunin (1880–1957) who had been the designer for a number of years for Diaghilev's Russian Ballet.[91] Polunin was invited to join the staff by Tonks shortly before he retired and such was the popularity of his course on Stage Painting that the number of students more than doubled in 1934 when he was assisted by Nevil Dickin, a former Slade student who was scenic director of Margate Repertory Theatre. 'All the several hundred costumes for "Tsar Sultan", "The Snow Maiden" and "Redhead" were entirely painted by the pupils of the Slade.'[92] The decorations for the Slade Dance and Cabaret were undertaken by Polunin's students; those in December 1936 for the third Charivari[93] were particularly successful. Both Schwabe and Laver attended. Schwabe thought the Cabaret presented by Polunin excellent; it was *A Secular Masque* by John Dryden in which Alan Carr (b.1914) looked and spoke 'with just the right amount of the tongue-in-the-cheek' as Mars, and Betty Stephen was Diana. Annette Scott, Schwabe noted, 'was very good throughout' as Venus; she had choreographed the masque with Betty Stephen. This was followed by a Burlesque Sketch by V.J. Polunin entitled *Beauties through the Ages*. In the first act female students appeared with their heads poked through the canvas of portraits in the manner of famous artists. Rosemary Allan (who married Gwynne-Jones in 1937) was Renoir; Schwabe thought one girl (Tillard) was astonishingly like Botticelli's *Primavera*. Camilla Wybrants was Raphael; he also thought the Goyas, Toulouse Lautrec, Cranachs were good. Schwabe's guests at his supper were the Provost and Mrs Mawer, the University secretary Douie,[94] who had been in post since 1927, the actress Viola Tree, the politician and diarist Lady Bonham Carter, his colleague Norman Janes (1892–1980) who taught wood engraving and etching and his wife Barbara Greg, herself a distinguished wood engraver and print maker, and Mrs Polunin (née Hart) a portrait painter and stage designer, and several others. To Schwabe's relief the evening passed off without incident thanks to Gerrard who did some good police work in organising the troops – six Beadles and a guardsman. At the close as people were leaving the building Roger Pettiward (1906–42),[95] who had left the Slade in 1932, got involved in a fracas and was hit on the nose. The Beadle stopped further trouble by immediately spinning Pettiward round three times very rapidly, leaving him with his back to his opponent.

Schwabe took the welfare of the students very seriously and went to great lengths to further their interests and careers. He proposed Olga Lehmann for the task of designing stamps for Newfoundland in 1933.[96] He was also responsible for her first professional commission in 1934, painting the scenery for Rossini's comic opera *La Cenerentola* at the Royal Opera House, Covent Garden.[97] Former students such as Christopher Perkins (1891–1968, painter and draughtsman) and Ithell Colquhoun (1906–88, Slade 1927–31) would seek his advice on how to make some money by art.[98] In June 1939 he went to Colquhoun's and Roland Penrose's (1900–84) show of surrealist paintings and 'objects' at the Mayor Gallery in Cork Street. He thought she had excellent draughtsmanship, craftsmanship and colour, while

the slightly morbid turn that she always had found expression in the most recent fashion in painting (though Schwabe believed that it was not very new). Schwabe recorded his impressions of the show:

> *There were dilapidated corpse-like figures, odd symbolic motives, and a very naked man, more or less naturalistic; also more naturalistic interior and some flowers. Mr. Penrose is not so efficient as Colquhoun. He scores by having labels stuck on the wall – 'I know why I am alive, but I don't know why I eat': 'Le monde est bleu, comme un orange'; 'These pictures are painted in oil and vinegar'; etc. Showmanship is evidently the most important side of his art, and the sillier the better, I suppose. Met Colquhoun in the Gallery and told her in mild terms what I thought of the show, giving her praise for what she has, but jibbing at the literature. She has, I am told, in the catalogue, which I did not see, photographs of herself nude.*[99]

Schwabe continued to provide testimonials for students and wrote several for Edgar Holloway (1914–2008). He described him as 'an able, accomplished and intelligent artist, with a sound knowledge of drawing'. Three years later in November 1939 Schwabe wrote of his 'high opinion of his ability as a draughtsman and etcher.' Holloway was declared medically unfit for service in 1941, Schwabe asked that should he be called up 'some channel may be found for the distinguished talent that he has; and that he may be made use of either as a draughtsman, or in map making, or in some direction in which that talent may not be wholly wasted.'[100] Neville Lewis with whom he had shared exhibition space at the Goupil in 1930 asked for a testimonial, explaining that, as Tonks was dead, he was driven to asking him. He was making an application for the Michaelis chair at the University of Cape Town. Schwabe in his testimonial said that he

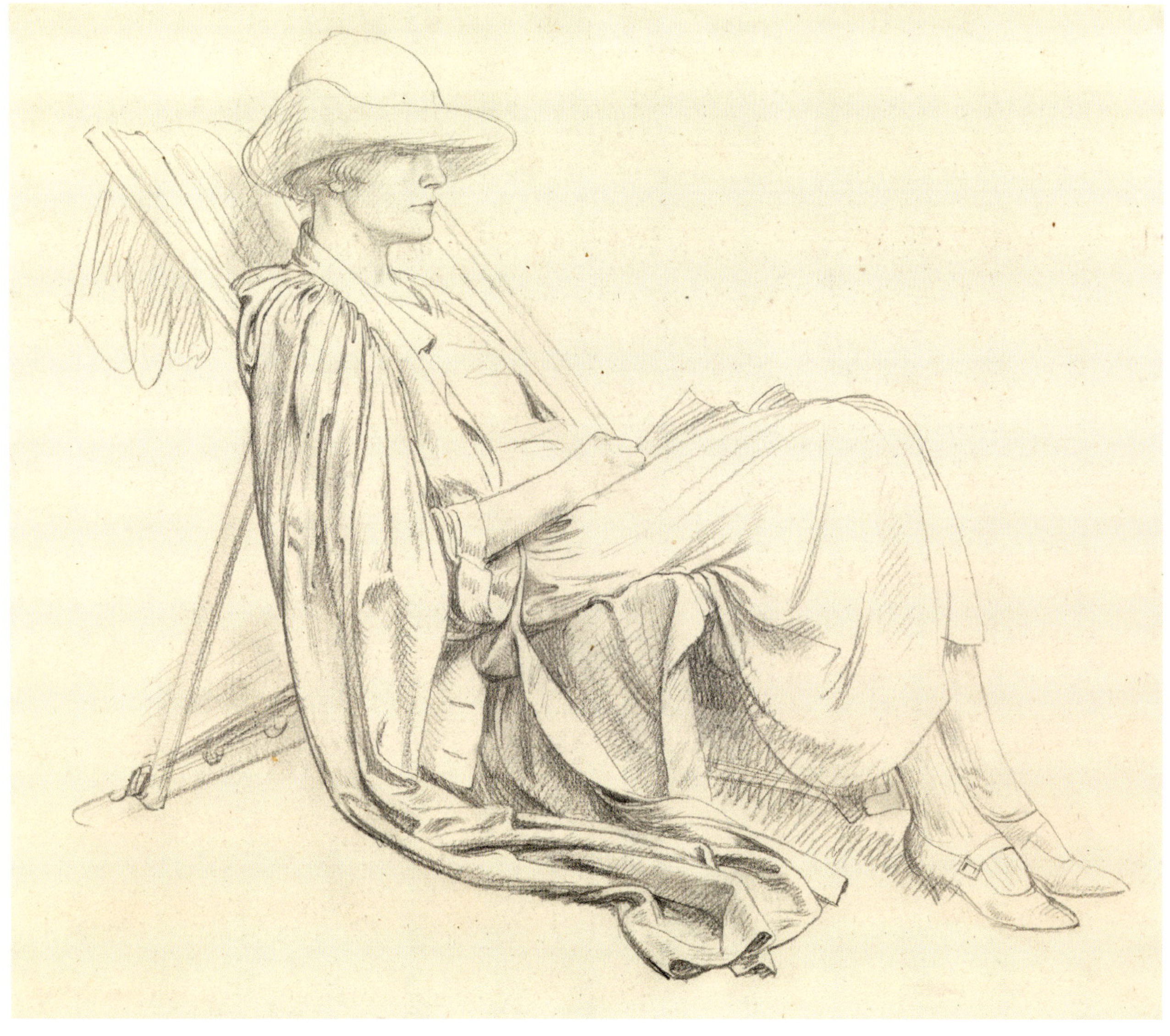

Katherine Mayer
pencil | 40 × 56 cm

was the most distinguished artist that South Africa had produced, which may not have been high praise, since the only others he knew were Gwelo Goodman (1871–1939) and Jan Juta (1895–1990).

Schwabe attended Tonks' funeral at Golders Green with Clause and the Charltons on 12 January 1937. He was introduced to Myles Tonks, a nephew, who also painted. Tonks' brother closely resembled him and when Daphne Charlton saw him she thought she had seen a ghost. Schwabe was driven back to the Slade by Gerrard whereupon he hung up a laurel wreath and press-cuttings with the reproductions of Tonks' pictures. The previous day Gerrard had cast a death-mask of Tonks. He had made the mould about 48 hours after death when the features had regained some serenity. Daphne told Schwabe there was some considerable difficulty getting the plaster of the death mask away from Tonks' head. It became a matter of force, Gerrard tugging for all he was worth.[101] Gerrard told Schwabe that:

> *Tonks was losing his hold over the students in his last three years at the Slade. They stood up to him more, and were impressed less by his mannerisms. He dreaded some sort of revolt, and complained that the modern young people, unlike those of his earlier time, wouldn't do what they were told. I have always thought it strange that a man who gave so much of his life to positive abuse of other people's work should be so hypersensitive as to withdraw from exhibiting his own on account of some adverse criticism. He did not show at the N.E.A.C. for years, chiefly because of that.[102]*

Schwabe visited Tonks' studio with Charles Collins Baker (1880–1959),[103] the painter and art historian, to pick out 45 or more drawings for the Slade School. Collins Baker, Schwabe noted, was very rightly

destroying some of the work – about half a dozen paintings, including an Adam and Eve in tempera:

> *it was a failure as a painting and never came to anything. It had a little look of Cranach about it. One or two large ruined pastels and a number of entirely unimportant drawings were also consigned to perdition. The moral of all this is not to keep too many of one's own drawings, but, though I have a firm determination to destroy a few hundred of mine soon, I know there will be ridiculous surplus of bad things.[104]*

The previous week Schwabe had gone through some of Katherine Mayer's effects who had died in February – drawings of all sorts, which he found interesting as they recalled many incidents of their Chelsea days. She lived at Trafalgar Studios in Manresa Road and had been a student at the Slade at the same time as Birdie and Schwabe and gained a prize for Fine Art Anatomy in 1906 when she 'had to draw people as though the skin had been taken off in various poses.'[105] She was in Schwabe's opinion very near to being an excellent artist and he thought that the things she did not show were frequently much better than her commissioned portraits. Schwabe reflected that he had known few painters with a better sense of character, particularly in children. He did not know how she died, but she had had mental breakdowns every month or so.[106] In happier days Schwabe had drawn her seated in a deck chair. Schwabe took an active part in hanging her memorial show at 97 Cheyne Walk where Whistler had had a studio. He was disappointed to find that the organisers had borrowed many pretty bad commissioned portraits of children and left out the drawings and studies he had selected, which would have given an intelligent critic a much higher opinion of her power as an artist. *The Times'* critic was not unsympathetic, describing her as a sensitive artist with a fairly wide range, commenting 'Portraits in water-colour are generally rather empty, but by virtue of her double sympathy, for children and for the medium, Miss Mayer made them remarkably full of expression, so that one feels the temperament of the individual child.'[107]

The Schwabe family and their friends the Bassetts spent the summer months in a guest-house in the small Dorset village of Cerne Abbas. They stayed at the Pitch Market, facing the Church door in Abbey Street, a half-timbered house, with a little fifteenth-century carving and two fifteenth-century fireplaces. For Schwabe holidays were a time for getting art work done and in Cerne and the neighbouring villages he found much material. They had holidayed in nearby Sydling in 1935 with the Wellingtons when Schwabe drew a little picture of the house with the portico, which Birdie liked, at the corner of Abbey Street in Cerne. Schwabe's preference was for working from the spot as he could check the detail more easily – he felt that working on it at home away from the spot made the drawing dull and mechanical. He and Birdie left Cerne on 20 September 1937 for London after Schwabe had climbed to the top of Cerne Church tower with their friend Minkie Pattison so that he could enjoy a final general view of the place that he liked so much. The following day he took his Cerne drawings to be mounted for the winter NEAC exhibition where they were modestly priced at 12 guineas each. At home he played about with a design for a banner for the Cerne Women's Institute, which he was doing out of friend-ship for Mrs Pattison. A previous design was rejected on account of the impropriety of the giant's figure. The infamous naked outline of the 'Giant' of Cerne is 180 feet in length cut into the turf on the slope of

Giant Hill overlooking the village and the valley of the river Cerne.

The start of the new Slade term was uneventful, the prize giving for the summer compositions going off well. Away from his usual routines – walking the dogs to Judges' Walk, taking a cold bath, the Slade, seeing the Provost and staff – Schwabe began a drawing of Mrs Noel Carrington in black, white and red chalks, with a little pastel added. Her head was as beautiful as he thought it, and the drawing went well in its first stage. She had sat for Gertler and Colin Gill. She and her sister, Margaret, were known as the beautiful Miss Alexanders. Noel Carrington said he should have drawn her sixteen years earlier but Schwabe thought she had 'worn wonderfully well'. The following month Schwabe began a drawing of Daphne Charlton but he found her a difficult and distracting sitter.

When Schwabe got the opportunity he would do a round of exhibitions in the afternoon. On Friday 12 November 1937 he visited Roy Beddington's (1910–95) show of water-colours, which Hagedorn thought too facile. He went on to two Degas shows, and thought Degas' *Spanish Beggar Woman* fine; he admired his colour and general control, especially in the later works, but there were occasional weak or empty pieces of drawing. At Tooth's there were some fine Pissarros, Boudins, Renoirs: and finally he went to the Duncan Grant show at Agnew's, with the big decorations which he believed were for the *Queen Mary*. He judged them remarkable, though the inconsistence or partial absence of planes he found worrying.

The annual South London Group Show was opened on 4 December by Thorogood. Schwabe arrived a little

late as he fell asleep in the Tube and got carried to
Balham instead of the Oval. Thorogood made reference
to Schwabe and his collection of works which were
a feature of the exhibition. A precedent had been established the previous year when a collection of Austin
Osman Spare's (1888–1956) drawings were shown.
George Holland (1901–87) wrote in the catalogue
that Schwabe did not indulge in showmanship:

> His natural reticence amounting almost to shyness, his sense
> of humour which always gives proportion and his essential
> rationality have conspired to keep him aloof from the 'sturm
> and drang' [storm and stress]. When the 'isms' and 'ists'
> explode in animated fireworks he tackles Torquemada[108] and
> solves the cross-word riddles with amazing facility. As director
> of studies at the Slade he quietly pursues his course providing
> that sound and solid base of training without which no structure
> of lasting achievement can be erected...
>
> Beneath the disarming geniality is an ardent spirit. Just as his
> work eschews the insincerities and sentimentalities that are the
> coinage of easy success, so, in his unsparing efforts wherever
> his energy is invoked... he brings the judgment of a fine and
> liberal mind...

Cerne Abbas
1939 | pen and ink and wash | 47 × 37 cm

The New Year brought good news. At his third attempt
Schwabe was elected an Associate of the Royal Society
of Painters in Water-colours (RWS); he had been rejected
in 1934 in favour of Albert Rutherston and Ronald Gray
and in 1935 by Charles Cundall, Leonard Squirrell and
Dorothy Coke. Schwabe submitted three works: *Family
Group*, *Kings Lynn* and *Cerne Abbas*. His proposer in March
1938 was William Lee Hankey (1869–1952) and
seconder Sydney Curnow Vosper (1866–1942, RWS
1915). Also elected were Daryl Lindsay (1889–1976),
Millie Fisher Prout (1875–1963) and Thomas Hennell

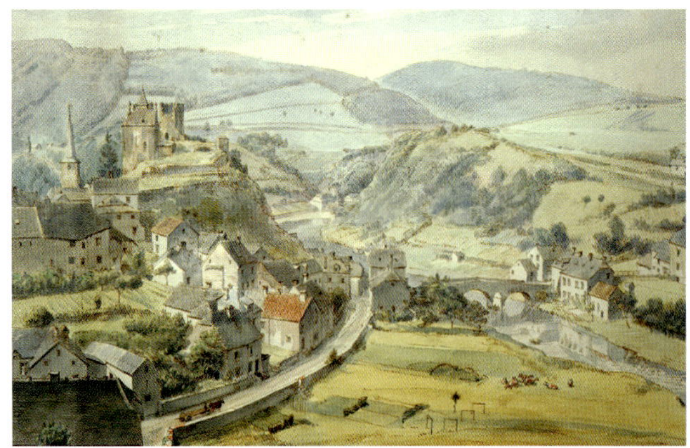

(1903–45), all with quite different styles. Schwabe was quite pleased though Charlton said it was not much of a show to belong to. The *Saturday Review* critic remarked that Schwabe 'is another careful painter, but he lacks the strong feeling for colour that Mr Ginner shows; his work is pleasing but uninspired'.

Schwabe was presented with his Diploma of Associate-ship from the RWS Council in June 1938. He had a long talk with the commissionaire who looked after the Galleries who said that buyers were now old stagers and that as they died off there were no young people to take their places; consequently sales were steadily declining. A few years previously, Members of the Society would have been horrified if one of their number sold a drawing for less than 20 guineas; Munnings had got £250 for one; now 8 and 10 guineas were usual, and not many sales at that. The photographic exhibitions had a 'bigger gate' than either the etchers or the painters.[109] Schwabe was elected as a full member of the RWS in November 1942.

Cerne Abbas was again the location for Birdie and Schwabe's summer holiday in 1938. They had as usual stayed in Dover over the Easter holiday where Schwabe struggled to finish his painting of the *Hotel de Paris*. The Schwabes stayed at Abbey Farm, Cerne for three weeks in August, being joined by Charlton and Ginger (Dr Joseph Bramhall Ellison).[110] The Schwabes' friendship with the latter developed from a chance acquaintance some twenty years ago when Birdie was in St George's Hospital, Tooting and Ginger was training as a medical student. They shared interests in the arts. Ginger invested a considerable sum of money in the film *The Robber Symphony*, billed as 'The First Surrealistic Picture'. After their return to Church Row, Schwabe

left with Max and Tony Ayrton for Sisteron in south-eastern France where they stayed at the Hôtel des Acacias. Schwabe had been abroad with Max before: in 1936 they had visited Esch-sur-Sûre in north-western Luxembourg where they spent the days drawing. A similar pattern was followed in Sisteron although fears about war were developing. Eddie Marsh later bought *Les deux Andronnes at Sisteron* from the National Society, which Schwabe had rejoined following a pathetic and flattering letter from the artist Bernard Adams (1884–1965). It seemed to Schwabe also flattering to have another picture bought by Marsh after all these years, particularly as Marsh made his purchases largely on the judgment of painters whose opinion he respected. Marsh went round the National Society with Fairlie Harmar (Viscountess Harberton 1876–1945) and Schwabe believed 'her unconscious log-rolling (bless her!) must have influenced him.'[111] Heber Thompson (1891–1971), when sending his cheque for the Artists' General Benevolent Institution, was also very complimentary about these same Sisteron drawings. They were in the best English tradition and deserved to take their place among the truly great. Schwabe thought this:

> frightfully kind of Thompson, who is sincere and honest as the day, but I wish I could swallow the last bit. Compliments were rarer when I was young. I have had several recently, to roll over on the tongue and savour privately. But too much of this sort of thing is bad, I'm sure. Eric Gill once introduced me to a man thus – 'This is Randolph Schwabe, a fine draughtsman'. I don't suppose I shall forget that easily.[112]

Back in London the war scare was at its height, with anti-aircraft guns and trenches in Hyde Park. People, notably Daphne Charlton, had been trying to persuade

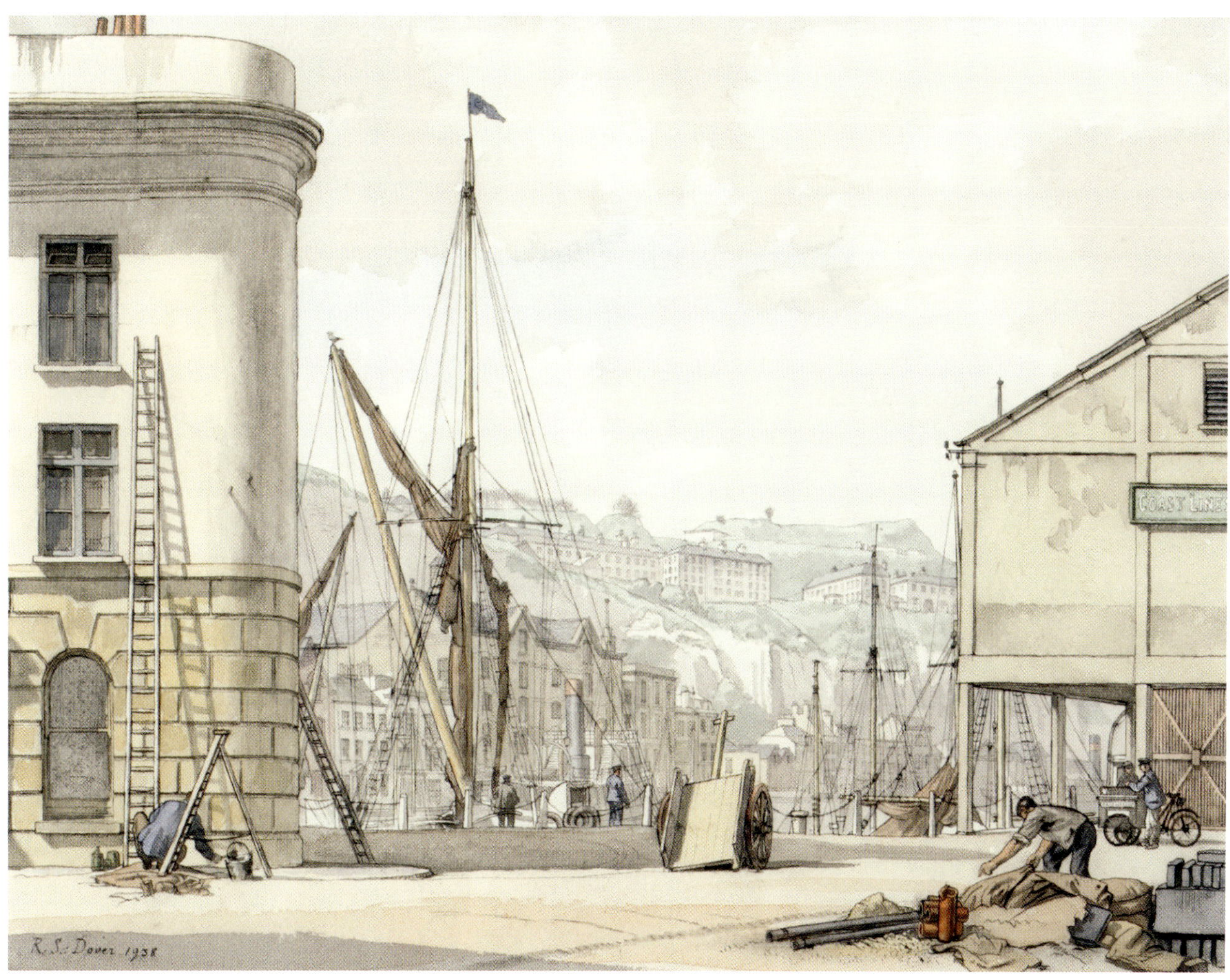

Hotel de Paris, Dover
1938 | ink and watercolour | 38.9 × 28.7 cm

Birdie to leave London. The Charltons had gone to Devizes. Alice Schwabe, on her return from Dover, joined an ARP unit and helped to distribute gas masks. Hagedorn had also been helping with the gas mask business, at Hampstead Town Hall. Notices were sent out postponing the opening of the Slade for a week till 10 October 1938. Durst reported at the Admiralty, was sent to Chatham but was given leave when things slacked off. A Foreign Office man told him that all German spies were recalled from England on 15 September. Lowinsky retired to the country with his family and a lorry containing his pictures and collections. He later was active in command of the Local Defence Volunteers at Garsington, just outside Oxford. On 8 October Schwabe recorded in his diary that he saw a balloon being filled in Grosvenor Square, part of the anti-aircraft barrage which was being tried out. Later he noted that the sky was dotted with balloons. When the Slade opened there were more students than the previous session, the numbers having risen from 218 to 239; as a result Schwabe received an automatic but unexpected addition of nearly £90 to his salary. His salary was also boosted by £250 as he had completed the posthumous portrait of *Sir John Rose Bradford*, consulting physician to University College Hospital and Past President of the Royal College of Physicians of London, which the Provost had requested. On Christmas Eve the Schwabes left by train for The Ancient House, Peasenhall in Suffolk to join the Tennysons to enjoy what was to be their last peacetime Christmas for some years.

Schwabe's diary for Sunday 19 March 1939 noted: 'Czecho-Slovakian crisis. People are more used to the idea of imminent war now, and there is less excitement than in Sept. and less depression.' On Tuesday 21 March

he wrote 'Provost definitely announced at the Professorial Board, that in case of war and evacuation of the College, the Slade would to go Oxford, to the Ruskin School' where his friend since their Slade student days, Albert Rutherston, was Ruskin Master of Drawing. It was Rutherston who had first suggested the move to Oxford, where he had been in post since 1929 following the untimely death of Sydney Carline. Rutherston 'brought to the school both the prestige of his personal reputation as a painter and designer, and the traditions and principles of teaching of the Slade School.'[113]

On 1 April thoughts of war were temporarily forgotten while Schwabe watched the Boat Race, at Ralph Edward's[114] (1894–1977) invitation, from Suffolk House, on Chiswick Mall. Cambridge beat Oxford convincingly by four lengths. The crowds were not as great as Schwabe had expected, which he attributed in part to its being Saturday morning and to declining interest in the Boat Race in this time of crisis. Mrs Lowinsky drove him back to Hammersmith Broadway as the Bridge was closed, having been damaged by an Irish bomb. Schwabe had seen the Race once before, when he had been seated on the roof of the poet Francis Macnamara's (1886–1946) house in Hammersmith Terrace with John, Innes, Dora Carrington and Ian Strang. It was seven years before he watched it again on a fine, rather misty morning from Edward's house, when Oxford won by three lengths.

Later that month Schwabe went to Rutherston's show at the Gallery in St James's Place, where Roland Pym (1910–2006) was also having a show. Pym had studied at the Slade under Schwabe from 1930–32

Slade Picnic, 1932: Ormrod; Charlton;
Daphne Charlton; Schwabe and Wilkie

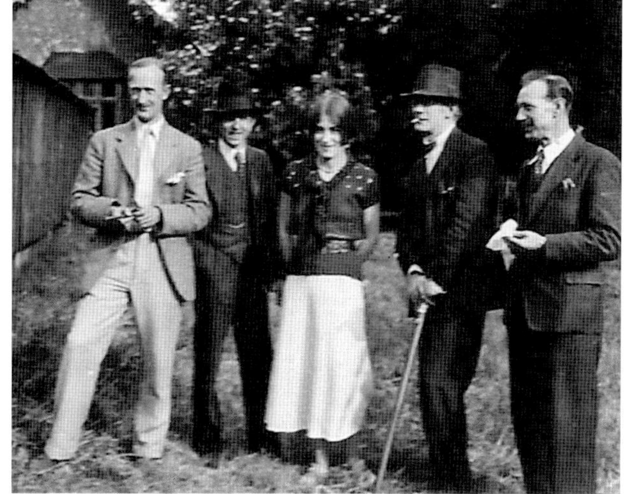

and specialised in theatre design. Schwabe thought him a clever decorator. Rutherston had sold a good few drawings but had marked them down to about 4 guineas each because the crisis made pictures seem trifling.[115] The next day they lunched together at the Athenaeum to talk over the proposal to shift the Slade to Oxford in the event of war, and spent a pleasant afternoon loafing about St James's and Bond Street. Schwabe thought Rutherston an excellent *flâneur*, interested as he was himself in all sorts of trifles. They looked into his exhibition in St James's Place, and another exhibition of drawings (including a very good Samuel Palmer) in the same street; and at the poet Samuel Rogers' (1763–1855) house and the back of White's Club for Gentlemen established in 1693, and at other buildings in that neighbourhood.

The Slade Picnic took place at the end of June at Wraysbury. In previous years it had been held at Rye House. Staff and students played cricket – Schwabe made 10 runs – and went bathing and dancing. The chief representatives of the School that year were Dodie Glass (later Masterman, 1918–2009), Peggy Rose, Paynter, Treffgarne, Parratt, Dingham, Riley and Miss Yeldham Taylor. The next day Schwabe presented prizes to Glass, Rose and Innes; this was as usual followed by a strawberry tea which that year was held under the Portico as rain threatened. One of the students, Reddall, was wearing Officer Training Corps uniform – a reminder of the fraught times.

Schwabe and Birdie frequently went to the theatre or to see a film in the evening – Saturday 8 July was no exception when they went to the Hippodrome in the West End. As they came out they were confronted by a black-out practice, with decontamination squads in

gas masks, washing away imaginary gas bombs. The proceedings lasted well into the small hours while sirens blew – all as realistic as might be. At the end of the month Birdie, Alice and Schwabe left for Cerne Abbas, again staying at Abbey Farm. They argued with Mrs Vincent about her charge of 1/- each for a bath, in addition to the three guineas a week. As Schwabe had a cold bath she let him off, but she was firm about the hot water, owing to the price of coal and the inconvenience of her hot water system, which landlord Lord Digby would not alter. Neither would he do much in the way of repairing the premises: the rain dripped through the ceiling of Schwabe's bedroom.[116] While there Schwabe received a telegram from Rutherston and on Tuesday 29 August he left for Oxford to see about Slade arrangements. He met Leonard Elton (b.c.1896), who had been Departmental Assistant at the Slade since the retirement in 1933 of Mrs Edith Green,[117] and had an interview with Veale, the University Registrar. He also inspected the empty Ruskin School premises, and the Ashmolean, which was being dismantled and the treasures sent to Wales and Chastleton.[118]

Schwabe returned to Abbey Farm to be met by commotion about the housing of six evacuated children from Haberdasher's Aske School. He heard rumours, confirmed on the radio at 11.30, of the bombing by the Luftwaffe of Warsaw and Krakow. He wrote in his diary on 1 September 1939: 'The balloon has gone up, as they say. Monstrous and almost incredible.' On 2 September they worked all day blacking out the house with curtains, black paper and other devices. In the evening 150 children and their teachers arrived in Cerne. The next day they all listened to Prime Minster Neville Chamberlain's radio message. It was, as Schwabe pithily remarked, 'War from now'.[119]

At the request of the Air Ministry, Schwabe went to London from Cerne to attend a committee for the selection of camouflage personnel. He found Jowett, Monnington, Ernest Jackson (1872–1945), the Air Ministry's Glasson and Kenneth Clark, as well as a secretary, Mallett at the Kingsway offices. There were masses of applications for camouflage work to sift through. The meeting carried over till the next day at the National Gallery, now completely cleared of pictures. Schwabe attended the meeting carrying his gas mask. As he travelled from Church Row to the National Gallery he was struck by the vulnerable points in the streets which were heavily sandbagged and the strips of paper pasted over shop and other windows to prevent the splintering of glass. Grimmond had told him that great quantities of sand were being excavated on Hampstead Heath and that fine groups of trees had been destroyed. The return journey to Cerne was no easy matter as there was only a skeleton staff at Paddington, and the Enquiry Office paid no attention to telephone calls.

Back in Cerne Schwabe worked on a drawing of Everett's shop and the portico house in order to forget about the shocking news of the Soviet Union invasion of Poland. On Monday 18 September he left for Oxford. One of his first tasks was to oversee Elton's search for accommodation for students. This was a challenge as house agents reported more demand in the previous month than in a whole year as Oxford was now the centre for various wartime activities. The Schwabes after much hunting settled on renting rooms from Mrs Brown in 7 Beaumont Street virtually opposite the Ashmolean Museum.

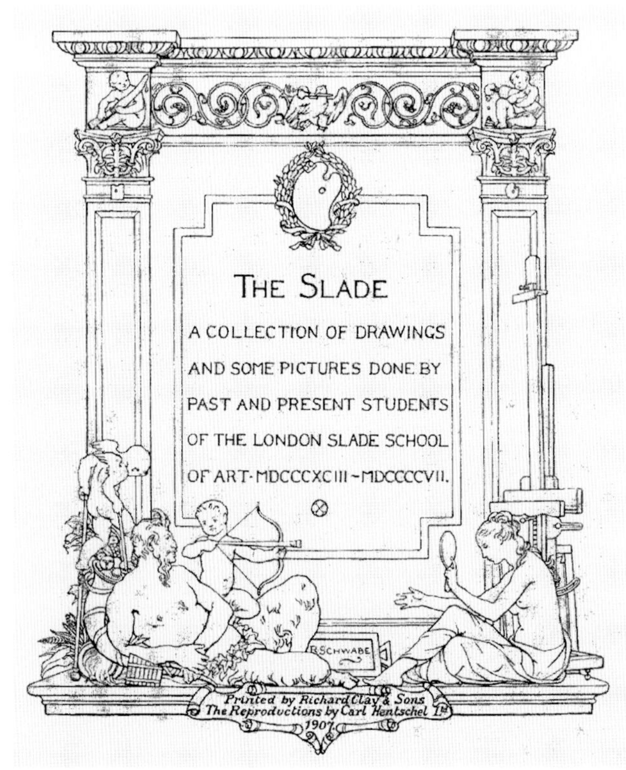

Title-page
c.1906

1 Spencer, G. (1974) *Memoirs of a painter*, p.22.
2 See www.aim25.ac.uk/cats/57/6023.htm accessed 2/1/2012.
3 It was the same show for which Augustus John did his big *Galway Peasants*, Schwabe diary 1930.
4 Schwabe, R. (1943b) 'Three teachers: Brown, Tonks and Steer', *The Burlington*, p.142.
5 Schwabe diary 1930.
6 Schwabe diary 1930.
7 Schwabe diary 1930.
8 Schwabe diary 1930.
9 Schwabe diary 1930.
10 Schwabe diary 1930.
11 Schwabe diary 1930.
12 Schwabe diary 1930.
13 Aitken, C. (1926) 'The Slade School of Fine Arts', *Apollo*, p.2.
14 Thornton, A. (1938) *The diary of an art student of the nineties*.
15 Schwabe diary 1930.
16 Gill, E. (1930), 'David Jones', *Artwork*, 23, Autumn, pp.171–77.
17 Gardner, J. (1983) *Elephants in the attic. The autobiography of James Gardner*, p.13.
18 February 1940 Schwabe wrote to the Prime Minister, in reply to an enquiry from his secretary about Walter Bayes and his proposed Civil List pension. Schwabe gave grounds for Bayes being granted it. Kenneth Clark also backed the proposal.
19 Short was knighted in 1911.
20 Rothenstein, W. (1932) *Men and memories: Recollections of William Rothenstein 1900–1922*, p.24.
21 Piper, J. (1950) Biographical and critical notes in *William Rothenstein memorial exhibition catalogue*, The Arts Council.
22 See Towner, D.C. (1979) *Recollections of a landscape painter and pottery collector*, p.26.
23 See Stevenson, J. (2007) *Edward Burra: Twentieth-century eye*, p.62.
24 Schwabe diary 1933.
25 *The Times*, 1/11/1927, p.12.
26 See Chris Beetles' entry on Badmin in the ODNB and his seminal monograph (1985) *S.R. Badmin and the English landscape*, p.14.
27 Schwabe diary 1930.
28 Strand, R. (2002) Obituary for Pullée, *The Guardian*, 27 Aug., p.18.
29 Binyon, H. (1983) *Eric Ravilious: Memoir of an artist*, p.26.
30 Speaight, R. (1962) *The portrait of an artist in his time William Rothenstein*, p.377.
31 Speaight (1962) Ibid., p.377.
32 The artist Barnett Freedman was a close friend of Mahoney; on learning his first name was Cyril he renamed him Charlie.
33 Schwabe diary 1930.
34 Stephenson, A. (1991) '"Strategies of situation": British modernism and the slump *c.*1929–1934', *The Oxford Art Journal*, 14, 2, p.30.
35 Schwabe diary 1930.
36 Schwabe diary 1930.
37 See 'The Rome Competition' in Sacha Llewellyn & Paul Liss (2010) *The unknown artist: Stanley Lewis (1905–2009) and his contemporaries*.
38 Schwabe diary 1930.
39 I am grateful to Richard Lowndes (2011) for allowing me to quote from his unpublished essay on *The ALS*, p.1.
40 Ana M. Berry (1928) 'A survey: Some younger artists and the A.L.S.' in *Design and Art*, p.46.
41 Berry (1928) Ibid., p.47.
42 See *Artwork*, 1924, 2, re The ALS travelling portfolios of pictures, pp.70–76 & pp.83-84.
43 Lowndes (2011) Op. cit., pp.6–7.
44 *The Preface and Catalogue of the 12th annual exhibition of the SLG*, December 1931. Artists and craftworkers in the area could apply for membership.
45 Collins, J. (1991) 'The origins and aims of the Contemporary Art Society' in A. Bowness et al. *British Contemporary art 1910–1990: Eighty years of collecting by The Contemporary Art Society*, p.17.
46 Recollections of Margaret de Villiers, 2011.
47 After four years 'the Society accepted its fate – an inability to compete with the long established RWS and Royal Institute, to one of which many exhibitors already belonged.' See Owen, F. (1994) 'Percy Hague Jowett and his circle'. *The Old Water-Colour Society's Club*, 63, p.77.
48 *The Times* 5/4/1924, p.8.
49 Information from the Hunterian Museums and Art Gallery Collections GLAHA 55441.
50 Interview with the author, Scotland 2009.
51 *The Times* 12/5/1924, p.19.
52 Charles Meryon (1821–68) ranks with Piranesi as one of the greatest architectural etchers.
53 Robertson, P. (Ed.) (2001) *The Chronycle: The letters of Charles Rennie Mackintosh to Margaret Macdonald Mackintosh*, p.22.
54 See the National Portrait Gallery.
55 I am grateful to Carole Hawkins for translating the catalogue.
56 Rothenstein, W. (1939) *Since fifty: Men and memories, 1922–38. Recollections of William Rothenstein*, p.154.
57 Daniel of the National Gallery had put Wellington up for the post and had been coaching him how to behave before a Committee, see Schwabe diary 1930.
58 Schwabe diary 1930.
59 Schwabe diary 1930.
60 Schwabe diary 1930.
61 Schwabe diary 1930.
62 Schwabe diary 1930.
63 Schwabe diary 1930.
64 Schwabe diary 1930.

65 Forge, A. (Ed.) (1976) *The [William] Townsend Journals.*
An artist's record of his times 1928–51, p.26.

66 Schwabe diary 1930.

67 Forge (1976) Op. cit., p.26.

68 Schwabe noted in his diary 1931 'McNab [Iain] says that the Slade
student (Westby) whom the Provost kicked out for the Clausen
business is working at his School [Grosvenor]. Thinks him
harmless but not much good. I didn't object to him personally,
but he had to go, of course.'

69 Pasted in typescript in Schwabe's *Newspaper Cuttings* book alongside
the article of 27 October 1930 from *The Daily Mail* was a suggested
heading for *The Daily Mail's* Apology: A KONODY OF ERRORS.
This was attributed to L. Elton.

70 William Rothenstein letter to Schwabe 18/5/1931.

71 Raverat, G. (1931) *Time and Tide*, 16 May, p.602.

72 Schwabe was for instance a member of the selection committee
for British Graphic Art in Bucharest (see *The Times* 18/12/1935)
and a judge for the Pewter Handicraft Competition (see *The Times*
24/9/1936) and the Central Telegraph Office Employees' Art
Exhibition (see Schwabe diary 1936), a role Orpen undertook
before him. He succeeded Bayes as Chief Examiner in Art for
the Board of Education.

73 See Chaplin (1998).

74 Rothenstein mentioned Schwabe's *Fructidor* to J.B. Manson as a
possible Chantrey purchase, but to no avail. Schwabe was neither
surprised nor hurt. See Schwabe diary 1933.

75 J.B. (1932) *Manchester Guardian*, 18 Nov., p.10.

76 *Morning Post* 14/11/1932.

77 *The Sunday Times* 4/12/1932.

78 Priv. Corr. to the author, from Margaret de Villiers, 20/3/2012.

79 See Holroyd (1974) p.48.

80 Her present 'daily help' was Selina Ruby Foot. See Schwabe diary
1932.

81 *Glasgow Evening News* 14/2/1933 article headlined 'Glasgow Should
Honour Charles Mackintosh. Architect With World Influence.
MEMORIAL EXHIBITION?'

82 This practice ceased in 1935 when elections became the
responsibility of the General Committee. See *The Athenaeum:
Club and social life in London 1824–1974.*

83 Schwabe diary 1936.

84 See www.aim25.ac.uk/cats/87/7253.htm and Schwabe diary
21/1/1938.

85 Laughton, B. (1971) *The Slade 1817–1971. A centenary exhibition*,
Royal Academy of Arts, p.9.

86 Schwabe diary 1935.

87 Schwabe diary 1936.

88 Paul Feiler interview with the author, Cornwall, May 2010
(henceforth PF interview 2010).

89 Margaret Thomas interview with the author, 2010, Suffolk
(henceforth MT interview 2010).

90 Schwabe diary 1937.

91 See Polunin, V. (1927/1980) *The continental method of scene painting.*

92 Laver, J. (1934) 'Designing for the theatre: continental methods
at the Slade School', *The Studio*, December, pp.261–66. He became
Keeper in 1938 succeeding Martin Hardie (1875–1952).

93 *Le Charivari* was an illustrated newspaper published in Paris from
1832–1937. The magazine *Punch* was subtitled *The London Charivari*.

94 Schwabe designed the book jacket for Douie's novel *The Lost Heritage*
in 1939. The cover which Schwabe charged Murray's the publisher
3 guineas for was reproduced in *The Times Literary Supplement* and
took up more space than the review. Douie resigned from UCL
on 31/12/1938 and his duties were taken over by E. L. Tanner.

95 Pettiward published humorous drawings under the pseudonym
of Paul Crum; a Temporary Capt. Beds. & Herts. Reg., he
was killed in a Commando raid on Dieppe, 19 August 1942.
He received some private tuition from Schwabe's brother
Eric aka 'Bill' while on Commando training in Scotland.

96 Schwabe diary 1933.

97 Granger , D. (2001) Obituary for Lehmann, *The Guardian*,
6 Dec., p.22.

98 Schwabe diary 1934.

99 Schwabe diary 1939.

100 Meyrick, R. (1996) *The etchings and engravings of Edgar Holloway.
A catalogue raisonné*, see Testimonials 1936 & 1939 & p.21.

101 Schwabe diary 1937. Schwabe never owned or drove a car.

102 Schwabe diary 1937.

103 See Collins Baker (1939) Tonks as an artist in J. Horne
The life of Henry Tonks.

104 Schwabe diary 1937.

105 Cecil Riley interview with the author, Cornwall, May 2010.
Riley taught at Warwick School from 1942-45. Students
according to Margaret Thomas had 'real corpses to draw from.'
(MT interview 2010).

106 Schwabe diary 1932. He noted that Mayer was 50 and looked
very well.

107 *The Times* 19/7/1937, p.12.

108 Pseudonym of Edward Powys Mathers the poet and translator/
linguist who composed crosswords for the *Observer* from 1926
until his death in 1939.

109 Schwabe diary 1938.

110 In 1932, in a landmark clinical trial, [at Grove Hospital]
Joseph Bramhall Ellison, a physician on the staff, discovered
that providing vitamin A to children with measles reduced
their mortality by 58%. See http://ezitis.myzen.co.uk/grove.html
accessed 13/5/2012.

111 Schwabe diary 1939.

112 Schwabe diary 1939.
113 Horton, P. (1946) 'The Ruskin School of Drawing and of Fine Art',
    The Studio, 132, 645, p.178.
114 Edwards was keeper of the Department of Woodwork at the
    Victoria and Albert Museum.
115 Schwabe diary 1939.
116 Schwabe diary 1939.
117 Mrs Green had for several years carried out the secretarial work
    of the School following the illness and retirement of her brother
    Koe Child in the summer of 1930 after 37 years of service. Elton's
    uncle D. S. MacColl, himself a former Slade student, suggested he
    apply for the post – see Chaplin (1998) Op. cit.
118 Elton drove Schwabe to Chastleton in Scott's van with the Slade
    pictures on 26/10/1940.
119 Schwabe diary 1939.

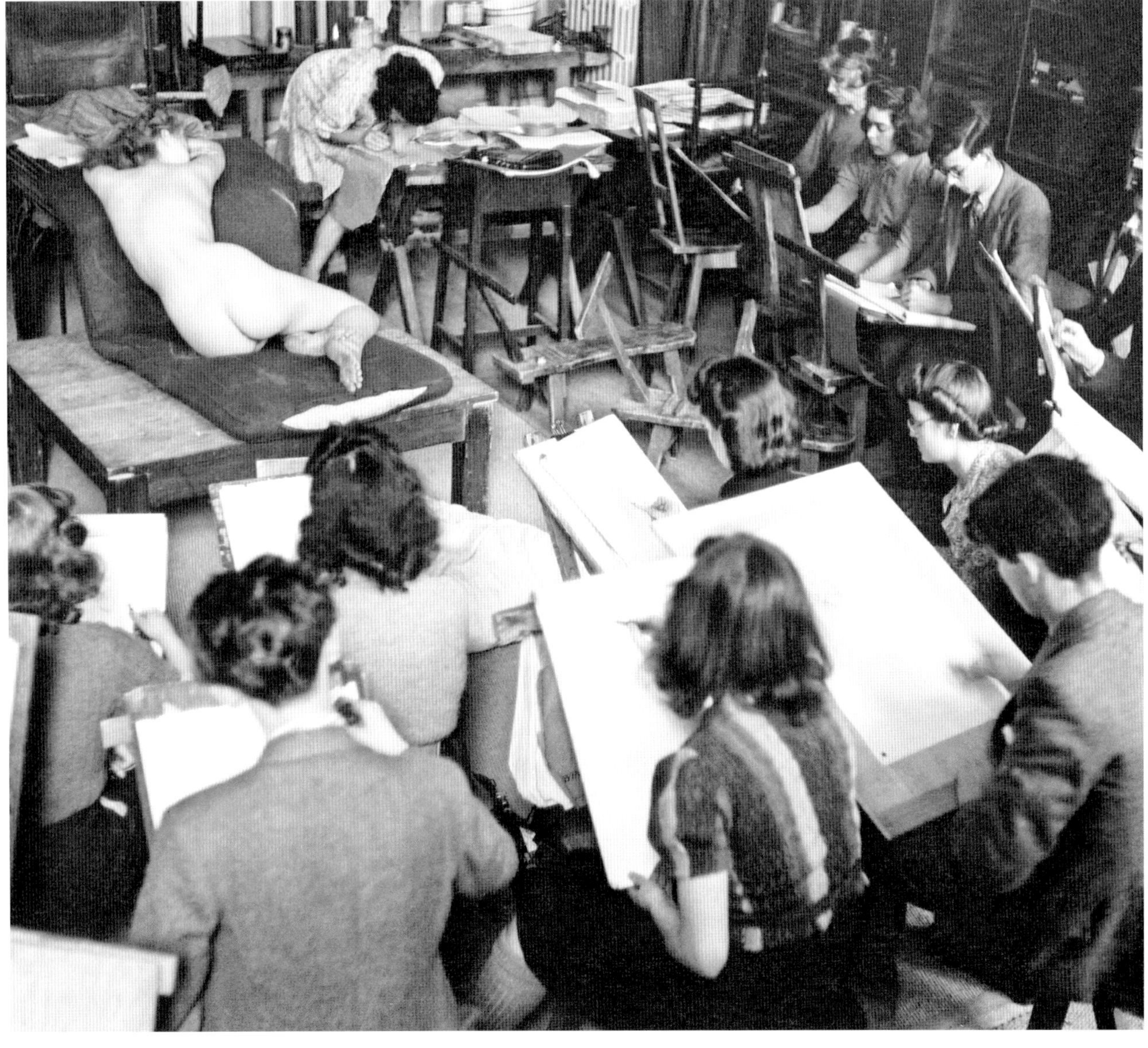

'The Life Room', *Picture Post*, 11 January 1941

SLADE AND THE RUSKIN

OXFORD 1939–45

On Monday 16 October 1939 the Slade-Ruskin School opened at the Ashmolean Museum. Over 100 students, men and women, new and old, were in their places and working within an hour. Schwabe thought it 'not so bad, considering all the difficulties, negotiated mainly by Albert [Rutherston] and [Leonard] Elton.'[1] The subjects to be taught were Painting, Drawing, Design, Engraving and Lithography. A life model would sit daily. Antique, Still Life and Head Painting would also be taught. Terms were to be of nine weeks as per the Oxford norm; accordingly termly fees were reduced to £7-7s. for full-time attendance. Part-time students would still be accepted. It was the practice of the Ruskin School for men and women students to work together: this was to be continued. Details of the teaching staff were to be announced later.

A few days after the start of the term Schwabe inspected the new design room in the unfinished Bodleian building where Albert Rutherston had started a small theatre class. The students had to take great care not to drop paint or mess up the new floor. The lavatories were not yet finished and in the interim the 'girls' had to use the Sheldonian and the men, the King's Arms.[2] Rutherston would on occasions take a few students to The Playhouse to do some practical work with Anthony Holland, the scenic artist.

At the weekend Schwabe returned to London to fetch some clothes, having none with him but those he took to Cerne in the summer. He called on the Ayrtons where he found Tony extremely pessimistic about the war believing that the interruption could be fatal to his chances of development as an artist. Later a Major in the Royal Engineers involved in camouflage, he

died of meningitis in Libya in April 1943. Ayrton was not alone in his pessimism – many artists who were ruined wrote to Schwabe for advice about jobs. Anthony Devas (1911–58), who went about the country painting portraits while he could, wanted settled teaching work. Cheston, who was in Bristol, was seeking something other than the mechanical copying of plans on which he was engaged. 'Tim' Brown, the Prix de Rome sculptor, sent what Schwabe thought was a conceited, illogical, conscientious objector's letter asking about teaching work: he had given up some work in the potteries on account of the 'stupidity' of business men.

The Slade-Ruskin collaboration of Schwabe, Rutherston and staff sought to encourage the students' development as artists in spite of the overcrowded teaching spaces in the Ashmolean and the shortage of materials. Exhibitions were organised from the outset. The first under the auspices of the University and Ashmolean authorities was supported by the Contemporary Art Society and featured the work of 50 British living artists in the Weldon Gallery of the Ashmolean Museum. The organising committee consisted of Sir Muirhead Bone (who lived in Oxford), Dr K.T. Parker, Keeper of the Department of Fine Art, Ashmolean Museum, Schwabe and Rutherston. The exhibition was to promote contemporary art and to assist younger artists in time of hardship. With limited wall space artists were invited to submit two unframed works of not more than 30 inches horizontal measure or one of a larger size; the Contemporary Art Society would provide a uniform moulding for all works free of charge and no commission would be charged on sales. The private view on 11 November was well attended. Among those who came were Kenneth Clark, William Rothenstein, Gilbert Murray (with whom Schwabe sat on the

Committee of the Whitechapel Art Gallery), Eddie Marsh and the Lowinskys. There was according to Schwabe 'trouble' with Paul Nash, who was to do an article on the show in *The Listener*. Schwabe said that Nash:

> *wants, for foolish reasons not unconnected with propaganda for Sur-Realisme and Paul Nash, to reproduce Ithell Colquhoun's 'Anchor', a surrealist 'machine', as the feature of the show. We nearly threw it out when hanging. Albert squashed this plan and got Nash to agree to reproduce [James] Fitton's 'Eve' instead.*[3]

This Nash did and in his article he reported that 'it had been selected by the organisers as representing the tone and character of the exhibition.'[4] Nash also informed readers that Stephen Bone (Muirhead's son), had painted the frames to harmonise with the pictures.

Shortly after the exhibition opened Schwabe was visited by H.M. Bateman (1887–1970) from Curridge, near Newbury, to ask advice about his painting. Schwabe thought he might have developed into a good painter instead of a caricaturist, and while he felt he did some pleasant things now, he did not think he could carry them very far. When young, Bateman had had lessons from an Antwerp painter, who in Schwabe's view had taught him little about tone and values. He suggested some private coaching from Gwynne-Jones who was also teaching at Reading one day a week. Schwabe took Bateman into his rooms in 7 Beaumont Street to show him some drawings of his own, and to compare notes, as they had been drawing similar subjects during the summer – barns, farm wagons and so on. He found him an able draughtsman, apart from caricature. Birdie, not knowing that he was the celebrated Bateman, was very favourably impressed by his personality and manners.[5]

In January 1943 Bateman returned to study at the Slade-Ruskin for five weeks of painting from the model.

Schwabe continued to undertake portrait commissions including one for the Cadbury firm of their chief engineer Arthur Hackett. The firm had other drawings of retired members of their staff which had been executed by Henry Payne (1868–1940), one of the Birmingham Group of artist-craftsmen. Schwabe was driven to Bournville to see the Payne drawings hung in the staff dining room, so that his might range with them in size and style. In the afternoon, he attended his first ever football match (West Bromwich Albion v Birmingham, played at the Hawthorns). There were about 10,000 people present whereas in peacetime there might have been 60,000. Cadbury paid Schwabe 16 guineas for each of his drawings, including those of Miss Catnach of the Catnach Press family, the first woman to be immortalised for the firm. Christmas was again spent with the Tennysons at Peasenhall, before the Schwabes travelled to Cerne for the New Year.

The New Year brought more students to the Slade than the previous term. Elton left towards the end of December 1941 going to the War Office, Ralph Nuttall-Smith taking his place. Gerrard had enlisted in the Royal Engineers, after lying about his age and was to go to France in the near future.[6] Schwabe was finding it 'for the moment, a whole-time war-time job'[7] and spent much time teaching. Biddy Picard (née Savage, b.1920) who attended Chesterfield School of Art before training in Oxford recalled how Schwabe would quietly 'mosey round'. She said:

> *he'd sometimes say you can do better than that, another day he'd sit down and do a little drawing. He'd point out quite a few things*

and then he'd perhaps do a little bit of a drawing to explain something in a top corner or somewhere. He was always around but as far as teaching goes, well basically you were teaching yourself by looking. Sometimes you'd get somebody would say something that just hit a moment where it was something you needed to know.[8]

Bernard Dunstan (b.1920) thought Schwabe 'too reserved to be what would now be called a "charismatic" teacher' but he felt lucky to have been taught by him as he had 'total integrity'. Schwabe's devotion to his *métier* and his 'lack of interest in fame or riches' provided a powerful and inspiring example to the young Dunstan.[9]

Schwabe in his rare free time would spend the short-pose hour from 3 to 4, drawing from the model Patricia (Pat) Koring, who became a close friend of Rutherston 'which significantly affected his life and work in old age.'[10] Picard described her as 'a very creamy pale blonde. We hated drawing her because she was a very uninteresting beautiful girl… Too perfect to be interesting.'[11] Dunstan described her as 'a svelte but passive blond' model.[12] There were also two 'fine figure models, Miss Duval, who has the head of a Watteau on the torso of a Greek Venus, and Miss Yeaxley, the Don's daughter'.[13] In February 1942 Schwabe and Rutherston looked to register their models Duval, Salle and Koring as in permanent recognised employment; otherwise they could be called up for some more obvious National Service; models were essential to the working of the School.

Another model Celia Dennis broke her arm after a fall in the School; Rutherston and Schwabe decided that the School would pay her compensation of £12 beyond her pay for three weeks. She had been one of Gertler's models and was probably the last person to see him alive before he committed suicide:

> *After she left [her usual portrait sitting], Gertler went back to the house and removed a mattress from one of the beds. Dragging it behind him, he returned to the studio, and after making sure the windows were tightly closed, stuffed it against the door. Then he turned on both the gas ring and stove, and lay down to await death.*[14]

Schwabe thought her 'A pretty, affected creature.'[15]

It was a particularly cold winter – the students skated on the Cherwell; elsewhere across the country there were many accounts of great blizzards with pine trees perishing under the weight of the ice and robins being found sheathed in ice, dead on branches. Schwabe was not put off by the cold as there was much to inspire his pencil and he continued with his drawings in St Helen's Passage and Pembroke Street.

The practice of visiting teachers was continued. Barnet Freedman, an official war artist, would arrive at the School in his army captain's uniform and Rothenstein 'visited occasionally, a tiny figure in unlikely squadron leader's uniform'.[16] Percy Horton, who succeeded Rutherston in 1949 as Ruskin Master of Drawing, was another visitor. Gwynne-Jones came to criticize the few Slade summer pictures that had reached them. No first prize was awarded as the consignment was so incomplete; nonetheless, Angela Baynes, Tony Baynes and Bartlett received £10 each, and Trice Martin and Irene Williams £5. While in Oxford Gwynne-Jones lectured on 'Realism and Naturalism in Modern Art' to the Slade students and a few others in the Ashmolean.

Tancred Borenius (1885–1948) had become the first Durning-Lawrence Professor of the History of Art at UCL in 1922, having been a lecturer since 1914. While the students found his lectures interesting his Finnish accent was a problem. Cecil Riley (b.1917, Slade 1936–39), a former prize-winning Slade student, operated the lantern slides for Borenius for the examination (which his girlfriend and later wife Joan Batty (b.1920) was taking). He recalled that when he studied History of Art in London:

> *you had glass slides, monochrome glass slides and [Borenius] lecture consisted of an old fashioned magic lantern with two things which caused a bright light and his lectures were – he put the slides up and he'd talk about them and you made notes and then we used to sit in the design room, as we called it at the Slade where old Ormrod used to operate, going through these slides and over and over again. Then the exam consisted of sitting in a darkened room with the projector, the slides on the screen and then when they came up you had to write about who did the picture and who was influenced by and what. And we were very naughty, we had some codes and if the painting was Signorelli's [c.1441–1523], somebody just whispered, skid on your belly or bottle of sherry.*[17]

Riley and his friends were not the only students to devise ingenious ways of passing the examination. Kyffin Williams (1918–2006) described how groups of his peers would memorise a different period and when the period flashed up on the screen they would identify it and the artist for their friends. 'Everyone took first class honours in History of Art.'[18]

Schwabe and Rutherston had given Riley permission to use the premises and studio to further his art. Schwabe and Charlton went to a show of work by Riley, Vera Leslie, Miss Fisher, Feiler, Tony Baynes, and Brayshaw, got up by themselves in a shed, up a wooden ladder, in New Inn Yard off St Aldate's.

The Annual Slade (and Ruskin) Dinner was held in the grand surroundings of New College Hall which slightly awed Schwabe's guests who wore morning dress; they included Basil Blackwell, the Priestleys, the Huskinsons, Lowinsky, Gwynne-Jones, the Charltons and some students (Parratt, the Emerys, Miss Grainger). Schwabe had invited J.B. Priestley (1894–1984) to speak. He had previously been much occupied with the première of his new play *The Long Mirror* at The Playhouse and kept on looking at his watch as he was giving out the prizes. Paul Feiler, the Chairman of the Slade Society, chided Priestley who did not much enjoy the reprimand.[19] Priestley's wife, Jane Mary Wyndham Lewis, who was working in the School, confided to Schwabe that they had sold some investments and were using the money to buy drawings. 'She offered to help good students of the necessitous kind in that way.'[20]

Throughout the war Schwabe continued with his various examining duties, traversing the length and breadth of the country, and with his committee work involving regular visits to London to attend executive meetings of the NEAC. He submitted three paintings, *Giants Head Farm, Cerne Abbas*; *Cerne in Winter* and *Keddle Bridge* to the RWS Annual Exhibition in spring 1940. Shortly after he exhibited *Sisteron, Provence*; a portrait of *Mr Randall Davies* and the recently completed *Pembroke Street, Oxford* at the Ashmolean Museum as part of the Contemporary British Drawings show organised in co-operation with the Oxford Arts Club. Rothenstein bought *Pembroke Street* for Carlisle Museum at the reduced

Pringsheim with Albert Rutherston,
Ashmolean Museum, Oxford
COLLECTION JANET AND DI BARNES

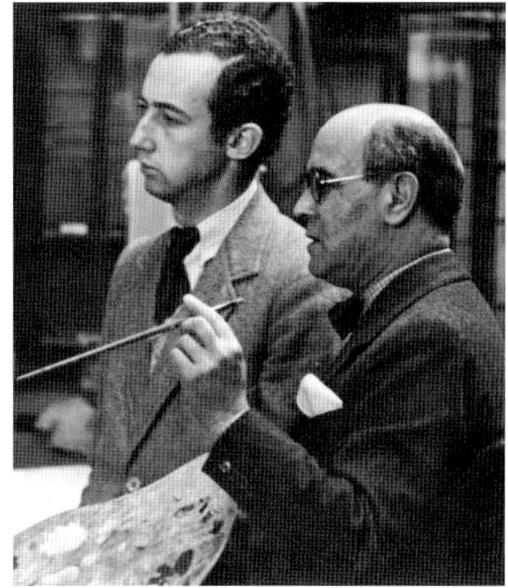

price of ten guineas. The catalogue, the cover of which featured a delicate vignette by Rutherston, explained that the exhibition was 'aimed at giving a comprehensive and representative survey of British draughtsmanship'. Lowinsky was irritated with Rutherston because he had not been included in the show but Schwabe thought this unreasonable as he had never exhibited a drawing in his life. The private view was not as well attended as it might have been although Paul Nash, an official war artist attended in Air Force uniform. Schwabe wryly observed that 'He had so many badges on him that people supposed he had designed his uniform himself.'[21] Parker bought one of Schwabe's drawings (*Sisteron*) for eight guineas for the Ashmolean Museum.

Plain-clothes policemen came to the School on the afternoon of 27 May 1940 and took away Feiler, who had been born in Frankfurt-am-Main and his cousin Pringsheim to be interned. Although the police were civil, Schwabe found it unpleasant and felt very sorry for the two men. Feiler's father, Erich Feiler, was Professor of Dentistry at Frankfurt University and his mother, Helene, née Pringsheim moved in liberal political circles. When the Nazis seized power in 1933 they sent him to school first to Zwolle in the Netherlands, then to Canford, Dorset.[22] Pringsheim's father was a distinguished authority on Roman Law; all four of his sons who were aged between 16–26 were deported without his or their consent.[23] As 'enemy aliens' they were taken to the police station in Oxford and then to internment camps in Huyton, near Liverpool and the Isle of Man. Due to be deported from Liverpool to Canada on 1 July aboard the liner *Arandora Star*, they were prevented from boarding by the sergeant who stood at the top of the boat and who

said to Feiler 'no more'. He pleaded to be allowed to be with his friends but the sergeant was adamant and said, 'no more, go back.' The next day the *Arandora Star* was torpedoed by a German U-boat off the west coast of Ireland and sank, with the loss of over 600 lives, including German and Italian internees, POWs and 'enemy aliens'. Feiler and Pringsheim left on the next boat with a considerable number of intellectuals and went from camp to camp, across Canada.

Feiler was first interned in Quebec where he recalled that his next door neighbour was Klaus Fuchs (1911–88), the German physicist, who later betrayed the UK to the Soviet Union and in 1950 was jailed for 14 years. After Feiler had been in Canada for about eight months he was told that certain categories of people would be released. These included professionals who would be helpful for the war effort; one of the categories was famous artists, in which he learned he had been placed by Schwabe who had been to London and signed a petition.

Feiler was sent back to England. 'So naturally, because I knew it was due to his [Schwabe's] plea that I was able to come back I was very keen to keep in contact with him.'[24] Feiler on his return took up a teaching post as art master at Eastbourne College which had been evacuated to Oxford and combined with Radley College. Exactly a year after he had last seen Schwabe he went on 27 May 1941 to visit him. Schwabe noted in his diary that Feiler 'thanked me warmly for the efforts I had made to get him out. It was a long business. He looks very fit, and is not resentful, knowing the conditions, and having come in contact with internees who really have Nazi sympathies.' Feiler found Schwabe to be a 'strange mixture of remote, very private and yet quite a public person in a way.' He would often see Schwabe at lunch socialising with his friends when he would invite him to join them.

Socialising was not always uppermost in people's minds; as Schwabe noted in his diary at the end of May 'Everyone is intensely worried about the War. The little success at Narvik comes as a small consolation for events in Flanders.' His sister-in-law wrote from Dover describing the scenes there during the Dunkirk evacuation as 'unforgettable'. Her husband, Tom Cobbe, a doctor, operated on the wounded for three nights.

The Slade Picnic in the village of Clifton Hampden, on the north bank of the River Thames, just east of Abingdon was called off by Parratt and Knaggs of the Slade Society as few people were in a mind to be festive. Parratt together with a good many male students including Heath, Treffgarne and Emery, were shortly leaving to join the Army. Some were conscientious objectors including the former student Cecil Riley who after attending a tribunal in Reading volunteered for the Anti-Gas Squad in Oxford. Bryan Wynter (1915–75, Slade 1938–40) and Hugh Lyell Mellor, who were friends of Riley's, were also conscientious objectors. Mellor appeared before a Lancashire tribunal. Judge Burgis said the applicant had most unfavourably impressed the tribunal, his life was selfish and shut and that he wanted to go on pursuing the comfortable, pleasant surroundings of Oxford. He was ordered to perform non-combatant service.[25]

The railings round the Martyrs' Memorial were removed on 1 July for scrap-iron for munitions. On the same day Schwabe's landlady cleared out her basement as a shelter in case of air-raids. They later

all received instruction in the use of the stirrup pump should they have to deal with incendiary bombs.

The Slade students were asked by Rutherston to volunteer as fire watchers in the Ashmolean. Gardner from the Home Guard, who had been a sergeant-major in the artillery in the last War, was responsible for looking after the Museum and a railing was built round the roof and students taken up to familiarise themselves with the layout. Biddy Picard would take her sleeping bag and sleep on the roof – 'where the great stone heads look down on Oxford.'[26] She recalled the beauty of the view of the towers and the bells as she watched the dawn light and the sun rise and savoured the smell in the early morning of oranges in the market and bread being baked. Picard also remembered that on one night Gardner put the History of Art slides on the screen in the lecture room to entertain the students until the 'all clear'.

As the term had finished Schwabe was busy at Beaumont Street completing his drawing of *Vanbrugh House* which he sent in October to the NEAC exhibition at the Suffolk Street Galleries in Pall Mall together with several of his architectural drawings of Oxford colleges. The RWS cancelled the exhibition, and *Vanbrugh House* was later bought by Parker for the Museum for the reduced price of eight guineas.

At the request of the Director John Rothenstein, Schwabe began in *situ* a drawing of the Tate Gallery which he thought had 'several bad architectural defects. The balusters are an ugly design, too'.[27] By the end of July it was finished – Schwabe had to put colour onto it as the Gallery could not buy anything that was not in colour unless from some private fund. The trustees paid Schwabe £20 for the completed watercolour drawing.

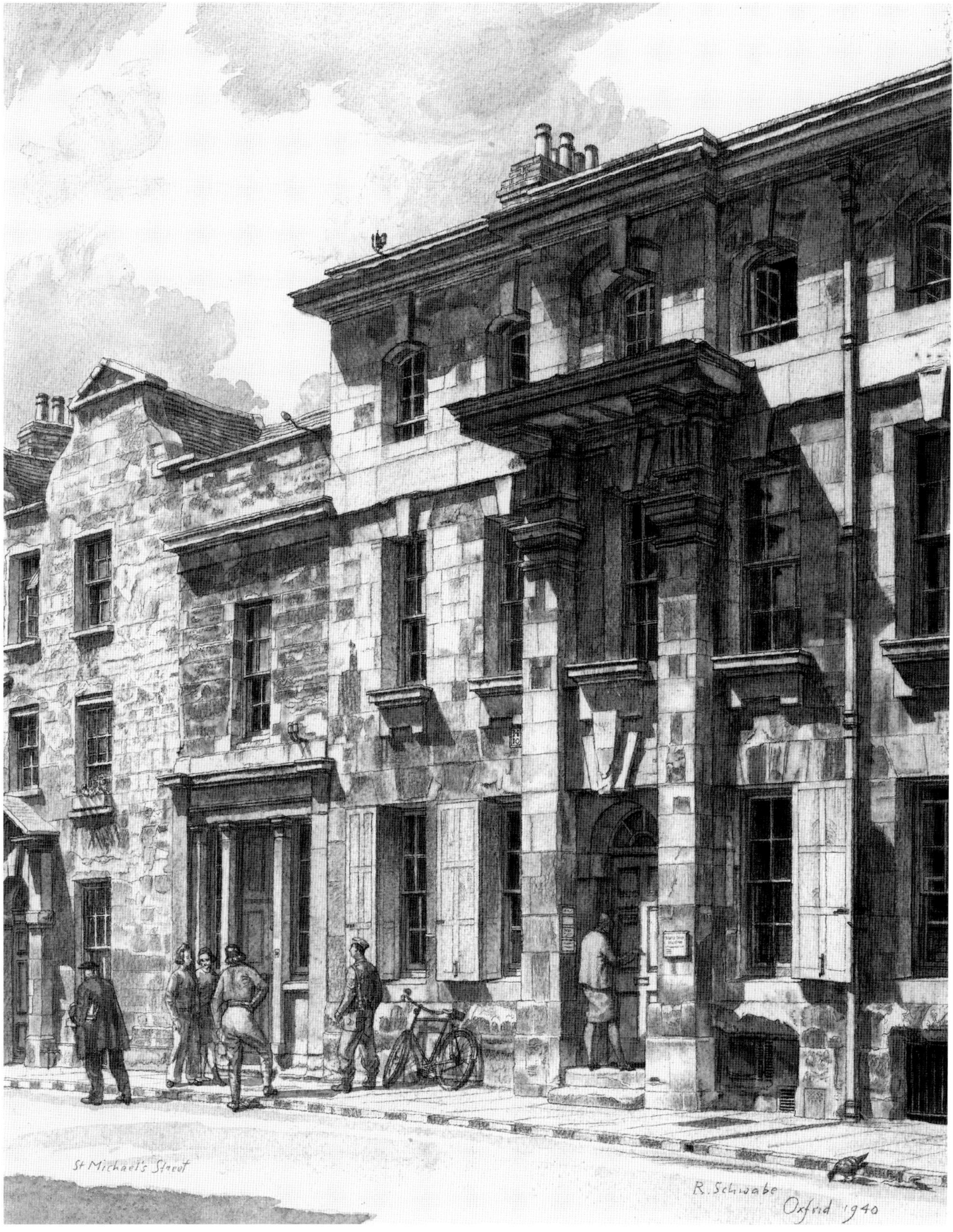

Vanbrugh House

1940 | black chalk and grey wash | 37.3 x 29.8 cm

Early January 1941 was so cold that even Schwabe did not go out to draw; instead he amused himself drawing in the Ashmolean Museum. The *Picture Post* sent the painter Ronald Ossory Dunlop ARA (1894–1973) to write a feature on 'The Life of an Art Student'. Joan Batty and Baynes were photographed at work in the Drawing Class. Dunlop wrote: 'They've seen how easily the old masters did it. They've seen how easily John and Orpen did. Now when they get down to it, they find drawing is a science, needing anatomical knowledge.' Schwabe later wrote a testimonial for Batty who had won a scholarship to the Slade:

> She has done well as a Slade student, her work is never perfunctory but is done with real interest and has a genuine personal quality. She has gone far with the study of drawing, painting and design and has a good sense of both form and colour. In the school sketch club and other exhibitions and competitions her productions have generally received high encomium and are certainly outstanding. She should have a stimulating influence as a teacher and has knowledge and feeling to support her.

Published on 11 January 1941 the *Picture Post* article immediately aroused the wrath of Charlton who sent Schwabe a copy of a most abusive letter he had written to Dunlop describing it as 'ignorance', 'downright dishonesty', 'inaccuracy', and 'bloody cheek'. Quite what parts of the lavishly illustrated four-page spread irritated Charlton are unclear. Perhaps he was irked by Dunlop's acerbic comments about the teaching methods of the Professors and how these varied:

> from almost complete indifference to a close and personal lecture to each student in strict rotation. Some give a very audible talk to one picked student, to which the others 'listen-in', whilst pretending to go on with their work. The headmaster or chief professor is usually little seen, but his influence over the school is felt by all. His ideas on how art should and should not be taught usually pervade the entire work of the establishment. But often more potent and powerful than the influence of the Head or the assistant professors is that of the 'big shots' amongst the students.
>
> Usually there are one or two outstanding personalities amongst the older students, who may already have earned a considerable reputation for themselves. These talented, creative students have a lasting effect on the rest and do a great deal of good if they are of the right type. They may do much harm if their egotism outweighs their real gifts.

Kyffin Williams believed himself to be talentless, yet he had real gifts, the realisation of which owed much to Schwabe. He entered the Slade in October 1941 having been discharged from the Army with epilepsy. Schwabe had interviewed him and although clearly surprised at his inability 'in his kindly way suggested that [he] should enter for a term to see how things went… older than most of the male students, [Williams] saw a lot of Schwabe and he became a very good friend.'[28] Schwabe had a passion for limericks and would share these with Williams. He even had one published in *The Times* about the German artist Menzel (1815–1905):

> There was an old fellow called Menzel,
> Who drew very well with a pencil,
> If he hadn't one, then
> He would draw with a pen,
> Or a brush, or with any utensil.[29]

For Williams his epiphany occurred during his second year when Schwabe told him that he could not draw and suggested that he see if he could paint. 'The more [he] painted, the more [he] began to realise that this

'The Life of an Art Student', *Picture Post*, 11 January 1941

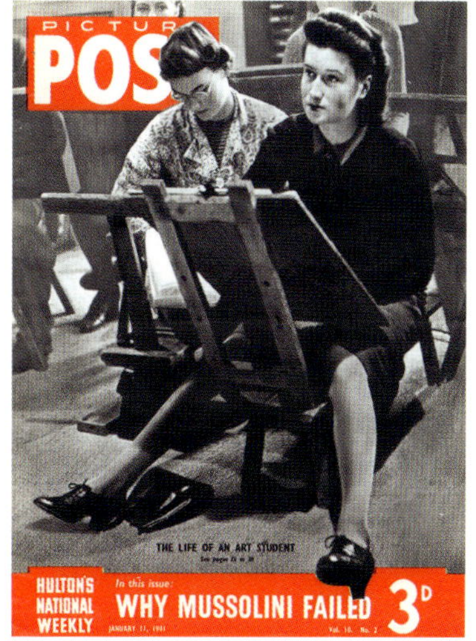

was [his] real means of expression.'[30] Williams subsequently was awarded a prize for portraiture and the Robert Ross Leaving Scholarship.

Many of the Slade students attended the opening of the Contemporary Art Society's exhibition in the Ashmolean on Saturday 15 February, 1941 and heard John Rothenstein's speech to the assembled throng. The exhibition comprised pictures by artists now working in or near Oxford, including Bone, Gwynne-Jones, Horton, Lowinsky, Nash, J. & P., Piper, Roberts, Rothenstein and Rutherston. Schwabe contributed several drawings, all of Oxford architecture, of which *Ship Street Backs* was purchased the following year from a NEAC touring exhibition in Bolton.

In spite of the aerial bombardment of London the Royal Society of Painters in Watercolours held their spring exhibition in Conduit Street. There were over one hundred and thirty paintings on view ranging in price from five guineas to £72 10s. *The Times* described the RWS as:

> *the home of two traditions, each of which has played a great part in English watercolour art ever since the eighteenth century.*
>
> *There is first, the use of water-colour as the ideal medium for the rapid catching of effects of colour or atmosphere, made out of doors and on the spot…*
>
> *The second tradition which flourishes… is that of careful drawings, often architectural, in pen or pencil, tinted more or less strongly with colour. Exponents of this method are such artists as Mr. Leonard Squirrell, Mr. Charles Ginner and especially Professor Randolph Schwabe, who, in 'The Ashmolean,' contributes a very fine piece of architectural drawing in a pleasant setting of lawn and cloudy sky…*

On 19 April 1941,[31] Baslow Church in the Peak District was the setting for the wedding of Alice Schwabe to Harry Jefferson Barnes (1915–82, known as Bysshe). Baslow was near the Barnes family home in Sheffield. Barnes,[32] a former student of Schwabe's, was at the time teaching art at the Royal Masonic School for Boys in Bushey, Hertfordshire. A modest reception at The Rutland Arms followed the ceremony 'where a reasonably plentiful collation was eaten and five bottles of champagne drunk… The doctors, professors, uncles and their wives, etc, all seemed pleased. No one had the temerity to put on a tall hat or tail coat, and the informality seemed suitable for a war wedding.'[33]

Schwabe made his first appearance on the Council for the Encouragement of Music and the Arts Committee (CEMA) at the National Gallery on 2 January 1942 to plan the spending of £750 allowed by the Treasury for pictures. Clark was in the Chair, Philip James (1901–74) was Secretary and the other members were Russell, Jowett, Miss Cazalet and John Rothenstein. Schwabe travelled to London for the April meeting with Eric Ravilious who as a war artist was in Royal Marines uniform and who had been taking his small son to school at Burford. He told Schwabe that John Nash (1893–1977) was known as a 'Wax-work' in his officers' mess but that Barnet Freedman was popular with the Navy. Just five months later Schwabe recorded in his diary 'News that Ravilious is missing, after his first operational flight in Iceland.'[34]

Schwabe had also recently been appointed with Walter Russell to act as overseas expert advisers to The Felton Bequests' Committee to advise on the purchase of English watercolours and drawings for the National Gallery of Victoria, Melbourne. In March 1942 they were instructed to discontinue purchases, owing to the war in the Far East.[35]

Back in Oxford there was trouble. The Keeper of the Ashmolean and of the Department of Antiquities, Edward Thurlow Leeds (1877–1955) was much vexed by the students' behaviour 'regarding the dignity of his museum, making a mess, whistling, and being generally ill-mannered and thoughtless.'[36] Edward A. Tunstall,[37] President of the Slade Society, called a meeting and Rutherston addressed the students. It was decided to be firmer on points of order.

In September 1942 the Schwabes were visited by Camilla Doyle (1887–1944), the painter and poet, who came over from Bampton Vicarage and gave them a vivid account of her fire-fighting experiences in the Close at Norwich where she had lived since 1934. She explained how she slept in her clothes and was a member of a team which during one of the big bombing raids on Norwich, prevented, by an hour's strenuous pumping and carrying of water, the fire spreading from one house to its neighbours. Her own house was much shattered and all the glass gone. Schwabe recorded in his diary 'Her eccentricity is less marked now than when we saw her last. She was always intelligent, and, I think occasionally her verses have the genuine thing in them.' Doyle had known the Schwabes since her student days at the Slade (1905–10) and had subsequently published a number of books of verse including *Poems* (1923) in which she had written the poem 'To Birdie (G.S.)'. The first verse was as follows:

*How well they chose who named her thus
In all her looks I see arise,*

*Change and return, the moods of birds
In various wise.*

Schwabe painted her portrait in 1923; Camilla Doyle took her own life in 1944.

Schwabe was disappointed on New Year's Day 1943 to get in only ¾ hour drawing in Turl Street because of rain. He went to the Ashmolean Library instead. The weather was inclement the following day with showers, but Schwabe was able to put in about 2½ hours in The Turl. By 11 January he had spent over 16 hours working on his drawing on his pitch just outside Lincoln gate. Such a drawing he calculated took 34½ hours to do, about 5 days' work in good conditions, and on this occasion he had to return to his pitch 13 times. He exhibited his meticulous drawing *The Turl, Oxford* at the RWS spring show in London, April 1943. His next drawing was of All Saints from The High.

The Slade term began on 18 January 1943 with, according to Schwabe, 'a pretty full house.' There were some new students and Charlton and Polunin came. Polunin executed with his girl assistants, Celia Venning, Mackertich and Jenny Snyders, the big decoration designed by John Piper for the British Restaurant[38] at Merton in Surrey. 'Based on buildings in the area [it filled] one entire wall, as well as the cased-in water tank in one corner, with a stage-like view of Merton Abbey, a sickle moon, and stars overhead.'[39] The task of interpreting the design was undertaken at UCL. Schwabe together with Polunin and his three assistants attended the opening of Piper's decoration on 7 April.

On the invitation of Sydney Sheppard (1877–1948), Schwabe joined the small informal Life Class at 27

Beaumont Street, run by Peter Greenham (1909–92) who taught in Magdalen College School. Greenham, an accomplished draughtsman and friend of Ernest Jackson's from his days as a student at the Byam Shaw School of Drawing and Painting (1936–39), had long hankered to be an artist. Rather secretive about his work, he did not show it to many people; nonetheless he went on to become a full member of the Royal Academy in 1960 and Keeper in 1964. The room where the small group of subscribers worked was underground, warmed by a fire and an oil stove, and with a good electric light on the model, but as Schwabe observed 'not such good a light on one's paper'.[40] Schwabe drew alongside Mr and Mrs Sheppard, Dunstan who had helped Greenham start up the class, Wynter and Daphne Dennison and another girl who was at Somerville. Diana Yeldham Taylor who did scene-painting at The Playhouse was the model, and Schwabe thought 'a very good one, too, better than most professional models in the beauty of her figure and in the way she poses.'[41] Another less experienced model 'had unwisely attempted a long-standing pose… She began to look pale and to sway slightly. As she tottered, Professor Schwabe slowly rose from his chair and moved forward without haste to catch her neatly, a large armful, laying her down gently on the floor in one flowing movement.'[42]

Schwabe sent two paintings to the Exhibition of Contemporary Paintings and Drawings which opened at the Ashmolean Museum on 6 March 1943. Fifty per cent of sales went to Mrs Churchill's Aid to Russia Fund and fifty per cent went to the artist. Schwabe submitted *Ringwould* and *Everett's Shop, Cerne Abbas*. The latter was sold for £8-8-0, and as a result Schwabe felt that he had presented £4-4-0 to Comrade Stalin,

or at least, to Mrs Churchill's fund. Polunin had to date put £100 in the bank to that end. Schwabe thought there were some good things in the show – a charming head by Ethel Walker, John's old drawing of the Slade, a good Gwynne-Jones landscape; also a second quality Duncan Grant, a good drawing by Jackson, and a slick portrait head by him in oil. The following month Schwabe sent *The Moustiers – Aiguines Valley* (14 guineas) and *The Artist's Wife* (10 guineas) to the Artists Aid China exhibition at The Wallace Collection, Hertford House, in London, organised by his great friend Ivy Tennyson. Winston Churchill in the catalogue foreword explained that the artists had agreed to contribute fifty per cent of the sale of their works to the United Aid to China Fund. The previous year in July 1942 Schwabe had sent work to the Artists Aid Russia exhibition where there were 900 paintings, drawings, sculptures on view. Schwabe also sent work to the Modern Pictures for the Red Cross exhibition at Christie's in September of that year.

Shortly after the start of the summer term Rutherston invited Chief Commander Pauline Gower of the ATS to come to the School, where she addressed the students on the work of topographical draughtswomen – work which could suitably employ some of the Slade-Ruskin girls. She, Rutherston, Griselda Allan (1905–87) and Schwabe lunched at The Mitre. Afterwards the Chief Commander returned to the School for discussions and Rutherston and Schwabe went with her to inspect the map-making department in New College, where those working included several ex-Slade girls.[43]

Towards the end of May 1943 Schwabe gave the journalist Stanley Parker a sitting for his drawing to accompany his interview for the *Oxford Mail*. The article was captioned 'Drawn and Quoted: Professor Schwabe or Oxford's Gain'. Parker, a self-taught artist from Melbourne, Australia had started his career on one of Keith Murdoch's papers. Schwabe thought he had a gift of likeness, although his drawing was rather heavy and coarse in order to make half-tone blacks for newspaper work. Parker thought Oxford the richer and brighter for the presence of the Slade students, and Schwabe exactly as he had expected an artist to be. He wrote:

That hair – it blew on the Wren-like dome of the head and clustered round at the attic column of the neck like leaves of grass; that tie – it fluttered beneath his chin like a bird: those hands and shoes, everything about him, so exotic to the man in the street so natural to him, proclaimed him to all for what he was. To all, that is, except himself. If he came face to face with himself in a full-length mirror it is ten to one he would give an absent minded bow, and one to ten he would not see himself at all!

Schwabe's family was well aware of his absent mindedness. On Birdie's birthday he:

went out and came home with a present. He had bought her a new coffee pot. After lunch he went back to work and in the evening came back with a birthday present for Birdie – a coffee pot. It was identical, bought from the same shop. He remembered his decision to buy this for her birthday but had no recollection he had already bought it.[44]

Parker closed his article by praising 'Mrs Schwabe, or Birdie as she is called amongst their friends'; he thought that she must be a genius for pouring oil on troubled waters. He believed that:

She understands the artist's temperament (being an artist herself) and she has made a great success of the most difficult role in the

world – the artist's wife. Randolph Schwabe does not appear to suffer from any of the fits of temperament peculiar to an artist – he is quiet and calm and gentle, with time for everything… Of course, he may always have been this way. But it is thanks to Birdie that he has remained so… It is Birdie's job to see that reputation grows. I think she will see that it is done.

Schwabe was also adept at dealing with troubled waters and although he had not served on the NEAC jury since the War began he and Muirhead Bone felt obliged to in October 1943 following difficulties the previous year. This time the other members were Connard, Ethel Walker, Millie Fisher, Dunlop, Clause, Cundall, Devas, Fairlie H., Beatrice Bland and Robin Guthrie. They finished the selection and rectified some injustices, including the rejection of a MacColl and a Stephen Bone on Tuesday 12 October. The following day he was back in London to help Dunlop, Connard, Clause and Cundall with the hanging. He found 'Poor old Ethel Walker (with her dog Peer Gynt) quite useless on these occasions, and only gets in the way.' He managed to persuade her to go home after lunch, having given her a valedictory kiss on the cheek in recognition of her being honoured with the award of the title of DBE.[45]

Schwabe was also involved with the hanging of the students' show in the Ashmolean, working with William Cole and Kyffin Williams, who was now President of the Slade Society. Dunstan had a large composition of nudes, some clearly based on June Miles and Daphne Dennison. Schwabe thought it a good effort. He and Rutherston wrote in the Foreword to the catalogue 'Most of the pictures and drawings…have been done out of school, in the student's spare time. Some are less experienced than others, all have to work under war conditions…

we feel that the Exhibition is full of vitality, imagination and promise…'.

As usual Christmas was spent with the Tennysons; Ivy was full of talk about the exhibition she was going to run in America in January. All were excited about the sinking of the German battleship the *Scharnhorst* off Norway in the Battle of North Cape on 26 December 1943.

In June 1944 Arnold Palmer and Kenneth Clark asked Schwabe to undertake some drawings for a 'Recording Britain' scheme that was being paid for by four London Home Counties brewers, Barclay Perkins, Courage, Watney and Whitbread. The Londoners' England Scheme was brought into being on the recommendation of the Central Institute of Art and Design and provided employment and commissions for 35 artists and resulted in 164 drawings and watercolours of London scenes and places of beauty and historic interest in the Home Counties. Bone was asked to do a drawing of a brewery, but, being teetotal, felt it was his duty to decline. Amongst those who accepted were Barbara Jones, Vincent Lines, A.S. Hartrick, Mona Moore, Ruskin Spear and Kenneth Rowntree. The Scheme formed 'part of a movement to bring the arts to the "pub"; for it [was] the intention of the four Brewers to show selections of these paintings in their licensed houses. It [was] hoped that this scheme [would] be the forerunner of a much wider plan for bringing art and the "pub" into even closer communion.'[46] The selection panel bought six out of the parcel of topographical drawings that Schwabe delivered to them, including *Judge's Walk, Hampstead*; *St Thomas's Street, S.E.1*; *Farningham, Kent*; and *Clerkenwell Green, with the Church of St James's*, which, at £15 each, he found very useful.

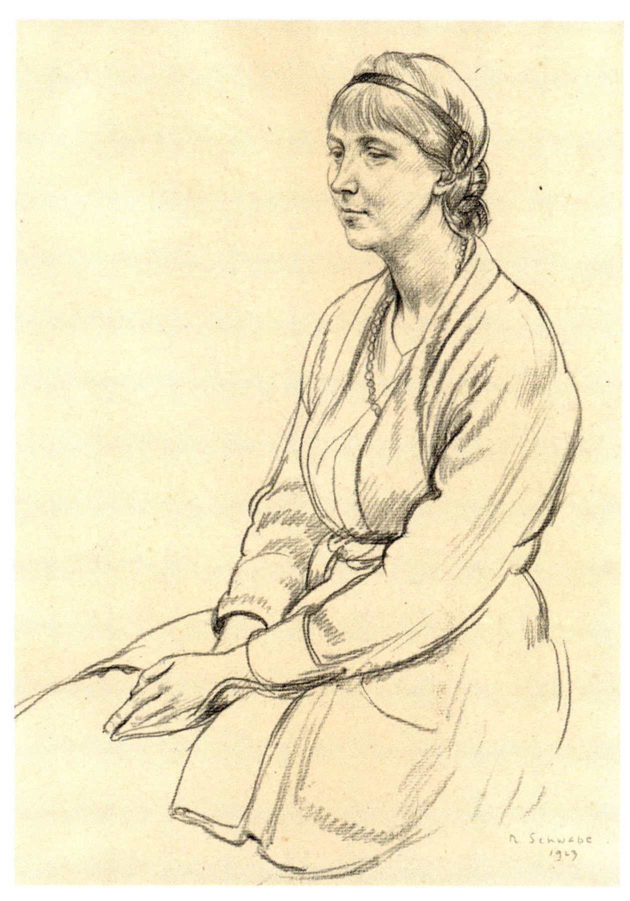

Camilla Doyle
1923 | pencil on pink tinted paper | 35.9 x 26.5 cm
NORFOLK MUSEUMS & ARCHAEOLOGY SERVICE
(NORWICH CASTLE MUSEUM & ART GALLERY)

Enwonwu
c.1945 | pencil | 11.8 × 22.5 cm
COLLECTION JANET AND DI BARNES

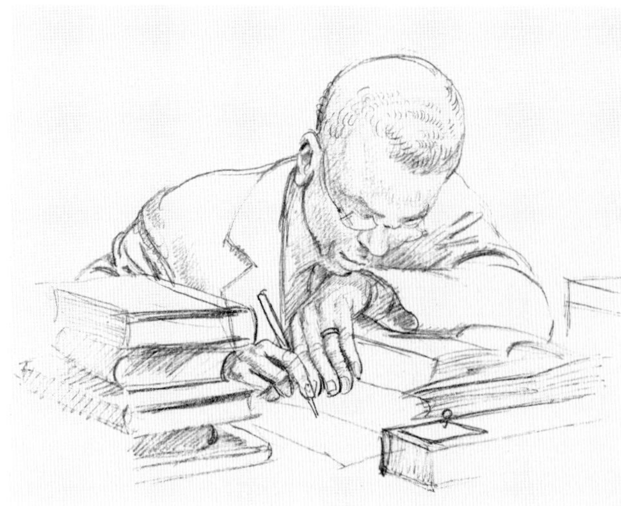

Augustus John opened the first exhibition in The Cogers, Salisbury Court, in February 1946, and said that 'artists have always been staunch supporters of the brewing industry. Now it was the turn of the brewing industry to acknowledge the work of artists.'[47]

Conditions for the artists and Londoners were difficult as Hitler had just launched the V1 Flying Bomb campaign targeted at the city. Schwabe recorded in his diary on 16 June 1944:

7.30 a.m. arrived Kings Cross. Breakfast at St Pancras. There had been an air-raid warning at 11 p.m., and some of the waitresses had been up all night fire-watching. The 'All-Clear' had not yet gone. (This was the first of the raids by 'robot' planes, supposed to be radio-controlled.)

Three days later he observed that:

Conversation runs much on the new German pilot-less bombing. Albert R. had one overhead in Burton Court during the week-end, which fell with a great explosion two blocks away near Ebury Bridge. The Maternity Hospital of St Mary Abbots in Kensington was hit. Paul Feiler narrowly missed one in the neighbourhood of Tottenham Court Road, seeing the houses rock as it burst… People estimate that the flying bombs come over London about every twenty minutes.

Oxford was comparatively tranquil and the Slade Picnic held in the pasture by the river above Godstow was 'a great success', over fifty persons attended, most of whom came in boats. There were a good many bathers and a well-organised supply of food and drink, and beer at The Trout about 7 o'clock. Rutherston and Kyffin Williams, Nuttall-Smith, Barbara Lloyd-Jones and Schwabe rowed home along Port Meadow.[48] By the middle of September 1944 street lamps were being re-erected in preparation for the relaxation of the black-out although it was not until April 1945 that they could show any naked light. Lawrence Dale called on Schwabe with a copy of his book, *Towards a Plan for Oxford City*, which contained 'a magniloquent inscription'[49] to him because the book included his drawing of *The Radcliffe Observatory*. He had completed the drawing some two years previously in April 1942 during a period of particularly cold weather.

The Provost of UCL came to the Slade in early December and spoke to the students in the Ruskin Life Room about the move back to London. In February 1945 Schwabe inspected the Slade wing, with a view to making arrangements for the School's return in October. The rooms were now used principally as students' common rooms, and the repairs had been very thoroughly done in those parts. The Exhibition Room (Duveen Room), however, had been destroyed by enemy action in 1941.

Having dealt with routine Slade affairs in the morning of 23 April 1945 Schwabe and Nuttall-Smith took Enwonwu (1921–94), the Nigerian student (who was backed by The British Council) on a long-promised educational visit to the village of Dorchester, with features of past ages. Schwabe recalled that they talked a lot about Norman and Gothic carving, the Picturesque and so forth. They looked at the Georgian bridge, the George Hotel, the landscape, thatch, tiles, half-timber and brickwork and the Abbey where St George's flag was flying – all quintessentially English. Schwabe said of Enwonwu that he was 'the first real negro I remember at the Slade: a cultivated, well-spoken man.'[50]

Schwabe recorded in his diary on 4 May 1945 that 'The War news is wonderfully satisfactory, as far as the approaching end of hostilities with Germany is concerned. The deaths of Mussolini and Hitler within a few days of each other make this time memorable.' Schwabe was engaged in drawing with Charlton, Greenham, Hector Whistler, June Miles, Dunstan and Wynter, with Miss Butler as model, when Victory Days were announced for 8 and 9 May. Flags appeared in the streets. Schwabe and Birdie spent Victory Day no. 2 quietly. About 10.15 p.m. they went out to look at the crowds.

> *St John's was flood-lit. There were dense, well-behaved crowds at Carfax, some groups carrying an effigy; others, one of their own number. A bonfire on top of the air-raid shelter in the Broad. By the Martyrs' Memorial, the base of which was piled with tiers of people, some St John's men were burning the A.R.P. ladders from the College, together with the props which had supported the arcade in Canterbury Quad against possible blast all through the War. A good blaze: the faces of the people lighted up by it, the sky black, the cold flood-lighting on St John's contrasting with the warm firelight. Trees silhouetted like stage scenery, lights — unaccustomed — in the windows of Balliol — a fine scene… everything good-tempered and well under control. I imagine there was no drink left in Oxford, which may partially account for the sobriety.*[51]

The beginning of July saw Schwabe and Gwynne-Jones sorting out the Slade-Ruskin prizes and certificates for painting. They considered the head paintings to be of a standard fully equal to that of the years just before the War. The life studies were less satisfactory: conditions had been difficult. The light, with the east sun pouring in in the summer, and the crowding of the rooms, was unfavourable.

The Slade-Ruskin tea-party took place for the final time in New College. Miss Tracey 'made an excellent speech of thanks' from the Slade students to the Ruskin staff – Rutherston and Griselda Allan who were given book-tokens and pieces of pewter (for Allan) as souvenirs. The Ruskin students gave Schwabe a book-token. Rutherston who was quite moved spoke in reply. Schwabe said 'There is no question that the association of the two Schools has been a happy and harmonious one; and we do owe a great deal to Albert, and Miss Allan has done her job well.'[52] Saturday 7 July was the last day of the Slade in Oxford. Several students came in to say farewell to Rutherston, of whom Schwabe said 'we all owe so much'.[53]

For Schwabe there was still much to do to facilitate the return of the Slade to London and its re-opening in October. He dealt with 27 letters at the Slade one August morning and there were still more to do! The Slade furniture was removed on 15 August, VJ Day, and towards the end of August Schwabe, following attendance at an Artists' Advisory Committee meeting, visited Nuttall-Smith at the Slade to see what progress was being made for the return.

On Sunday 9 September 1945 with much regret the Schwabes left Oxford for London, to stay with the Tennysons in Drayton Court, London. They were in effect homeless; 20 Church Row had been sold as it was riddled with dry rot and uninhabitable, their furniture having gone into storage. For Schwabe and Birdie there was much uncertainty about their future housing. They went to see Towner at Christ's Hospital, Horsham, where for the past two years he had been in charge of the art school, to discuss the possibility of living in 8 Church Row with him and his mother or staying with the Tennysons as they seemed to wish. They eventually decided to stick with the Tennysons. Fortunately, Ivy's food supplies were often supplemented by parcels from America and she still had a small reserve of wine for her dinner parties.

'Schwabe's greatest triumph was his control of the School during the war years, when it moved to Oxford.'[54] That 'he was able to hold the school together, and indeed to manage to teach anything, during such a difficult period'[55] says much about his leadership and the valuable support that he received from Albert Rutherston at the Ruskin School. Undoubtedly the students and the School benefited from its continuous functioning and Oxford was the richer and brighter for the influx of art students.

THE SLADE, LONDON 1945–48

On Monday 1 October 1945 the Slade reopened 'with its traditions and its character intact.'[56] The end of hostilities witnessed an influx of students and it was expected that there would be an even greater demand for admission as the process of demobilisation progressed. By the start of the second term of the 1945–46 session there were 254 students enrolled (91 men and 163 women), in sharp contrast with the numbers at the Slade-Ruskin in 1944–45 which totalled 107 (22 men and 85 women). The Slade was cramped and overcrowded, materials and accommodation for students in short supply, and it was difficult to get models. Schwabe on his second day back in Gower Street was confronted by about fifty girls on the stairs, unable to find places to paint or draw. Schwabe with the assistance of Charlton and Brooker, back after his long absence in the Army in

Africa and India, managed somehow to deal with them. He brought the Provost over to see the state of affairs.

The end of the first week saw Margaret Alexander (b.1902) teaching Lettering to her packed class at the Slade for the first time in six years; the Sculpture Department (under Gerrard) reopened after its enforced closure due to the lack of suitable studios in Oxford; classes in Engraving with Janes also reopened; and all the staff reported back after doing War Service or work of national importance with the exception of Borenius who was seriously ill. Bartlett continued as Assistant to Polunin in the Theatrical Scene-Painting classes. The teaching of perspective was revived and taught by Nuttall-Smith who was now Departmental Assistant and Tutor to Fine Art students. Understaffed, Schwabe later appointed three visiting teachers – Rodrigo Moynihan, William Coldstream and Rodney Burn – 'to give periodical lessons to supplement the work of the regular staff, who found it difficult to give adequate instruction to every one of the large number of students in the life rooms.'[57] Charlton was not overly impressed by Moynihan's appointment; he and Wilkie were concerned that the drawing side – the Slade's fundamental strength – was in danger if painting was too much emphasized. Charlton also thought that any money that could be found for additional salaries should go to raising the pay of the present teachers.[58] The issue of visiting teachers was to cause disagreement amongst the staff which Schwabe found most unpleasant but fortunately they did not 'have a lot of this sort of thing'.

Schwabe reported to the RBA Galleries in Suffolk Street on 9 October to serve on the New English jury – it was a long day as there were over 1,500 pictures to sift through. The ninety-seventh exhibition featured

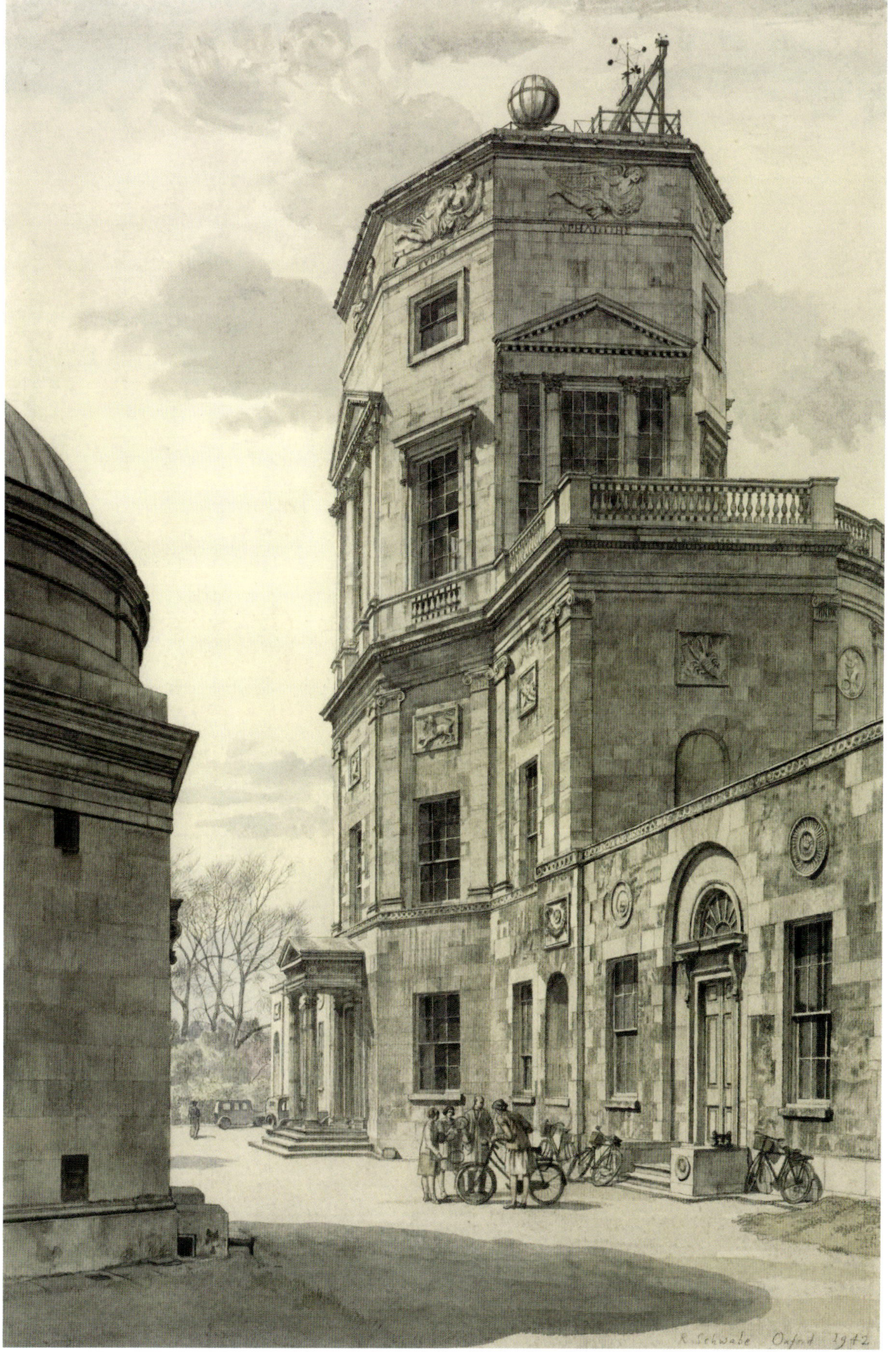

several memorial groups of pictures by recently deceased members including Sir William Rothenstein, Fairlie Harmar, James Bolivar Manson (1879–1945), and Joseph Southall. Of the living exhibitors *The Times'* critic praised the seniors, in particular Sir Muirhead Bone and Randolph Schwabe who both showed some good drawings. Schwabe exhibited six works including *The Barn, New College, Oxford*; *Cashelnagore* (Birdie had recently met Mary Kennedy who had offered to lend the Schwabes their house at Cashelnagore) and a sketch of his first grandchild *Janet*. There were no sales. He sold one drawing of a farm at Curbar at the RWS exhibition the following month; Schwabe also served on the RWS Council with 'the excellent Flint in the chair' and remained on the NEAC executive.

Back to his pre-war routine Schwabe engaged in a round of exhibitions going with Birdie at the weekend to the Victoria and Albert Museum to see the Royal effigies and other sculpture from Westminster Abbey on display for the first and possibly only time. There was also an opportunity to see a show of the late Edward Johnston's calligraphy, which included William Rothenstein's drawing of Johnston, which Schwabe thought exactly like and very expressive. Schwabe liked Johnston (1872–1944) 'with his odd ways, his humour and his great voice, of unusual carrying power. He was a valuable influence and an excellent performer.'[59] His textbook *Writing and Illuminating, and Lettering* first published in 1906, was one of the best Schwabe knew.

Schwabe continued to serve on the Artists' Advisory Committee, helping with the hanging of pictures at the Royal Academy and later allocating the war record pictures to various collections. The November meeting brought news that Hennell was reported missing,

'probably killed, in Java, in an insurrection of the Indonese at Surabaya. He seized a Sten gun and fought them. The rest of his party retired into an hotel.'[60]

The Slade term was not without incident. Raymond Mason (1922–2010) and Leo Davy (1924–87) who had commenced their studies in Oxford were in trouble for defacing the work of a fellow student Fletcher. Davy had gone so far as to burn one of Fletcher's paintings, for which Schwabe thought he would 'have to be sacked'. As far as Schwabe was concerned he did no work in the School – he did attend lectures in philosophy which 'remained his life's preoccupation.'[61] Schwabe interviewed Leo Davy and asked him to discontinue his attendance. After Davy left Fletcher set upon him in the corridor, hit him in the face, shook hands and declared that honour was satisfied. Davy was concerned in a perfectly decent way when he talked to Schwabe that his friend Mason should not be blamed. Schwabe sent Mason to Pye, the Provost, who did not expel him; but insisted he make a written apology to Fletcher.[62] Schwabe had previously done much to support Mason who had held an impromptu exhibition of his paintings at the entrance to the Ashmolean. Schwabe accepted him and paid his fees. 'A little later, he also did Mason the service of suggesting that he lacked a certain "fluidity of touch" as a painter and should try his hand at sculpture.'[63]

Schwabe was also direct with Mason's fellow Slade student Philip Brown (b.1925) telling him 'Really, Brown, you must try and draw more like the Old Italian Masters.' Brown, a medical student, had been interviewed by Schwabe at the Ashmolean before starting the course in London, and recalled telling Schwabe that he was not able to work anymore – he

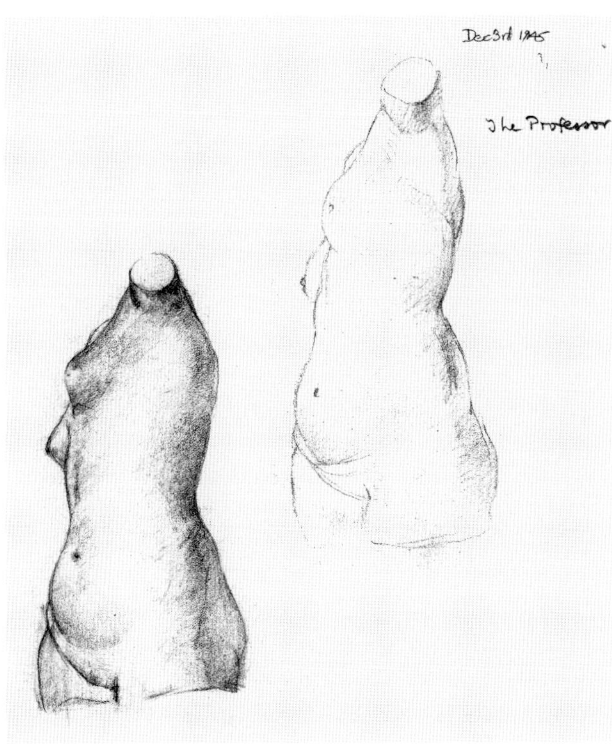

Philip Brown, 'Life Drawing', 3 December 1945,
with demonstration drawing by Randolph Schwabe

had found the pressure of the examinations too much
– and that he had been advised to avoid intellectual
pressure. Schwabe 'sort of took a pace back when [he]
suggested that art wasn't intellectual'; it was, Brown
said on reflection, 'quite a funny thing to say to the
professor'. Schwabe, 'a meticulous white-haired old
gentleman with side-whiskers, gold-rimmed spectacles
sporting a black bow-tie', was by then 60 years of age.[64]

Brown made notes on his own life drawing of
Schwabe's comments:

> *Think before drawing <u>every</u> stroke.*
> 1. *Makes sketches in between the parts.*
> 2. *Go from one important point to another then fill in between
>   trying to make position in space right.*
> 3. *Look back from model a lot to bind pieces together.*
> 4. *Feel pose.*
> 5. *Always finish a drawing.*

Schwabe with his needle-point pencil had earlier
completed a small precise and delicate demonstration
drawing alongside Brown's faltering attempt at drawing
a woman's naked torso.

Schwabe's sales from exhibitions improved in 1946.
He sold two drawings at the New English: one a study
of June Miles done at one of the Oxford evenings and
a pen drawing of three nudes done from the same
model and making a group. By the close of the
exhibition he had sold two more.

Schwabe attended a meeting in early March of the
Rome School Faculty of Painting at Lowther Gardens.
It was the first meeting in seven years. Only the
Monningtons and Schwabe of the pre-war members

attended. Five had died since the last meeting: Colin Gill, Charlton Bradshaw, Ernest Jackson, D.Y. Cameron and Dermod O'Brien.

In June the Slade received instructions from the Government that, of any new admissions, 90 per cent must be ex-service people. The School was already full until 1948. Later that month Schwabe judged the Slade work for prizes with Charlton, Gwynne-Jones and Brooker; they agreed that there was some good work, 'perhaps back to pre-War standards', but they decided that the figure drawing was not quite worth a First Prize. The first post-War Slade Picnic was a success. 'Charabancs for over 80 people. Lunch at Chessington Zoo. Tea at the Inn at Shere.'[65]

The start of the new term was busy for Schwabe – there were now 300 students (132 men and 168 women) enrolled. One problem was overcrowding; two weeks into term he and Charlton met with the leading men students to discuss arrangements for allotting painting places. The Slade dance passed off smoothly. There was a cabaret, with a Royal Box in which Schwabe sat. He thought the can-can very good although somewhat spoiled by one of the girls, slightly drunk, falling over every time she attempted a cart-wheel.

In the New Year Schwabe attended the private view of work by Eduardo Paolozzi (1924–2005), at the Mayor Gallery; Paolozzi had worked with him and Rutherston in Oxford. Schwabe did not care for Paolozzi's drawings. Paolozzi had transferred to the Slade when it reopened as 'he wanted to "make-things"' and sculpture was taught there; at the Ruskin he had had to be content with making collages away 'from the formal experience of being instructed in life

drawing by… Schwabe'.[66] Paolozzi 'embraced European modernism, especially the art of Picasso and the surrealists, developments disapproved of by… sculpture master, A.H. Gerrard, with whom [he] clashed.'[67]

The Slade Society organised an exhibition of drawings, paintings and sculpture by Slade students at Walker's Galleries in New Bond Street which the Provost opened on 12 February 1947. Schwabe wrote the foreword:

> *This Exhibition is not the first of its kind. One of similar aims was held in 1933… and during the War period of evacuation [the students] were enabled to repeat the venture (in 1942, 1943 and 1944) at the Ashmolean… In general, these Exhibitions made a good impression. Though promise has not always been fulfilled, some of the artists who exhibited a few years ago have already come into the public eye and are making reputations. It is hoped that the present occasion may help to produce a fresh crop of talent… Variety and the absence of a cliché style may at least be claimed. Though all the exhibitors are now working in the School, there is little of a recognizable School mannerism, since, the students mostly accept the point of view that what they learn academically is confined to questions of technique and craftsmanship, with the exploration of good traditions: which does not prevent a response to the feelings and aspirations of our own period and a lively expression of personality.[68]*

The exhibition was attended by 200 visitors per day during its three-week run.[69] This was despite the cold and dark and post-War fuel economies. The coal crisis had led to the Government restricting domestic electricity to 19 hours a day. The Slade had, so far, been allowed to use the electric heaters to keep models warm.

In April 1947 Schwabe started a drawing of Sydney Shovelton, Secretary of King's College, in his big room looking on to the quad. Schwabe found him a pleasant gentleman, coming from Manchester, and familiar with persons and things that Schwabe remembered such as the building of the Ship Canal, the presence of the De Traffords in Trafford Park, the fine old trees there and the farms at Barton, where Schwabe's father and grandfather Ermen lived. He sent four drawings priced from £20 to £50, including 'the precise architectural drawing of St James's Church, Dover'[70] (£20) to the NEAC spring exhibition which was held in Bristol because of the difficulty of finding a suitable venue in London. He also exhibited with the NEAC at the winter show – it was to be his last – when he again sent several drawings from his holidays in Dover.

Some much-needed improvements were made to the Slade buildings including the installing of fluorescent lighting in two of the life rooms. Two new concrete huts were build in the quad but in the hot summer they dripped pitch continuously from the ceilings. Schwabe provided the Examiners with overalls as a precaution.

Shortly before the start of the new term Schwabe visited the Tate with Albert to see the re-hanging of the work of Hogarth, Blake, Turner and Constable. Schwabe found it an impressive show. Even he (and he was always told he had no imagination) had his imagination stirred.

January 1948 heralded Schwabe's final term at the Slade. The Beadle had lit the fire in his room in anticipation of his arrival. At the end of the day Schwabe took 'tea at the Club, that oasis of peace, where [one] is not always obliged to speak to anyone.'[71] Barnet Freedman who also enjoyed being a member of the Athenaeum came as a visitor to the Slade, followed a few days later by Rutherston.

Schwabe continued to spend time in the Life Room drawing, which was almost a religion to him and part of his very being. When teaching he would go round some of the students' paintings, recognising that increasingly most *wanted* criticism and would ask for it. As on previous occasions he wrote a brief fore-word to the Slade Exhibition at Walker's Galleries, and characteristically modestly wrote:

Though it is true that I have been consulted about various matters in connection with the show, I am not responsible for it: I wish to give full credit to the Slade Society for almost everything that has had to do with the initial incentive and the organisation. The Society is a democratic body which usefully controls many unofficial activities in the Slade School: it does its work well.

A suitable spirit of independence seems to me to characterise the work shown. There is espirit de corps, and something in common due to a basic training, but adventure is not repressed, neither is personality stamped upon. It would be difficult to discover in the exhibits anything that could be called a 'Slade mannerism'. On the other hand, slavish imitation of fashionable modern movements is equally uncommon.[72]

Friday 12 March 1948 was Schwabe's last day at the Slade. In the morning he attended a Committee of Management of the Courtauld Institute. He had little interest in the proceedings, but attended out of a wish to be civil to Anthony Blunt.[73] He lunched at the Athenaeum and returned to the Slade.

Two days later in the early hours of Sunday morning he suffered a serious heart attack. Despite taking what he described 'as a long rest' he never set foot again in his beloved Slade – he died on 19 September 1948, drawing to the end.

1 Schwabe diary 1939.

2 Schwabe diary 1939.

3 Schwabe diary 1939.

4 Nash, P. (1939) 'Letter from Oxford', *The Listener*, Nov. 11, p.1065.

5 Schwabe diary 1939.

6 Gerrard, Schwabe noted in his diary on 30/7/1940, 'is a great success as a camouflage officer'.

7 Schwabe diary 1939.

8 Biddy Picard interview with the author, Cornwall, May 2010.

9 Dunstan, B. (2006) *The paintings of Bernard Dunstan*, p.12.

10 Martin (2005) Rutherston, ODNB.

11 Picard (2010) Op. cit.

12 Dunstan (2006) Op. cit., p.11.

13 Schwabe diary 1940.

14 MacDougall, S. (2002) *Mark Gertler*, p.326.

15 Schwabe diary 1940.

16 Aitchison, D. (1989) 'The Slade School of Fine Art at the Ashmolean Museum, 1939-41', *The Ashmolean*, 15, p.5.

17 Interview with Cecil and Joan Riley (née Batty) by the author, Cornwall, May 2012.

18 Skidmore, I. (2008) *Kyffin, a figure in a Welsh Landscape, the biography of Sir Kyffin Williams, RA, told through conversations with the artist and his friends*, p.66.

19 PF interview 2010.

20 Schwabe diary 1940.

21 Schwabe diary 1940.

22 See Chronology in *Paul Feiler: Elusive space relief and paintings*, The Redfern Gallery (2010), p.75.

23 Laffitte, F. (1940/88) *The internment of aliens*, p.81.

24 PF interview 2010.

25 *Manchester Guardian* 31/7/1940 – pasted into Schwabe's cuttings book. 'From around 1943 Wynter and… Mellor, worked as keepers in the laboratories of Oxford University's Department of Human Anatomy, tending the animals there for vivisection' (Bird, M. 2010, *Bryan Wynter*, p.32).

26 Picard, B. (2005) *A life's work*, p.7.

27 Schwabe diary 1940.

28 Williams, K. (1993) *Across the Straits an autobiography*, p.139 & p. 141. Williams joined North Company of Oxford Home Guard and commanded a platoon.

29 *The Times* 20/12/1944. Schwabe in his diary 20/12/1944 explains that Lessore quoted his limerick on Menzel to Iolo Williams (1890–1962, journalist, author and art historian), 'who published it in *The Times* today'.

30 Williams (1993) Op. cit., p.148.

31 19 April was also the anniversary of Birdie's and Schwabe's wedding in 1913.

32 Barnes was appointed Assistant Master of Painting & Drawing at Glasgow School of Art from Jan. 1944. He took over as Director in 1964 when Douglas Bliss retired. While at Bushey, Edgar Holloway in 1941 did an etching of his colleague Barnes.

33 Schwabe diary 1941.

34 Schwabe diary 1942.

35 Russell retired. Clark was appointed in 1945 – the brief was extended to 'watch for opportunities to purchase Old Masters, contemporary works and examples of French Impressionist School.' See Lindsay, D. (1963) *The Felton Bequest: An historical record 1904–1959*, p.82.

36 Schwabe diary 1942.

37 Tunstall wrote an article in *The Burlington* magazine with fellow student Antony Kerr in Feb. 1943 on 'The painted room at the Queen's College, Oxford'.

38 The Government's non-profit-making British Restaurants opened in early 1940, by 1943 there were 2,160; they provided a place for a coupon-free meal a day which had been cooked by volunteers (see Burnett, J. 2004, *England eats out: A social history of eating out in England from 1830 to the present*).

39 Spalding, F. (2009) *John Piper. Myfanwy Piper. Lives in art*, p.188.

40 Schwabe diary 1943.

41 Schwabe diary 1943.

42 Dunstan (2006) Op. cit., p.11.

43 Schwabe diary 1943.

44 Margaret de Villiers interview with Di Barnes, 2011.

45 Schwabe diary 1943.

46 See the catalogue for the exhibition 'The Londoner's England' held at the Suffolk Galleries, Pall Mall 23 Oct.–10 Nov. 1945.

47 *The Times* 9/1/1946, p.6.

48 Schwabe diary 1944.

49 Schwabe diary 1944.

50 Enwonwu returned to Nigeria in 1948 and took up the position of Federal Arts Adviser.

51 Schwabe diary 1945.

52 Schwabe diary 1945.

53 Schwabe diary 1945.

54 Freeman, J. (1979) *Made at the Slade. A survey of mature works by ex-students of the Slade School of Fine Art, 1892–1960*, p.3.

55 Freeman, J. (1979) Ibid., p.3.

56 Forge, A. (1961) 'The Slade (3): To the present day', *Motif*, 6, Spring, p.46.

57 See UCL Annual Reports.

58 Schwabe together with other UCL Professors had his salary raised to £1,500 a year the following February. He wondered how that compared with £1,000 before the War, regardless he doubted if they were as well off now as they were then.

59 Schwabe diary 1945.

60 Schwabe diary 1945. See chapter 5 'War artist' in M. MacLeod

(1988) *Thomas Hennell: Countryman, artist and writer* and Clarke (2008).
61 Buckman, D. (2006) *Artists in Britain since 1945*, p.389.
62 Schwabe diary 1945.
63 Peppiat, M. (1982) *Raymond Mason: Coloured sculptures, bronzes and drawings 1952–82*, p.6.
64 Brown, P. & G. (2002) *Pages from our life*, p.3 and interview with the author, Eastbourne, March 2012. Brown particularly enjoyed at that time calligraphy under Margaret Alexander and was awarded first prize at the end of the year. He went on to forge a successful career as a painter and stained glass artist.
65 Schwabe diary 1946.
66 Spencer, R. (Ed.) (2000) *Eduardo Paolozzi: Writings and interviews*, p.10.
67 Spencer (2004) Paolozzi, ODNB.
68 I am grateful to Keyna Emerson (b.1922) for the loan of the catalogue. Keyna was a student at the Ruskin 1939–41 and after serving in the WRNS returned to study at the Slade 1945–47.
69 See UCL Annual Reports, p.139.
70 See *The Times* 22/5/1947.
71 Schwabe diary 1948.
72 Schwabe was too ill to attend the exhibition which ran from 28 April–11 May, 1948.
73 Schwabe diary 1948.

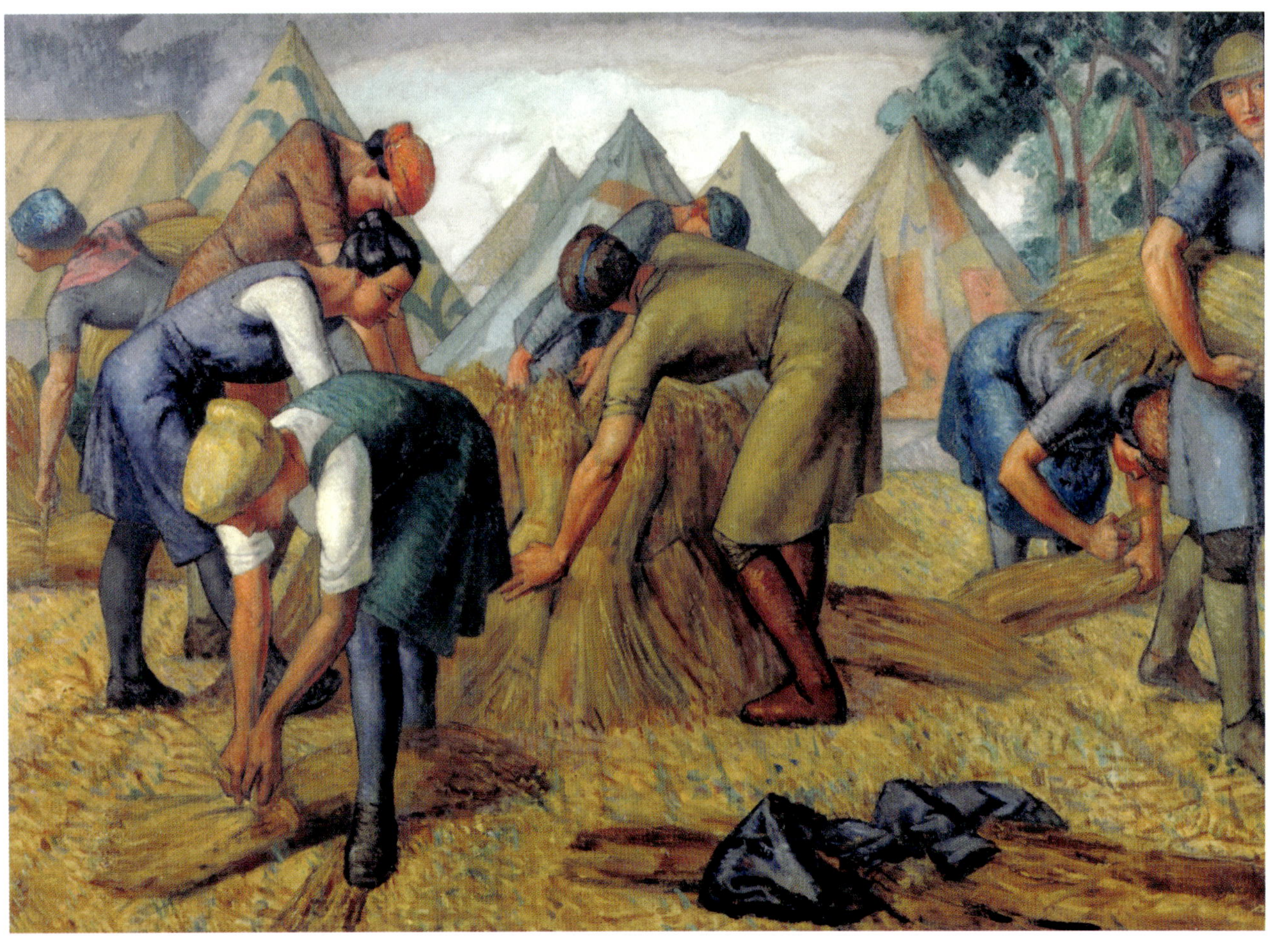

Voluntary Land Workers in a Flax-Field, Podington, Northamptonshire
1919 | oil on canvas | 106.6 x 152.4 cm

WAR ARTIST

THE FIRST WORLD WAR

During the First World War the British Government employed artists at home, and on other fronts, primarily for propaganda purposes. With the formation of the Ministry of Information in March 1918 the Canadian-born minister, Lord Beaverbrook, increased the number of official war artists. The British War Memorial Scheme was established to create a lasting record of the sites and stages of the war. When the Ministry of Information closed, the Imperial War Museum took over its responsibilities towards artists.

Schwabe was contacted on 27 March 1918 by Alfred Yockney (1879–1963), former editor of the *Art Journal*, now employed by the Ministry of Information, to ascertain if he were free of military obligations and could put aside any private work to undertake work for the Ministry. Schwabe's friend Francis Dodd, whose brother-in-law was Muirhead Bone, had some months earlier put Schwabe down as an artist available to do official work. He had told Schwabe that he would 'get some pay, have a good time have to work hard & be free of the recruiting officer, it may come off, but I feel sure something or other will mature.'[1] Robert Ross (1869–1918), one of the 'penumbra of art advisers'[2] to the Scheme (including Bone), was also instrumental in getting Schwabe employed. Schwabe replied by return to Yockney stating that he would be very pleased to put aside any private work and expressed the hope that the scheme would mature. He explained that he had no military or other war obligations. Schwabe who had a weak heart, frail physique and uncertain health had been rejected for the Army on 31 May 1916 and again on 4 August 1917.

Yockney asked Schwabe if he could suggest a subject. Muirhead Bone had proposed that his subject might be *The St Paul's Watch at Night*, a scene from the upper part of St Paul's. Yockney was anxious to know if this idea appealed or whether some other theme would be more congenial. Schwabe expressed a willingness to undertake the subject which he understood was to be carried out on a considerable scale.

Schwabe completed the Ministry of Information form on 17 June while staying at Wolmer Farm House, Marlow Common in Buckinghamshire, and supplied information about his nationality and that of his father and mother so as to obtain a permit to work at St Paul's Cathedral. In the past when applying for other permits, Schwabe had been questioned about his mother's nationality. She was technically German although her father Godfrey Anthony van Ermen was born in Brabant in 1807 before settling in England in 1837; he was naturalised in 1863. His first cousin Cuthbert Ermen was Resident in the service of the Rajah of Sarawak, a British protectorate in Borneo, and Godfrey Ermen, who had enlisted in the Royal Engineers in 1915, was at that time in Mesopotamia. Another first cousin was Captain Godfrey of the 6th West Riding Regiment, who died from acute influenza on service in 1915 in Skipton. He went on to point out that his father's family had settled in Manchester and Cheshire over a hundred years previously.

Schwabe had one or two interviews with Yockney which led him to believe that the St Paul's work was to commence shortly and as a consequence he shelved other lucrative work. On 15 August he met Henry Rushbury[3] who, unaware of these circumstances, informed him that it was proposed that he (Rushbury) should execute for the Ministry a picture of *The St Paul's Watch at Night*, the size to be 5ft by 3½ft. Schwabe proposed an alternative subject, the work of the Women's Land Army, which interested him equally. He believed it was essentially a war subject and came well within the scope of the proposed war record. He was ready to start work at a day's notice as he was anxious not to waste time, as the harvesting period, which offered special opportunities for study, would soon be over; he asked Yockney to put the matter before the Committee and favour him with an early reply before he involved himself in expense and trouble.[4]

THE WOMEN'S LAND ARMY

By early September 1918 Schwabe, who had been staying at the Hind Hotel in Wellingborough, Northampton, had gathered sufficient material to enable him to do 'a series of pictures of the more important or unusual activities of the Women's Land Army [WLA].'[5] The subjects included timber felling at Whittlewood Forest in the south of the county, the work of a flax camp, work with sheep and horses, and activities at Burghley Park Training Centre. He also suggested to Yockney that a recruiting meeting in London was another possibility. Yockney, having got approval from the Committee who thought it would be good propaganda, replied that 'The arrangement suggested was that you should work under the total output scheme and the first payment for your services [£30] would become due at the end of this month.'[6]

The first painting Schwabe completed was the yet untitled picture of German prisoners of war assisting Land Girls with the harvest in the late summer of 1918, probably at Rushden Farm, some three miles

from Podington, Wellingborough.[7] Schwabe explained to Yockney that 'What the blighters are doing is making a straw stack after the corn has been threshed.'[8] The composition is noteworthy, particularly the close proximity of the Land Girl to the German soldier, as the Government had prohibited their working alongside Land Army women and the *LAAS Handbook* required recruits to promise 'To avoid communication of any sort with German prisoners.' Schwabe also submitted a drawing of Miss Gwynne-Jones, Alan Gwynne-Jones' sister, who was a forewoman in the WLA. Schwabe's naming of the sitter prompted a rebuke from Yockney as it might cause difficulties with the censor and the request that in future such studies should be anonymous.

Schwabe executed his big painting of a flax camp in a studio on Kings Road, Chelsea, a short walk from his home in Cheyne Walk, which he rented for the task at 10/- per week from 11 September–31 March 1919. He was working with his friend and best man, Darsie Japp, who had served in the Royal Field Artillery during the war, reaching the rank of Major and being awarded the MC. The camp was in Podington, one of several in Northamptonshire as flax culture had been revived to supply the demands of aeroplane manufacture and specifically fabric to cover the aircraft's wings. The title settled on was *Voluntary Land Workers in a Flax-Field, Podington, Northamptonshire*. The women are tying the flax plants in small sheaves by twisting a few stems round them just below the seed bolls while others stook them in much the same way as wheat. In the background is their camp of old army camouflaged bell tents, supplied by the War Office, in each of which seven girls would be accommodated for about two months, under semi-military discipline. Schwabe also painted *Thatching Flax for Aeroplanes* which depicts two Land Girls perched precariously on top of the rick on ladders, thatching. Schwabe contributed 21 works, in various media including two large oil paintings, smaller drawings and studies in pencil and wash, chalk, charcoal, and one in pen and water-colour of women working on the land. At the end of his eight months or so of working on these important documentary records of women's work he received £266 14s. 6d. in payment.[9]

THE SECOND WORLD WAR

By the Second World War Schwabe was 54-years-old and 'an established [and vastly experienced] academic draughtsman. His meticulous architectural drawings made him an ideal recorder of bomb damage.'[10] On the afternoon of Saturday 16 November 1940 Schwabe was drawing a cast for his private satisfaction in the Ashmolean when his daughter Alice brought over a telegram from E.M. O'Rourke Dickey[11] (1898–1977), secretary of the War Artists' Advisory Committee (WAAC) at the Ministry of Information, London. It requested that he make a drawing or drawings of the ruins of Coventry Cathedral before the debris was tidied up as it was the Committee's experience that damage by bombing was at is most spectacular when seen soon after the event. He was to be paid travelling expenses and maintenance at the rate of £1 a day for every 24 hours he was away from home for study of his subject. Such was the urgency that Dickey could not tell Schwabe the fee as that would be subject to the approval of the Committee.[12]

BOMB DAMAGE

During the eleven-hour bombing raid, code named Moonlight Sonata by the Germans, on 14–15 November

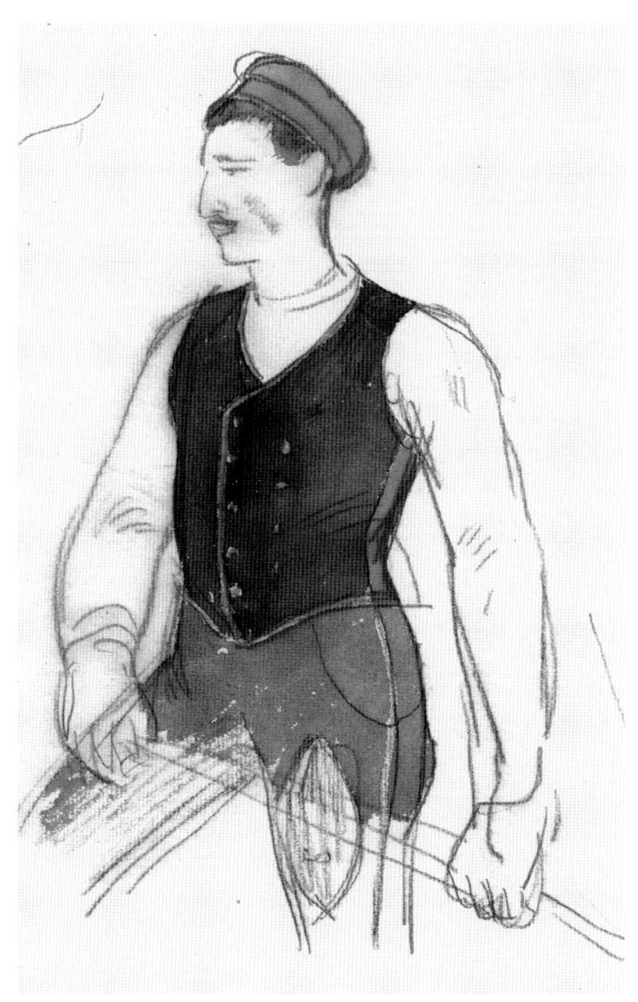

Study for 'The Women's Land Army and German Prisoners'

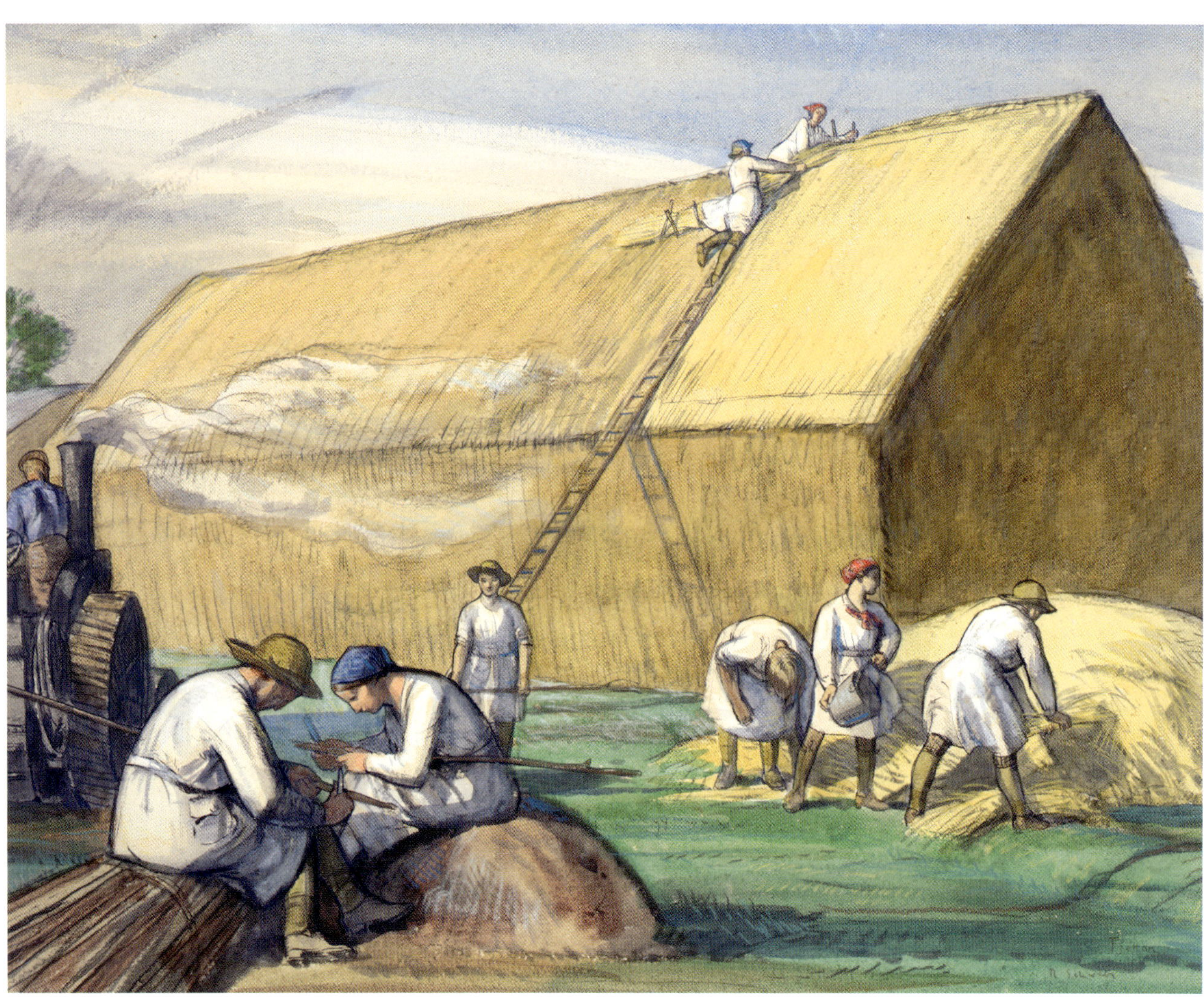

Thatching Flax for Aeroplanes
pen and watercolour | 44.4 x 57.7 cm
© IMPERIAL WAR MUSEUMS

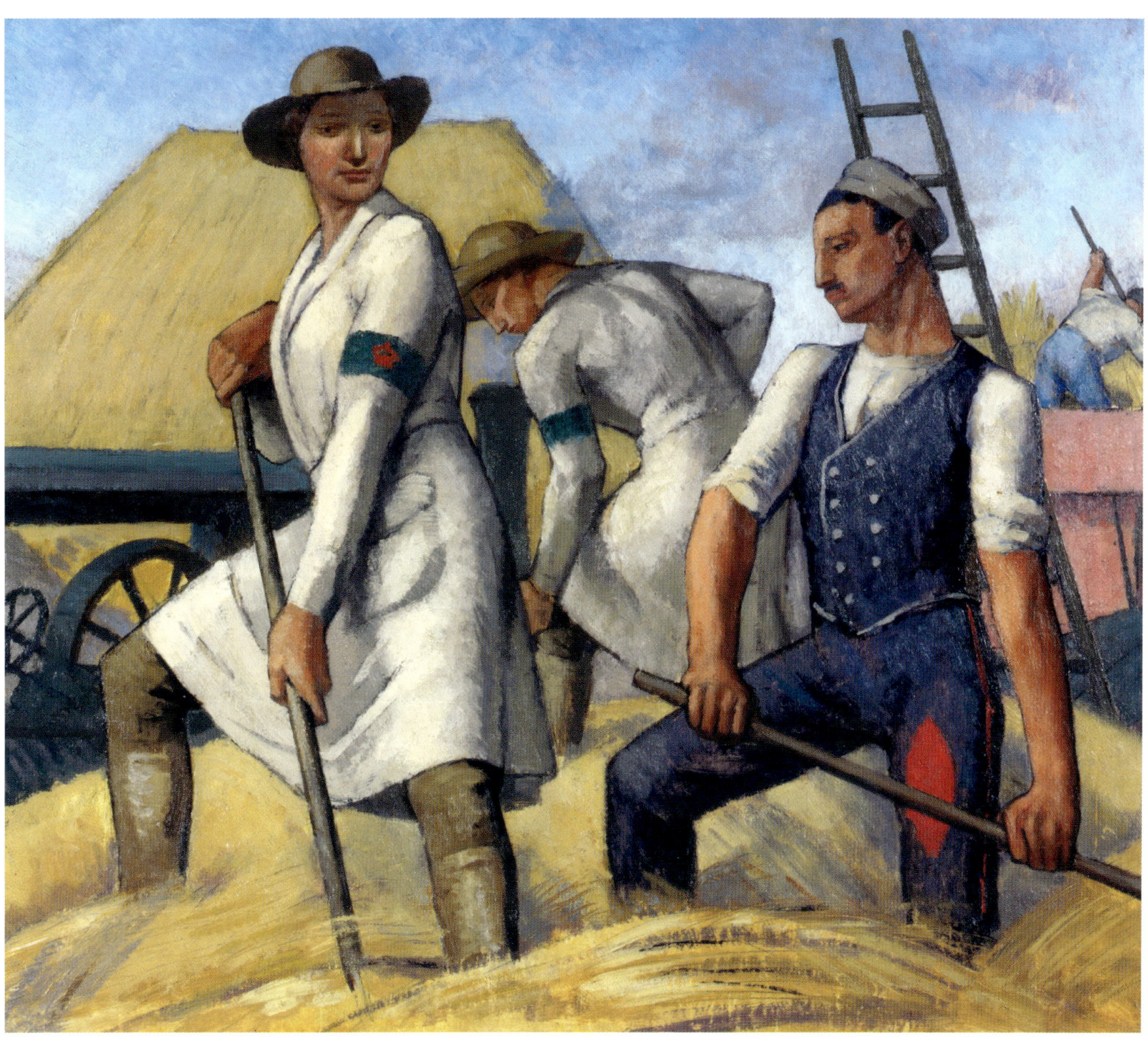

The Women's Land Army and German Prisoners
1918 | oil on panel | 48.2 x 57.1 cm
© IMPERIAL WAR MUSEUMS

1940, over 500 tons of high explosives were dropped on Coventry.

> *The first wave of Heinkels was over the city by about 7.20 p.m. and dropped more than 10,000 incendiaries which started eight major fires and a mass of smaller blazes. Soon the red glow in the sky could be seen by the incoming German planes even before they had crossed the coast in endless waves of bombers that kept coming all through the night.*[13]

As the devastated city burned, so too did the lead and timber roof of the medieval cathedral (St Michael's) until all that remained of the gutted cathedral was the tower, together with its spire supported by flying buttresses. Across the city 568 people died and nearly 1,000 were injured. It was Coventry's Guernica.[14]

Schwabe arrived in Coventry a week after the bombing; the train connections were still bad with the result that he had to take a bus for the last part of the journey from Leamington. John Piper, recalled from a short holiday by Clark, chair of the WAAC, had arrived the morning after the bombing when the ruins were still smoldering to make notes and studies for the paintings that he later worked up. His intent and approach was quite different to that of Schwabe's. Piper's finished painting was 'for propaganda purposes,…immediately reproduced as a postcard. It sold widely and was seen as an expression of British resilience.'[15]

Clark, replying to a memorandum from Dickey about which artists should be asked to record architecture which had been 'disagreeably messed up,' stated:

> *In our records of air-raid damage we must distinguish two kinds: records in which the real motive is the original excellence of the architecture; and damage which is picturesque itself. The former should be done by architectural draughtsmen such as Schwabe; the latter by the artists with a sense of pictorial drama like Sutherland and Piper.*[16]

In Coventry, Schwabe called at the Ministry of Information, in the Council House, which was 'besieged by all sorts of applicants for all sorts of social services and help.'[17] He was taken to the Chief of Police for an extra permit. Schwabe was able to get into the Cathedral ruins, which he found had to some extent been tidied; while there he observed 'gangs of sappers pulling down a building fronting the west end of the Cathedral, using steel ropes and having a tug-of-war with it.'[18] Unable to commence work, he was driven to Birmingham and put up at the Imperial Hotel, where he had stayed before when doing the portraits for Cadbury. Also staying were a party of neutral journalists – Swiss, Finnish, Hungarian, Danish, and Swedish. Schwabe, as ever sociable, joined the party after dinner, although he was aware that an air raid had begun – it was 'the heaviest night of the Birmingham Blitz [and the raid] started 600 fires'[19] and lasted until 5.50 a.m. (11 hours). With classic understatement Schwabe recorded that it was 'Very heavy indeed'– comparable, he was assured, to the worst of the London raids:

> *Incendiary bombs dropped in Temple Street, outside the hotel, early on, and at the back of the hotel too. Later there were heavy explosions and the hotel shook. Bombs fell pretty close. About 2 o'clock I rather foolishly went to bed, and got some sleep in the lulls between attacks. Intermittent gun fire and bombing lasted, with only short intervals, till the 'all clear' sounded.*

The following day he saw just how serious the damage was in Birmingham as he was driven to Coventry by a

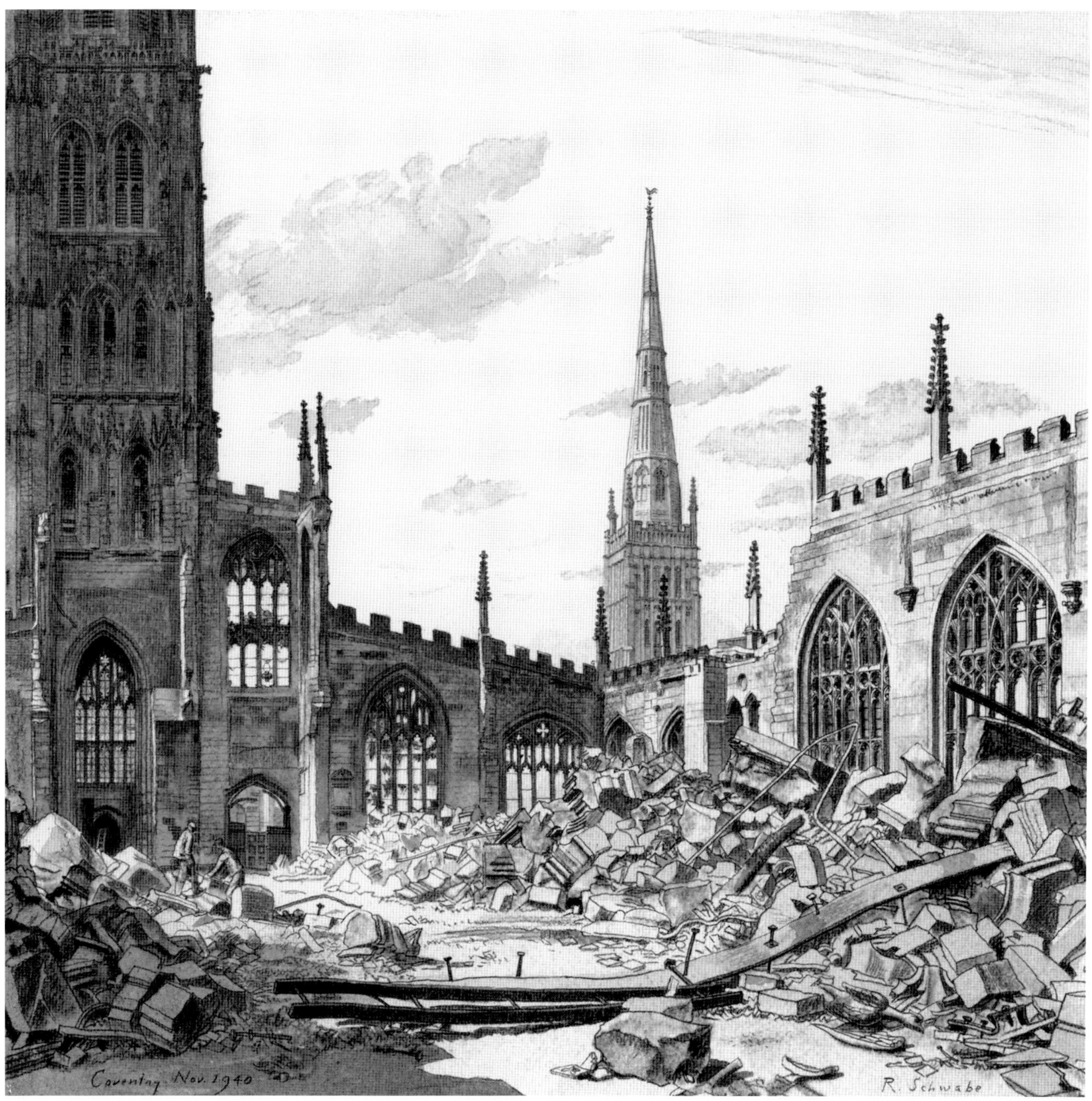

Coventry Cathedral
1940 | pencil, conté crayon and wash | 37.5 × 37.1 cm

very circuitous route; the ten-mile journey took two hours, as many roads were blocked. He recorded in his diary that:

> *Whole rows of cottages are gone, factories, warehouses and commercial buildings knocked down or burnt out. The Cathedral still stands. New Street Station was hit. We had no water in the hotel this morning except what was left in the bedroom water pipes – no tea for breakfast, but food and fruit juice. Queues of people in the streets fetching pails of water from available sources.*

In Coventry he called on the Chief Engineer, to get the Cathedral key, as the place was locked up and was sent on to the Provost, the Very Rev Mr Dick Howard. He was at a funeral; his wife invited Schwabe to wait by her dining room fire (her upper windows were smashed). Having got the key he worked for three hours before he had to leave on account of the return journey to Birmingham. Fortunately it was a peaceful night with only German reconnaissance planes overhead.

The following day Schwabe worked without interruption for four hours. He saw the Provost in the Cathedral who told him that 'as long as he lives the spire (which he admires greatly) will stand, and the church rebuilding will begin as soon as feasible.'[20] Schwabe also noted:

> *Production stopped dead in Coventry for some days after the big raid. About 10% of the people in the factories are back at work now, and the percentage is rising: perhaps it may reach 50%. The old Alvis works are gutted, and there is a bad hole in the road near there. Water has been laid on again to-day in parts of the town. People, on the whole, don't look as miserable as one expects. Coventry Art School is said to be re-opening tomorrow; and, of a row of 15 or 20 wrecked shops that was pointed out to me, the only one re-opened was one for the supply of artists' materials!*

He worked for two further days *in situ*; the notices on the shops 'We are blasted well open', 'More open than usual', 'You should see our Berlin branch', appealed to his dry sense of humour. Schwabe returned to Oxford on 27 November having deposited the key and a volume of marriage registers that he had picked up in the ruins of the Diocesan Registry. He finished the Coventry drawing that week-end, having, including travelling, been fully engaged on it for five and a half days; he was concerned about the arrears that must be made up at the Slade. Schwabe's painstaking and topographically accurate pen-and-wash drawing shows the interior of the Cathedral 'piled high with fallen masonry. A rough path has been cleared towards the west door, but the way is blocked by a twisted roof girder and fallen stones; two… figures are shifting rubble near the base of the tower.'[21] He received a fee of 15 guineas on account on the assumption that he would make a further drawing, perhaps of another subject to complete the comparison.

On 2 January 1941 Dickey sent a telegram to Schwabe, this time wanting him to draw City ruins as soon as possible. Schwabe left Oxford for London two days later and went to the Home Office in Whitehall, to the Ministry of Home Security, where he was interviewed by a Mr J.T.A. Burke, who gave him a letter of authority in addition to the permit from the Ministry of Information. The following day he walked out from the Strand Palace Hotel where he was staying to look at the City. He was relieved to find that most of the familiar landmarks were still there; although St Mary-Le-Strand was damaged and St Bride's gutted, the steeples of both by some quirk of fate were still standing. The church by the Guildhall had gone as had the one in Coleman Street; services were going on in the less damaged ones. Many warehouses in St Paul's

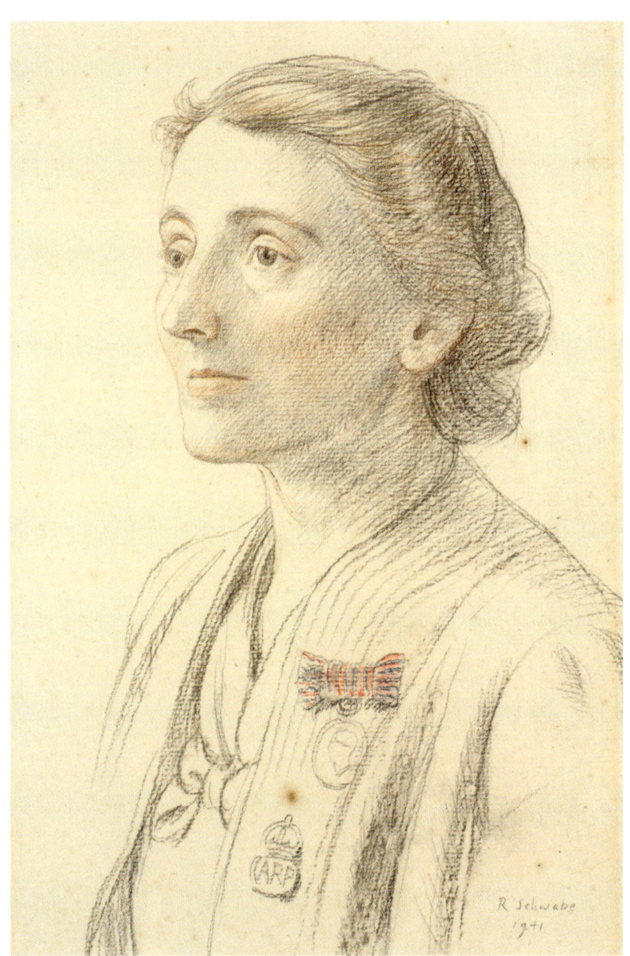

Miss Hollyer GM
1941 | pencil and chalk | 37.1 x 23.5 cm
© IMPERIAL WAR MUSEUMS

Churchyard were burnt out, but St Paul's as far as
Schwabe could see was unscathed. Schwabe looked to
find a window from which he could draw the roofless
Guildhall, but there was none. He decided to make the
best of it and draw in the open, inside the building but
under cover to shelter from the snow shower and slight
drizzle. He began work about 1.15 and carried on till
after 4; as he drew he could hear the dynamiting of
unsafe buildings. The monuments inside the Guildhall
were smashed and cracked from the heat of the flames.
The Library was mostly saved. He returned to his pitch
the following morning and worked until just after
4 p.m. when the light was too poor; by a similar time
the next day he had finished the drawing as far as he
could on the spot. Having finished the drawing of
the Guildhall, Schwabe submitted it for censorship.
The fee was 15 guineas.

Later that month he went for his 'first sitting on
the Artists' Advisory Committee of the Ministry
of Information.'[22] He was something of a reluctant
member but he served dutifully for the next five years.
The Committee at the National Gallery was Russell,
Gleadowe, Dickey, Muirhead Bone, Peake of the Air
Force and Crowe of the War Office. Clark was absent
with 'flu. They looked at a lot of pictures and drawings
submitted for purchase, and some that had been
commissioned.[23] Two weeks later the Committee met
again. The discussion, among other matters, was about
the desirability of making pictorial records of the
changes in military uniform; there was no enthusiasm
for this. Schwabe said *sotto voce* to Gleadowe that he
would not be very keen to do the job even though
he had done diagrams for two books on costume.
Gleadowe said he knew that Schwabe had, and that
'Kelly and Schwabe' (*A short history of costume and armour*)

was one of the most thumbed works in Winchester School Library, where there were two copies, both in tatters.[24]

The Artists' Advisory Committee took advantage of Schwabe's absence from the May meeting to recommend that he be commissioned to draw the Commons sitting in Church House in Westminster. The letter informing Schwabe of the commission was marked SECRET 'because the fact that the Commons are sitting where they are is not for publication and must be strictly regarded as confidential.'[25] Schwabe declined, explaining 'I am not such a free agent as some other artists – I have my duties in the School, and just now other commitments such as examining work… If it can be held over till July, I will do my best… The obstacles are not willfully made.'[26]

On 3 January 1945 Schwabe was able to make a drawing of the Royal Hospital, Chelsea as by chance he was in London for a meeting of the Artists' Advisory Committee. The bomb had fallen that morning at 9 a.m. He was taken to the Home Office to get a pass signed by the Inspector General of the Ministry of Home Security and then worked on the site for about 1½ hours making notes of the scene on some minute paper supplied by the Ministry. The result was *V.2 Damage at the Chelsea Pensioners' Hospital, London SW3*, which Clark thought was highly satisfactory and meritorious of the 12 guineas fee.[27]

HOME FRONT HEROES

At the WAAC meeting in July 1941 Clark suggested Schwabe for one of the portrait drawings of women war heroes. This he accepted and several days before the end of August he went to the National Gallery to see the little room west of the main entrance allotted to him as a studio in which to draw Wendy Pauline Hollyer, GM. Prior to that he had inspected the exhibition of fireman artists at Burlington House and found it a good show, with interesting work by artists new to him – Dessau, Rosoman, Uden, Heppell, Hailstone and others.

Miss Hollyer arrived, before Schwabe, with her mother. Schwabe liked his sitter, 'quite straightforward and frank, easy to talk to, though a little nervous, rather dowdy in appearance, and at first sight a plain, rather red-haired, freckled girl of about 30, though after a study of her features they appear to have some distinction.'[28] Schwabe didn't think he had made a very good beginning, but hoped that he might pull it round at the next sitting. After two hours further work at the National Gallery it was finished. The half length portrait of Miss Hollyer turning towards the left wearing with not a little pride her George Medal, the ribbon which is depicted in colour, was passed by the censor and Schwabe received a fee of ten guineas.

Hollyer, a member of the ARP (Air Raid Precautions) and a telephonist was working in the Report Centre at the Town Hall, Croydon, when a heavy calibre bomb completely demolished it during the evening of Sunday 24 November 1940. There were five telephonists in the Message Room, three of whom were killed instantaneously and two ultimately rescued alive, one of whom was Hollyer. Trapped under tons of debris, and severely injured with wounds in the neck from a large window frame and other woodwork which was 'blasted' across the Message Room, she was able to communicate with the Rescue Party personnel who

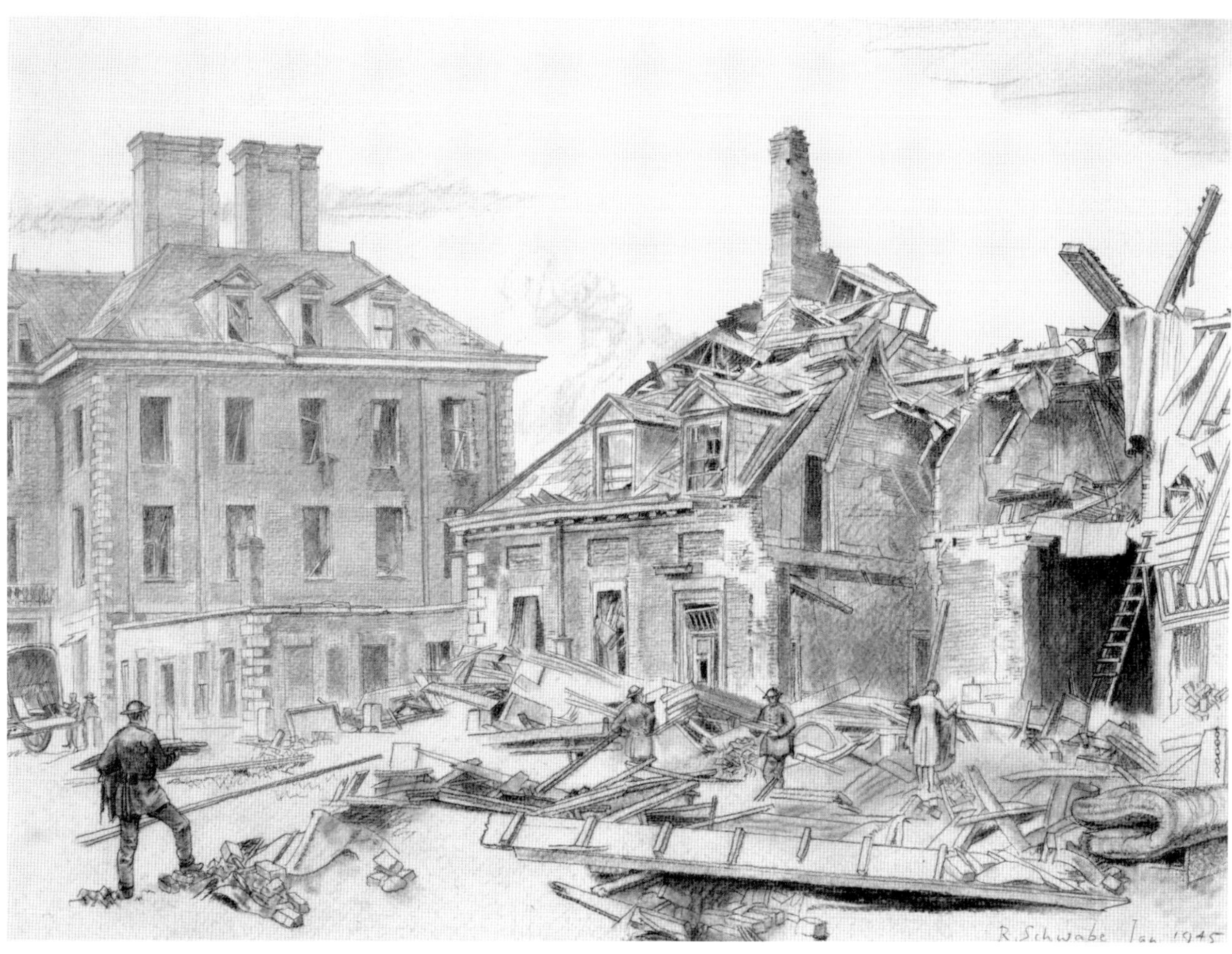

V.2 Damage at the Chelsea Pensioners' Hospital, London SW3
1945 | pencil drawing | 31 × 41 cm
© IMPERIAL WAR MUSEUMS

administered morphia. While still pinned under wreckage, she managed to reach the telephone and accepted a message. Refusing to leave her post, she then tested the other telephones and, finding some of them in working order, cleared sufficient space to carry on. This she did throughout the evening and night until she was relieved the following morning. Both Hollyer and her rescuer Dr Oscar Holden, the Borough Medical Officer were awarded the George Medal.[29]

Six months later Schwabe was contacted by Dickey and asked to undertake five portrait drawings of sitters nominated by the Ministry of Home Security. For this work he was offered a fee of 50 guineas. The first two subjects were Post Office people. In March 1942 Mr Kenneth George Giblett, GM of the Post Office service in Bristol sat in the life-room in the Ruskin School, where Schwabe found the light excellent. He drew from 10–1, and 2–4. Schwabe described Giblett as 'A youngish fellow, with some sort of good looks and good bony structure; quiet and refined, unselfconscious when sitting, easy and modest in manner.'[30] The following day after a further ninety minutes work he completed the pastel of Giblett, who was very civil about it, and apparently pleased. Giblett, a skilled workman in the engineering department, at the Post Office, was awarded the George Medal for his role overseeing the Post Office Fire Brigade during a heavy raid on Bristol, in particular attending fires at stores adjacent to the Post Office.[31]

Schwabe next drew Mr Samuel Frank Pople, GM (c.1897–1947), also of Bristol, an ex-soldier once in Tientsin, now a telephonist. Pople told Schwabe that the Germans were not more than 300 feet away at

times in the Bristol raids; also that he did not deserve a medal any more than any one else, certainly not more than his wife, who had to stay at home all alone. Mrs Pople came with her husband, 'she looked at the portrait and said – "That's you, Frank" and expressed herself as satisfied (thank the Lord)' wrote Schwabe.[32] Pople, a Night Supervisor at Bristol Post Office, was awarded the George Medal for his role in rescuing valuable equipment.

Early on the morning of 4 July 1942 Schwabe began his pastel drawing of Police Constable Francis Henry Dart, BEM (b.1911) of Swansea, who arrived in a very smart full-dress uniform with silver buttons, modelled on the Guards. He told Schwabe that as a boy he worked:

> in a coal mine, his father having been a miner too. His father's advice was to chuck that career, as there was nothing in it, so he joined the Constabulary, in spite of being offered a Scholarship which might have taken him to a Welsh university. He was well treated in the coal-mining firm, and went on with his education, while with it, so that he might be qualified as a possible overseer or manager. An intelligent man, of fine physique. His medal was for conspicuous courage in air-raids.[33]

Schwabe finished Dart's portrait the following morning.

A few days later Schwabe went to Liverpool for his final portrait commissions of two police officers. He was told that the city's worst 'blitz', for nine days or nights, on end, was in May 1941 but since then it had been fairly quiet. He was struck by the traces of the bomb and fire damage and how much the Cathedral had grown since he last came to Liverpool to make drawings for the *Manchester Guardian*, 15–18 years

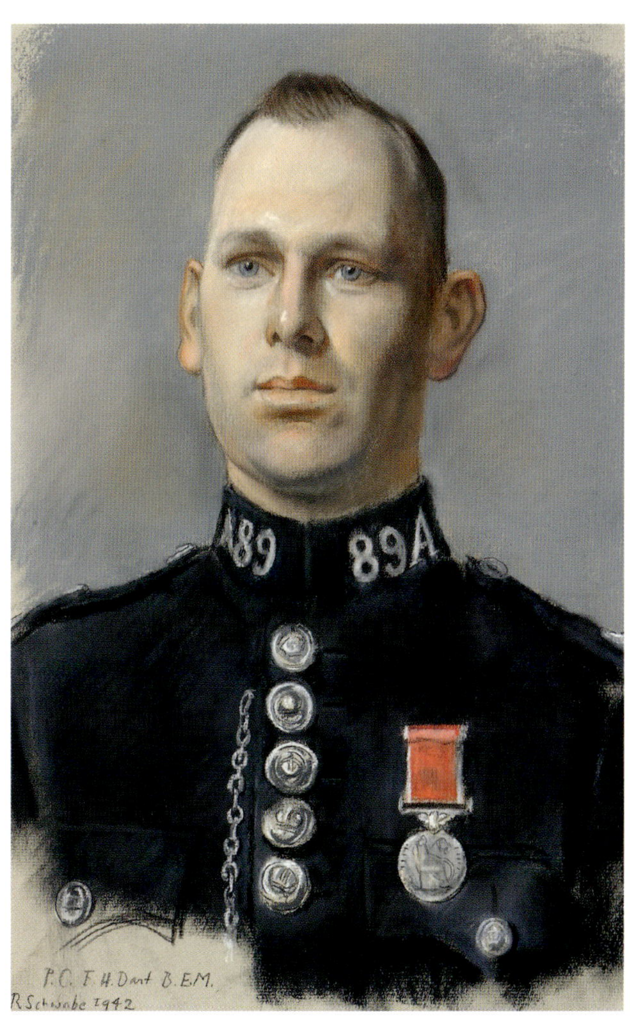

Police Constable F.H. Dart BEM
1942 | chalk pastel on paper | 41 × 31 cm
© NATIONAL MUSEUMS LIVERPOOL, WALKER ART GALLERY

previously. The houses alongside it, opposite the tower, were just a heap of rubble.

Schwabe worked at the Art School, in Hope Street, where Huggill, the Principal, put a studio at his disposal. At 10 a.m. Chief Superintendent Edward Nichols of Liverpool Police Force and Sergeant Thomas Alker of the Manchester Police Force came. Schwabe started to draw Alker, 'a fine fellow, once a coal miner. Much the same story as PC Dart of Swansea.'[34] He drew him from 10.15–12.45, and again from 2–4.30; the light was good, which helped Schwabe finish the portrait.

The *London Gazette*[35] had the previous year reported that Sergeant Alker, during a heavy air raid when some works premises were set on fire, organised a party of men; and while an Auxiliary Fire Service unit fought the flames, he arranged for the removal of motor tyres from the burning building. At the same incident a fire was discovered near an ammunition store and, showing total disregard of danger to himself, Alker went on the roof of a tool shed and extinguished the flames, thereby saving the ammunition.

Schwabe drew Nichols from 9.30–4; he had received the George Medal for rescuing a prisoner trapped in his cell at Walton Jail, Liverpool after it had been struck by a high explosive bomb, in September 1940. Schwabe thought him:

> *An excellent man, he has risen from an ill educated (since then self-educated) youngster to a rank equivalent to Lieut. Col. His attitude to me was genial yet respectful — he addressed me always as 'sir', rather to my surprise. A brave fellow (as they all must be, to get their distinctions), religious, simple and fond of gardening.*[36]

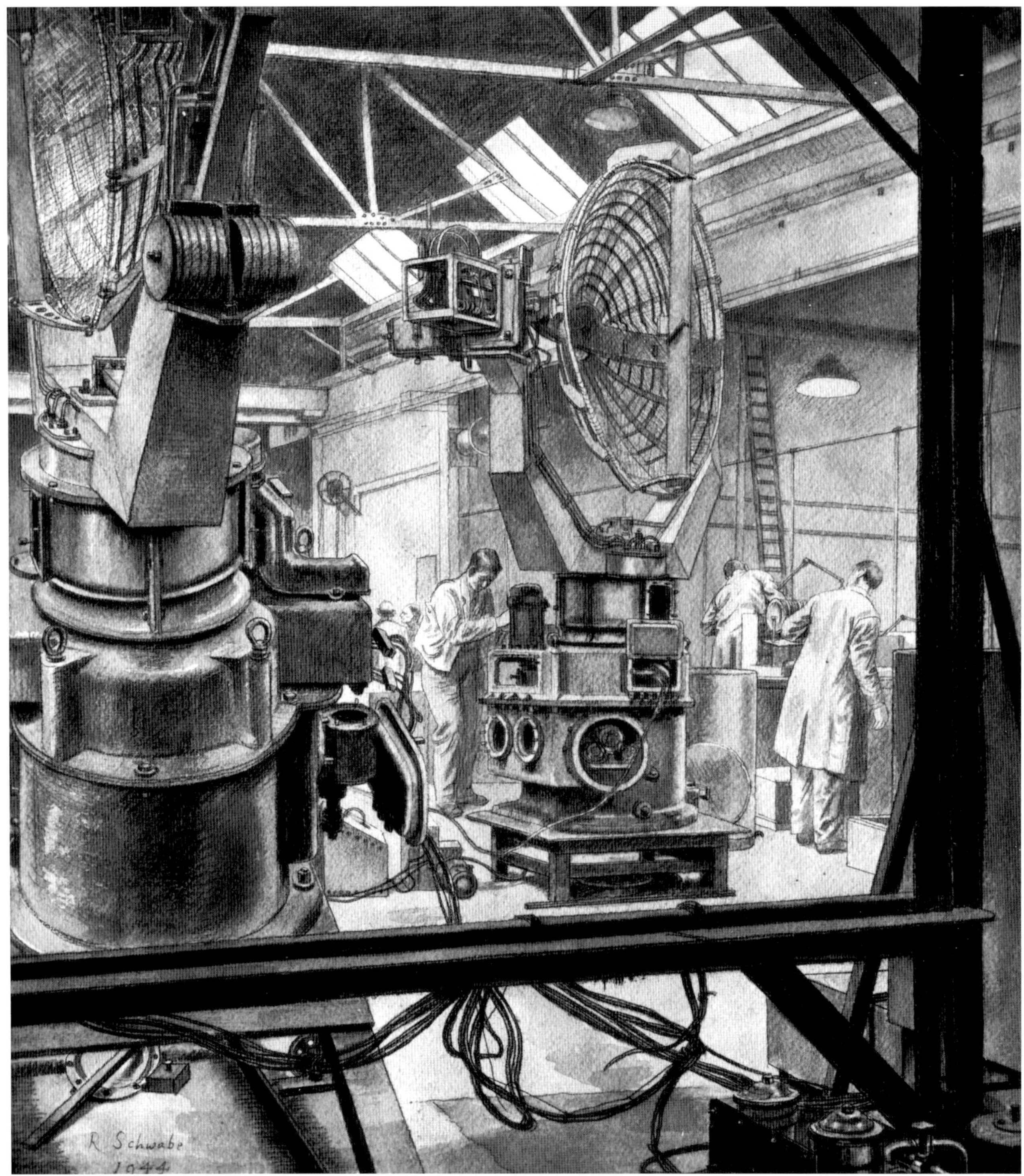

AUK
1944 | black chalk and watercolour | 42.5 x 37 cm

During a break from the sitting for lunch, Schwabe took the opportunity to walk down to Pier Head. He watched the Wallasey ferry-boat arrive, packed with hundreds of people; and a liner putting off; he saw that the Harbour Board and Cunard offices and the Customs House remained amidst ruin upon ruin. The shawled women and the mill hands in the streets reminded him of his childhood.

MANCHESTER'S WAR INDUSTRIES: A PICTORIAL RECORD

In September 1944 Schwabe was contacted by Lawrence Haward (1878–1957), Curator at Manchester City Art Gallery, asking if would care to undertake a drawing of some industrial scenes which would be paid for by the firm concerned and presented to the Gallery's war collection. Haward 'wanted to have records not only of the fighting forces' achievements but also of the industrial effort behind the scenes'[37] and, where possible, these were to be undertaken by artists with a Manchester connection. Schwabe certainly had a Manchester connection; indeed he had told Hubert Worthington (1886–1963) Professor of Architecture at the RCA that he felt it was his *alma mater*. Schwabe was also a member of the long established Manchester Academy of Fine Arts, having been proposed by Ethel Henriques (1886–1936) in 1932.

Schwabe left Oxford for Manchester on 1 October; Hagedorn and Dodd had also agreed to make drawings for Haward. He went to the Ferranti factory at Hollinwood, near Oldham to draw radio-location gadgets. The following month he took his drawing *AUK*[38] for censorship to the Ministry of Information who declined to pass it, as the AUK radio-location instrument was still on the secret list having only recently been fitted on warships. Haward was disappointed as this likely meant it would have to be 'submitted again later on, say on the declaration of an Armistice, in order to get permission to show it to the public.'[39] He informed Schwabe that:

> *Vincent Ferranti himself and the other directors who saw the drawing… were all delighted with it and were particularly interested in spotting familiar details. The head of the department, whose name I forget, but whom you saw when you first went into the workshop, pronounced everything to be exactly as it should be and he was much interested in the life-like attitude of some of the figures which you had introduced.*[40]

The boiler-makers Adamson's of Dukinfield were the location for Schwabe's next factory drawing in January 1945; Clause and Cundall had earlier been up doing similar drawings. He found the factories spacious and thinly peopled – which was quite different from the crowd at Ferrantis.[41] At Adamson's they handled mostly heavy stuff at which not many workmen could work at a time. Schwabe thought the boys handling molten rivets looked very young – he guessed, under 14.[42] He spent three days drawing on the spot; *Pin-Riveting a Lancashire Boiler* was exhibited at the City Art Gallery in October. *The Times'* critic described it as 'an admirable monochrome drawing… which shows how well an engineering subject suits this distinguished architectural draughtsman.'[43]

1 Undated letter from Dodd to Schwabe, the month is indecipherable, the day recorded is 17. Private collection.

2 Harries, M. & S. (1983) *The war artists. British official war art of the twentieth century*, p.86.

3 Rushbury eventually produced some thirty works for his series *London in Wartime*.

4 See Randolph Schwabe, Imperial War Museum, First World War Artists' Archive, File Number 287/7.

5 See Randolph Schwabe, IWM, Ibid.

6 See Randolph Schwabe, IWM, Op. cit.

7 In Clarke (2008) I suggested the location was Church Farm, Podington. Since then a Schwabe sketch of the German POW has been located on which he had written Rushden Farm. German prisoners lived at Rushden House in the coach house and stables and worked on the land.

8 Randolph Schwabe, IWM, Op. cit. The painting had been finished earlier but there was some discussion (30/8/1919), as to the title that should be recorded in the catalogue of War Pictures.

9 See Malvern, S. (2004) *Modern art, Britain and the Great War*, p.180.

10 Summerfield, A. (1989) *The artist at war*, p.22.

11 Dickey studied at the Westminster School of Art, becoming Professor of Fine Art at Durham for five years before being appointed Staff Inspector of Art at the Board of Education in 1931.

12 Randolph Schwabe, Imperial War Museum (IWM), Second War Artists' Archive, File Number GP/46/34 (A). Dickey to Schwabe 17/11/1940.

13 Gardiner, J. (2010) *The Blitz. The British under attack 1939–1945*, p.302.

14 The *Birmingham Gazette* on 16 November carried the headline 'Coventry – Our Guernica' cited in Campbell, L. (1996) *Coventry Cathedral: Art and architecture in post-war Britain*, p.9 and see F. Spalding (2009) *John Piper. Myfanwy Piper. Lives in art*, p. 179 where she makes the case that the comparison with the destruction of Guernica was not entirely just.

15 Spalding, F. (2003) 'John Piper and Coventry, in war and peace', *The Burlington*, July, p.493.

16 Clark to Dickey, 29/11/1940. IWM, Op. cit. Second World War File.

17 Schwabe diary 1940.

18 Schwabe diary 1940.

19 Gardiner (2010) Op. cit., p.305.

20 Schwabe diary 1940.

21 Campbell (1996) Op. cit., p.13.

22 Schwabe diary 1941.

23 Schwabe diary 1941.

24 Schwabe diary 1941.

25 Dickey to Schwabe, 22/5/1941. IWM, Op. cit., Second World War File. The original idea of recording events at the Commons came from Harold Nicolson.

26 Schwabe to Dickey, 25/5/1941. IWM, Op. cit., Second World War File.

27 Gregory, WAAC Secretary to Schwabe, 11/1/1945. IWM, Op. cit., Second World War File.

28 Schwabe diary 1941.

29 See www.london-gazette.co.uk/issues/35095/supplements/1344/page.pdf and www.museumofcroydon.com/asset_arena/pdf/p1/61384_map.p1.pdf (accessed 9/5/2011).

30 Schwabe diary 1942.

31 Pers. Comm. from Julia Carver, Collections Officer, Fine Art, Bristol Museum & Art Gallery, 26/4/11 and the Supplement to the *London Gazette* 14/2/1941.

32 Schwabe diary 1942 and Carver (2011) Ibid.

33 Schwabe diary 1942. See *The London Gazette* 25 April, 1941 for details re Dart's bravery and devotion to duty in rescuing people from bombed-out buildings while the enemy attack continued and bombs fell nearby.

34 Schwabe diary 1942.

35 *The London Gazette*, 21 March 1941.

36 Schwabe diary 1942.

37 *Manchester Guardian*, 22/9/1945, p.3.

38 'The painting… is of the Type 277 British naval radar. This radar served as surface search radar…and as an "approximate" height-finder and low-flyer detector. The antenna was known as outfit AUK…radars were given a Type designation… but the radar disk or scanner was given a separate nomenclature'. Dr J.R. Bullen letter to S. Martin, Fine Art Department, 24/2/1992. Manchester City Art Gallery archives.

39 Haward letter to Schwabe, 24/11/1944. Private collection.

40 Haward letter to Schwabe, 8/12/1944. Private collection.

41 Schwabe illustrated *The Tinkers of Elstow* by H.E. Bates (1946) which told the story of the Royal Ordnance Factory managed by J. Lyons and Co. for the Ministry of Supply during the Second World War.

42 Schwabe diary 1945.

43 *The Times* 26/10/1945, p.6. The location of *Pin-Riveting* is unknown.

ILLUSTRATION AND DESIGN

Schwabe is an ideal decorator of books because, in addition to being a fine draughtsman and a fine artist (terms by no means synonymous), he understands every form of reproduction and the necessity for the design to balance with the page. Further, he is an encyclopaedia of all kinds of knowledge relating to costume, to Nature in its manifold forms of expression, to the history of art, literature and nations, and, not least important, welcomes criticism and works with the producer.[1]

THE BEAUMONT PRESS

Thus wrote in 1927 the dance historian and critic, specialist publisher and bookseller, Cyril Beaumont (1891–1976), in a glowing tribute to Schwabe, who was associated with him in the production of more than a dozen books of different character. For over a decade Schwabe fastidiously designed 'initial letters, title pages, full-page illustrations and many smaller decorations.'[2] The fine and delicate lines of his varied contributions were ideally suited to realising the Beaumont Press's motto *Simplex Munditiis* (Elegant in Simplicity). Beaumont established the eponymous private press in 1917 for the purpose of affording distinguished contemporary writers the opportunity to have their work published in their lifetime. Each edition consisted of a limited number of copies on hand-made parchment vellum signed by the author and artist and a larger number of copies on hand-made paper, all bound in decorative paper boards. Schwabe's first contribution in 1921 was to provide the cover design, title-page decoration and 15 other decorations for Beaumont's thirteenth book *Crossing: A Fairy Play* by Walter de la Mare with music by C. Armstrong Gibbs. The decorations by Schwabe were in black and Beaumont thought they 'reflected admirably the wistful note of the play, which gave them an elusive charm.'[3] The book was priced at £2 5s., 264 copies

were for sale, 56 signed copies cost four guineas each. The numerous experiments and revisions and the large number of designs made it Beaumont's most expensive book in the series. In spite of the cost the book sold well and Schwabe supplied wood-cut decorations for Beaumont's next book *After Berneval: Letters of Oscar Wilde to Robert Ross* which was priced at a more modest £1.1s. and £2.10s. Vyvyan Holland, Oscar Wilde's son, who had supplied Beaumont with the letters, rejected Schwabe's original title page design of the Bay of Naples in southern Italy from the viewpoint of Virgil's tomb. Beaumont thought he possibly disapproved as adverse comment might be evoked by the association with Virgil. A compromise was reached and Schwabe 'replaced the outline of the tomb with a clump of bushes'.[4]

Schwabe approached his next venture, *To Nature* (1923), a book of new poems by Edmund Blunden (1896–1974) with much enthusiasm as he had a great regard for his poetry. It was a time-consuming task as he contributed 34 exquisite initial letters (an innovation for Beaumont's series) which gave 'place to a scene in miniature, a tiny interior or landscape' in harmony with the mood and period of each of the poems. These met with Blunden's approval who said 'Mr. Schwabe's little pictures have my warm praise and gratitude'.[5]

Beaumont entrusted Schwabe with the task of designing a title-page decoration and a head and tail-piece to accompany each of the seven essays by Arthur Symons in *The Café Royal* (1923), the seventeenth book. Schwabe and Birdie, along with a myriad of other artists and their models and writers, would frequent the Café Royal at the Piccadilly end of Regent Street having dined at a nearby chop-house. Schwabe 'with

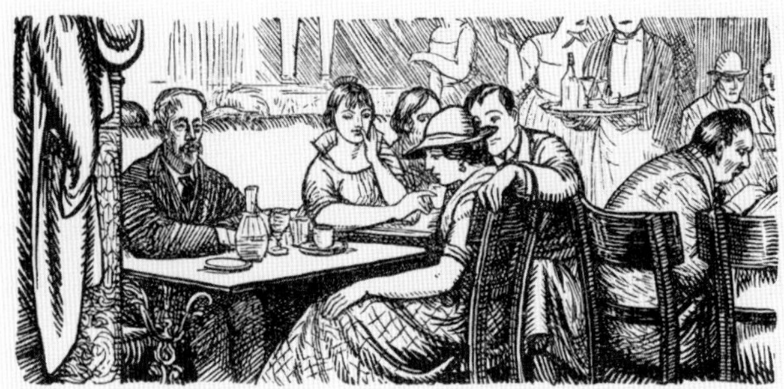

The Café Royal
1923

FIRST RHYMES

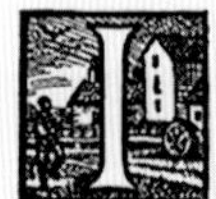
N the meadow by the mill
    I'd make my ballad,
Tunes to that would whistle shrill
And beat the blackbird's ringing bill—

WATER MOMENT

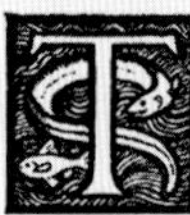
HE silver eel slips through the waving
    weeds,
And in the tunnelled shining stone recedes;
The earnest eye surveys the crystal pond

THE LONG TRUCE

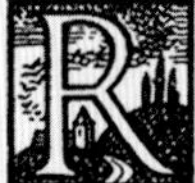
OOKS in black constellations slowly wheeling
Over this pale sweet sky, and church bells
    pealing
The homely pilgrims to the fount of healing;

Initial letters for *To Nature* by Edmund Blunden
1923

his dark cloak, well-shaped tall hat, and ivory-knobbed cane'[6] strolling into the Café Royal in his debonair fashion accompanied by Birdie 'with her sleek black head, clear, ivory skin and long limbed angular grace… two natures so brilliantly complementary'[7] they did not look out of place. 'Amid the smoke haze that shed a bloom over its rococo ceiling and mirrored walls'[8] they met their friends and chatted across its marble-topped tables. The Café 'acted as a powerful magnet to younger painters eager to rub shoulders with the artistic great of the day.'[9] Symons, also a habitué of the Café Royal since 1894, in his opening essay recalled Augustus John who was often to be found there and the 'radiant conversations' they had 'on the soul in art, on the flesh and the spirit and the beauty of absinthe…on serpents, gypsies, Russian ballets…'. Schwabe in the head-piece for the essay depicts the heavily moustachioed Symons seated with his friends about to partake of an absinthe. *The Genius of Marlowe*, the fourth essay, led to much intense discussion between Schwabe and Beaumont at 75 Charing Cross Road. In his memoirs, *Bookseller at the Ballet*, Beaumont recalled Schwabe's studious features as they wrestled over designs for the head-piece. While Beaumont acknowledged that Schwabe took full advantage of the symbolical treatment which the essay lent itself to, he did not like at first the proposed scheme. Schwabe sent him another which he believed was a vast improvement, accompanied by one of his typical letters in which he explained:

> In the new one there is more interest, and I have tried to keep in mind characteristic people like Jost Amman [c.1539–91] and the Stammbuch artists. It could, of course be enriched with more 'colour', but the question of weight with type comes in then. Don't you think it is better left like this? I hope you will approve…

Seasonal head-pieces for *The Curwen Press Almanack*
1926

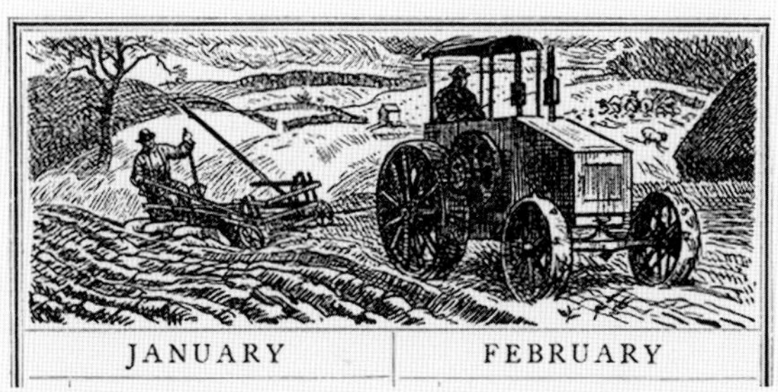

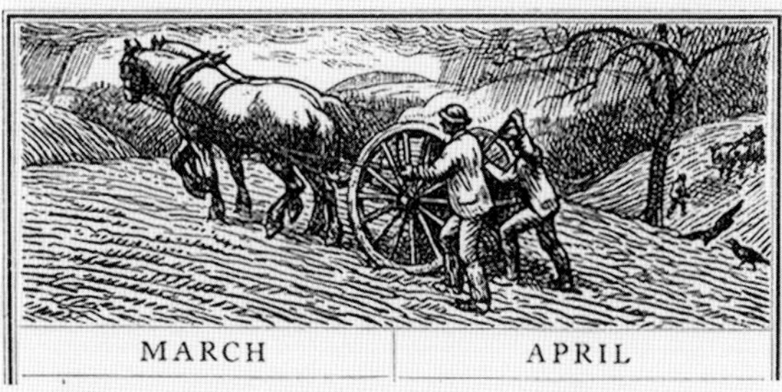

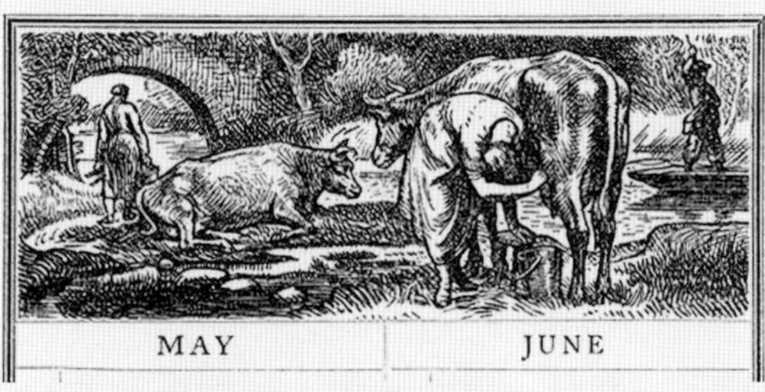

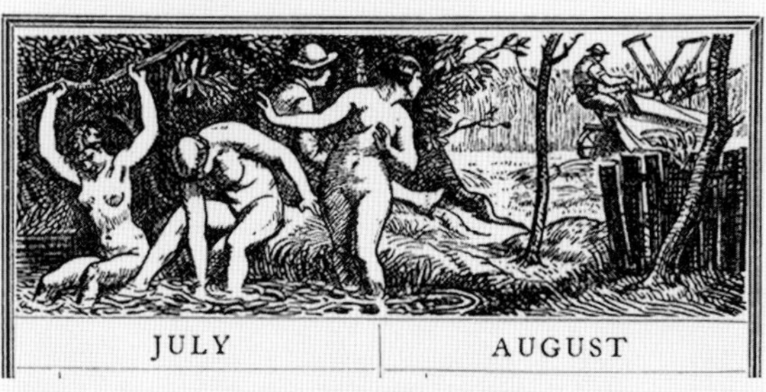

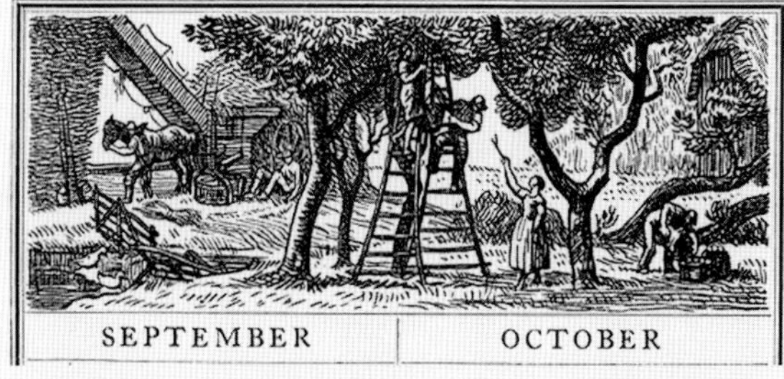

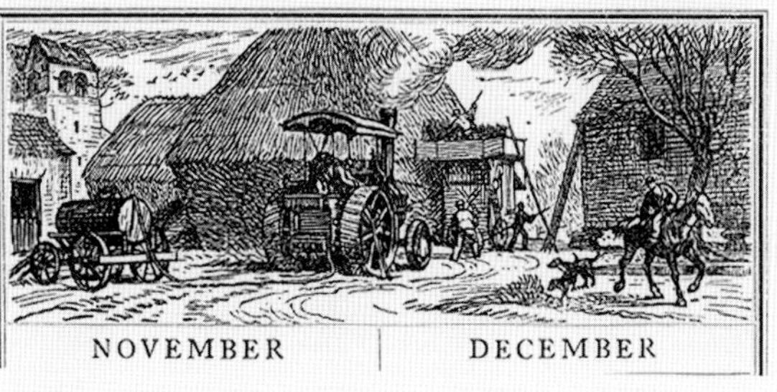

*I have been scouring the country for the Deadly Nightshade,
and have found some. From the material object and a botany
book a pattern has resulted which I rather like myself, only
I am not sure about it on your rather yellow grey paper.*[10]

Beaumont approved the revisions which retained the
pair of bombasted breeches which was an allusion to
those characteristics of padded, inflated style which
Schwabe found in both Symons and Marlowe. He
found the required shade in an Ingres paper on which
Schwabe's design was printed in green, violet and black.

Schwabe's decorations embellished *Madrigals and Chronicles*
(1924) a collection of unpublished poems by John
Clare (1793–1864). Blunden wrote the preface and
commentary and in a letter to Beaumont expressed his
admiration for Schwabe's designs which were inspired
by a study of Thomas Bewick's (1753–1828) woodcuts.
He said of Schwabe's portrayals of country life, which
foreshadow his work for *The Curwen Press Almanack*[11] to
which he contributed six finely executed seasonal head-
pieces of agricultural scenes, in 1926, 'there's strength
in them, which suits Clare – his gentleness was deeply
powerful.'[12]

Blunden and Schwabe again combined their complementary talents in Beaumont's nineteenth book
Masks of Time (1925) which comprised thirty-five of
Blunden's poems dealing with peace and the impact of
war. Schwabe's design for *Part Two* (the war poems) was
stark, cut on wood, the gas-masked skeleton conveying
with the minimum of line the horror and brutality of
war. Blunden considered it 'a master work, for which I
thank Schwabe with all my heart. I do not think it too
bold, for it is clear and active in detail. A candid mind
will not rebel against truth's light from the clouds.'[13]

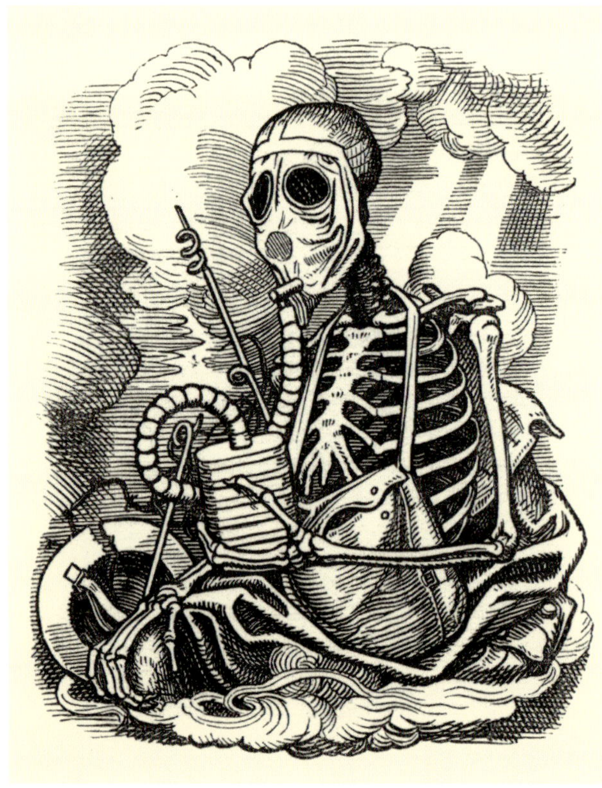

Illustration for *Masks of Time* by Edmund Blunden
1925

Schwabe designed the title-page for *The Letters of J.E. Flecker to Frank Savery* (1926).[14] He wrote to Beaumont from Petersfield, Hampshire where he was visiting Alice, a boarder at Bedales School, to explain that the design for the Cedars on the title-page would engage his attention when he was back in town; however he made notes of the Cedar outside his window. The cover was by Claudia Guercio (1904–81);[15] the book contained no decorations.

Henry Williamson's (1929) *Wet Flanders Plain* took the form of a Diary of a Nine Day Visit by a soldier returning to the battlefields where he had fought. Schwabe's cover design of The Menin Gate Memorial to the Missing evokes the tens of thousands of soldiers who were slaughtered like cattle in Ypres Salient.[16] The lion *couchant* is looking away from the city to face the battlefields. On the side columns the inscription 'Pro Patria' 'Pro Rege' ('For Country' 'For King') is visible. In front of the Gate, which was opened in July 1927, are small parties of tourists, some in uniform, in the foreground a one-legged veteran with his trouser sewn short at the hip and crutch to support him under his right arm. The cover design in black, red and grey is striking with rifles intermingled with farm implements. There were no decorations accompanying the diary entries.

A Summer's Fancy by Edmund Blunden was Schwabe's next commission from Beaumont. He was glad of the work as he was 'a little tired of being a sort of office boy'. It gave him 'an incentive to do something that is interesting and worthwhile.'[17] Schwabe started work in February 1930. He discussed with Beaumont a synopsis of the illustrations to propose to Blunden. They met at *The Nation* office where Blunden was

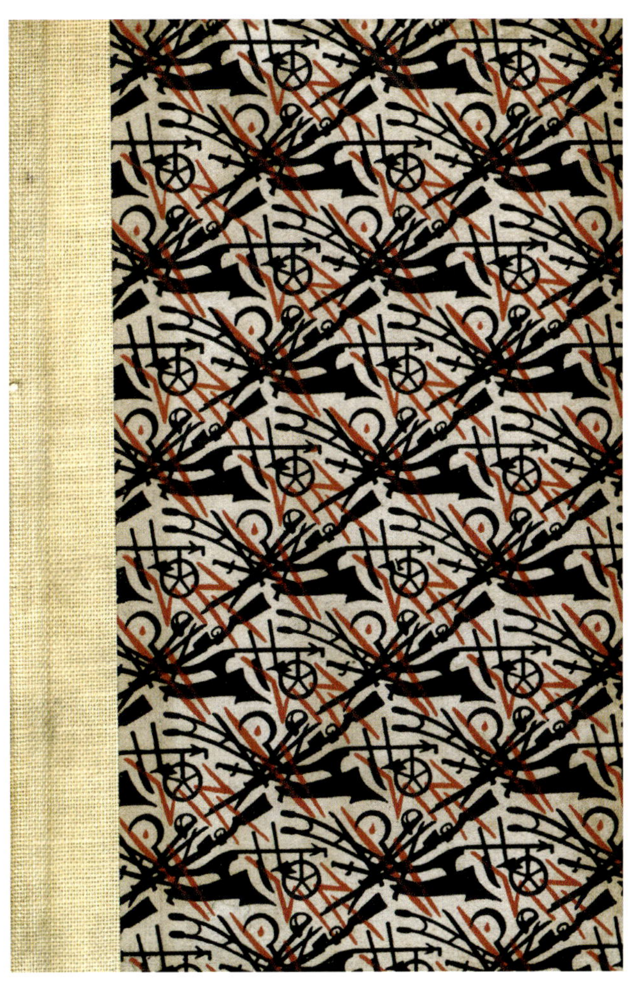

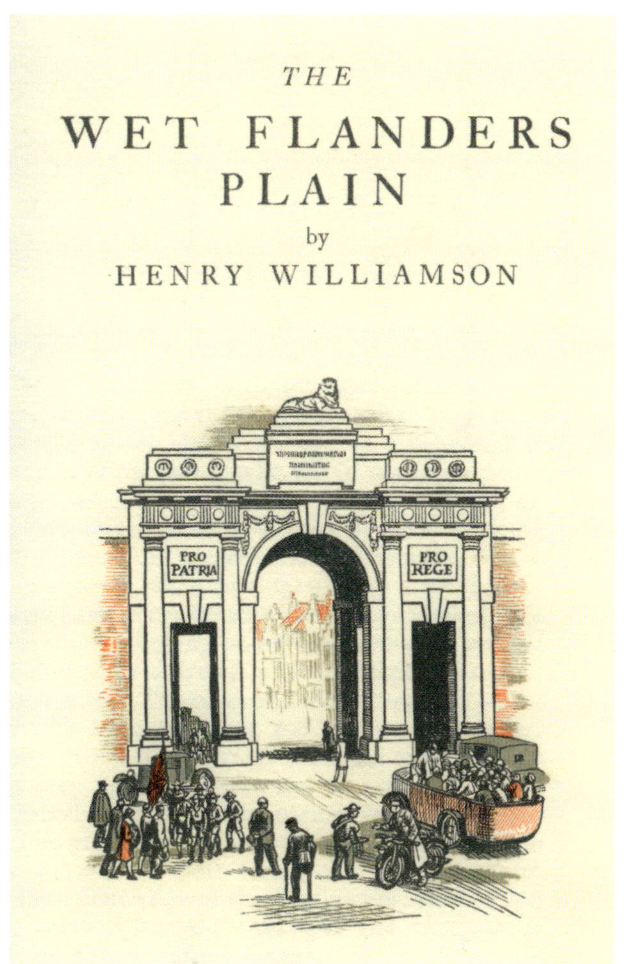

Cover and title-page for *The Wet Flanders Plain*
1929

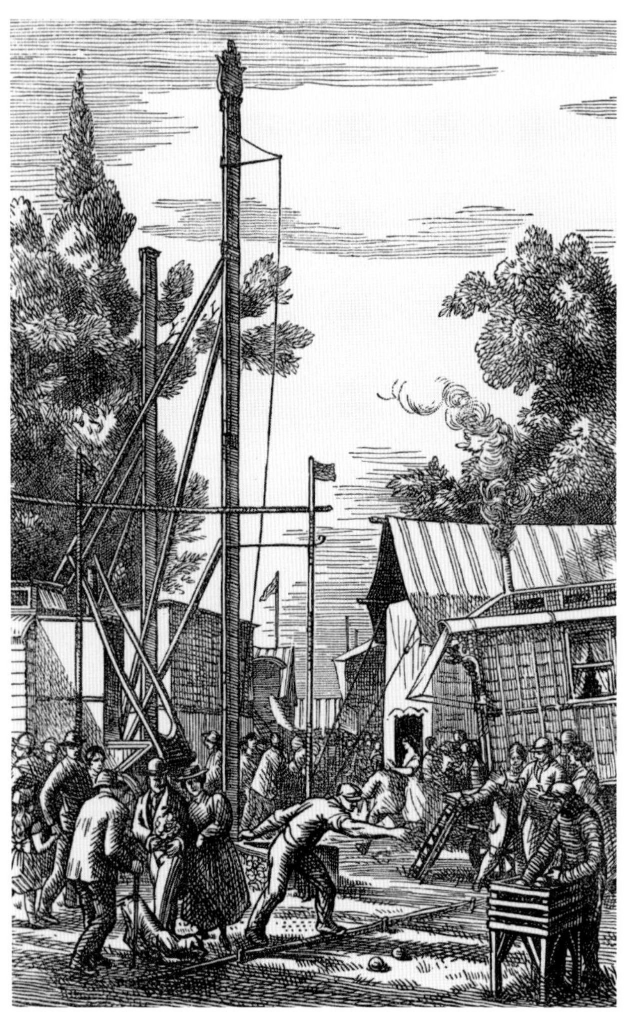

Illustration for *A Summer's Fancy* by Edmund Blunden
1930 | pen and black ink

literary editor. Blunden accepted the proposals and sent Schwabe picture postcards he had annotated of Yalding in Kent, the scene of the poem written in 1922, and books with pictures of the district. He examined these and the poem with a view to the illustrations and noticed one or two changes in the verses as now set up; he informed Beaumont, who told him privately that Blunden's wife, to whom parts of the poem were addressed, had been 'carrying on' with another man while he was lecturing at the Imperial University of Tokyo in Japan, and that he was much broken up by it.[18]

Schwabe took advantage of his regular Easter holiday in Dover with Dora and Tom Cobbe (Birdie's sister and her husband) to take the train to Yalding to look over the terrain. He thought it had 'many beauties' and he made some useful notes about the church and town bridge, including the tumbling-bay, for the Blunden illustrations. He worked intermittently on these over the next month and was able to send one to Beaumont by the middle of May, having made some slight revisions of tone in the manner of the popular Victorian engraver Birket Foster (1825–99). Schwabe hoped the wood engraver would be able to follow the drawing. He was aware that sometimes he got too minute, without achieving as much difference of tone as he wanted.[19] Beaumont liked it. Schwabe then worked on a full-page drawing of a fair scene followed by one of the weir. He too was pleased with the proofs of the new wood block which he thought had been very well cut – the engraver received about £8 for each block while Schwabe asked only £12 for the job.

Schwabe 'went to the War Museum to cultivate an atmosphere and procure facts for the Blunden illustration'[20] of giant guns going through a town

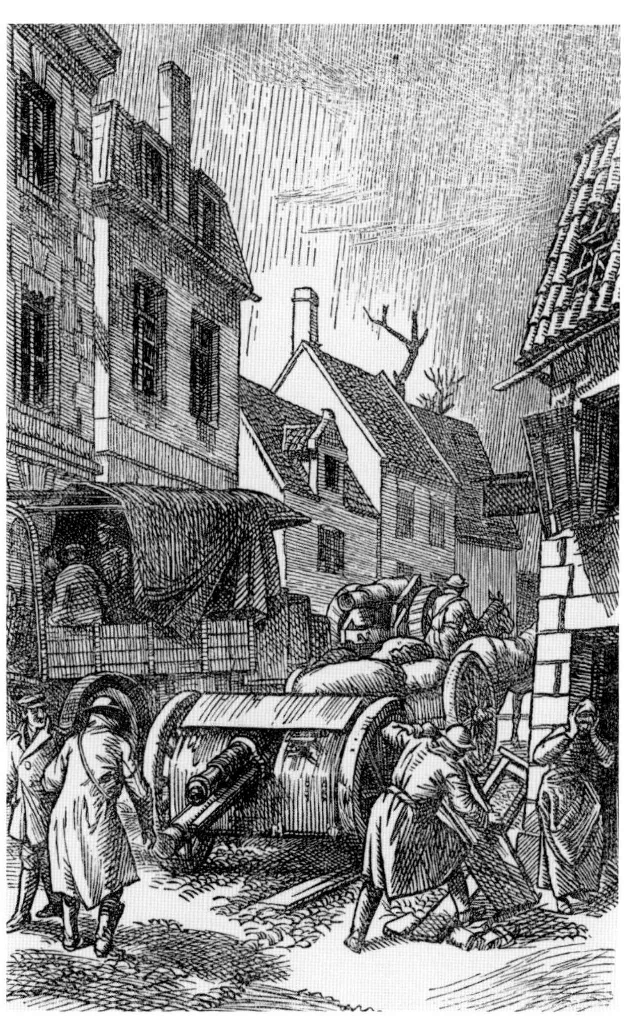

Illustration for *A Summer's Fancy* by Edmund Blunden
1930 | pen and black ink

in Flanders. The author thought the outcome 'not at all bad' and a 'truthful record' although he found the houses 'a trifle on the Georgian side.' He acknowledged that he seemed overly concerned with matter of fact but he liked 'either that or good outrageous wildness'; nonetheless he thought that Schwabe's drawings 'were delicate and thorough'.[21] Schwabe's final task was the book cover; he had been keen to relinquish the task but Beaumont thought 'it would be a pity to run the risk of the harmony of the book being disturbed through supplying a cover by another hand' particularly as Schwabe had taken such care with the drawings which in his opinion were 'an improvement on *Madrigals*, which is saying a good deal.'[22] Beaumont wanted something in two or three colours, to include 'some small repeat of floral motifs suggesting of Summer in the Country, cornflowers and buttercups, or buttercups and daisies, but you will know, perhaps blue-bells and something else would be nice.'[23] The book was printed throughout in black, as it seemed to Beaumont that Schwabe's drawings were full of colour in themselves. For the title-page Beaumont selected a Nicholas Cochin type as it always suggested summer to him, though he did not know why.[24] The book was one of the exhibits in the Fifty Best Books Exhibition of 1931 organised by the First Edition Club.

Schwabe met Blunden for the first time in November 1943 in Oxford where he was tutor in English literature at Merton College; Rutherston introduced them at the opening of a propaganda exhibition 'The Spirit of France' in the Ashmolean Museum. Schwabe thought Blunden not as striking a figure as Masefield (who made the opening speech) whom he had met some forty years earlier in William Strang's St John's Wood studio, on one of his Sunday evenings at home.

Schwabe and Blunden talked about Yalding and his drawings of that village; Schwabe was sorry to hear that the 'High Houses' in Yalding had been pulled down, because no one would put up £500 to save them from destruction and the old bridge had been damaged by a tank.[25]

Blunden's *To Themis — Poems on Famous Trials with Other Pieces* (1931) was the final book issued by the Beaumont Press. Schwabe provided the cover design in black and yellow of emblems of the law, the title-page decoration and frontispiece. These were 'vastly to [Blunden's] liking'.[26]

THE GOLDEN AGE OF THE RUSSIAN BALLET

Schwabe also collaborated with Beaumont on a number of specialised books about ballet. Looking back in the 1930s he recalled:

> the great days of the Russian Ballet and the Theatre Movement about 1912–1920: how we lived through it and were rich without realizing how exciting and interesting it really was: though, goodness knows, Birdie and I were excited enough about the first Ballet season the Russians gave in London.[27]

Schwabe wished he had kept a diary then as it cost him an effort now to remember the names of some of the dancers of whom he had drawn portraits.

Diaghilev began a season of ballet in London on 2 November 1921 with the production of Tchaikovsky's *The Sleeping Princess (La Belle au Bois Dormant)* at the Alhambra Theatre, Leicester Square. Schwabe was commissioned by Beaumont to undertake decorations for *The Sleeping Princess* as part of his series *Impressions of the Russian Ballet*. Schwabe spent much time behind the scenes at

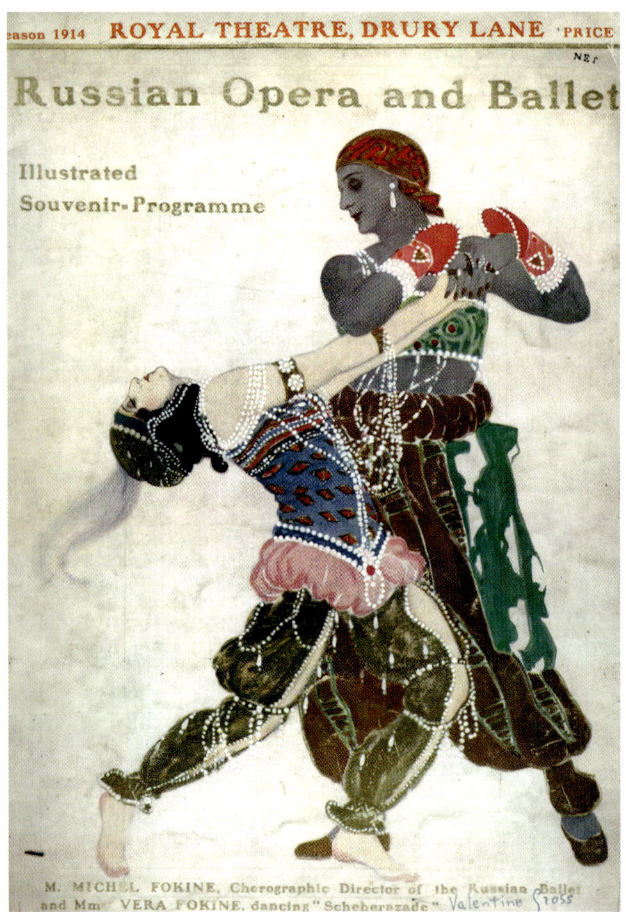

Russian Opera and Ballet programme cover
1914

Cover for *A Manual of the Theory and Practice of Classical Theatrical Dancing*
1922

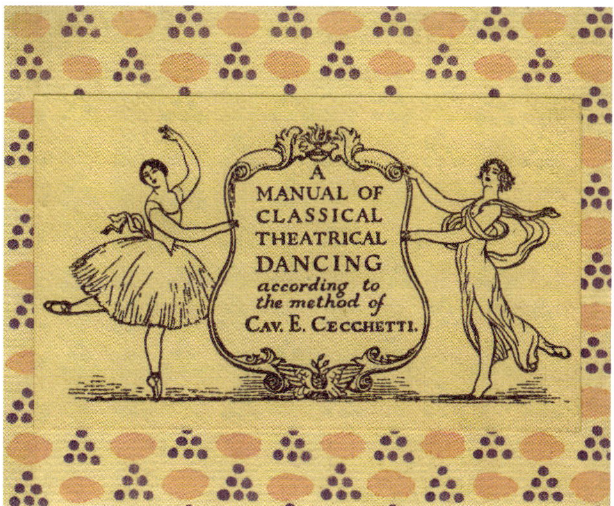

rehearsals enthusiastically making preliminary sketches while his young daughter Alice watched the dancers entranced from the stalls – she had wanted to be a ballet dancer and Cecchetti, the dancer and choreographer, said she should but Schwabe would not let her – he thought it would be too much hard work.[28] Alice vividly remembered both her excitement when she first saw Stanislas Idzikowski (1894–1977) in his most famous role as The Blue Bird fly across the stage and her bitter disappointment later when she met him wearing a suit rather than his bird costume, which reduced her to tears.[29]

After one performance Beaumont took Schwabe back stage to the dressing room of Bronislava Nijinska, sister of Nijinsky to make a drawing of her as the Lilac Fairy:

> *they chose the pose in which she holds her wand between her clasped hands. As the narrow room made it difficult for Schwabe to see his subject in the right perspective, Nijinska quickly took the things off her dressing-table and posed standing on the top of it. The 'sitting' was varied with little rests, during which Nijinska talked about ballet, a conversation so interesting that we lost all count of time, until we were sharply reminded of it by the abrupt turning off of the lights in the dressing-room.*[30]

The part of the Lilac Fairy was alternately danced by Lydia Lopokova (1892–1981).

Beaumont was so impressed with the manner and spirit of the teaching of the Italian ballet master Enrico Cecchetti (1850–1928), that he thought it should be preserved and codified. He approached Idzikowski, one of Cecchetti's best pupils to collaborate on producing *A Manual of the Theory and Practice of Classical Theatrical Dancing* (1922) 'which played a decisive role in the making of

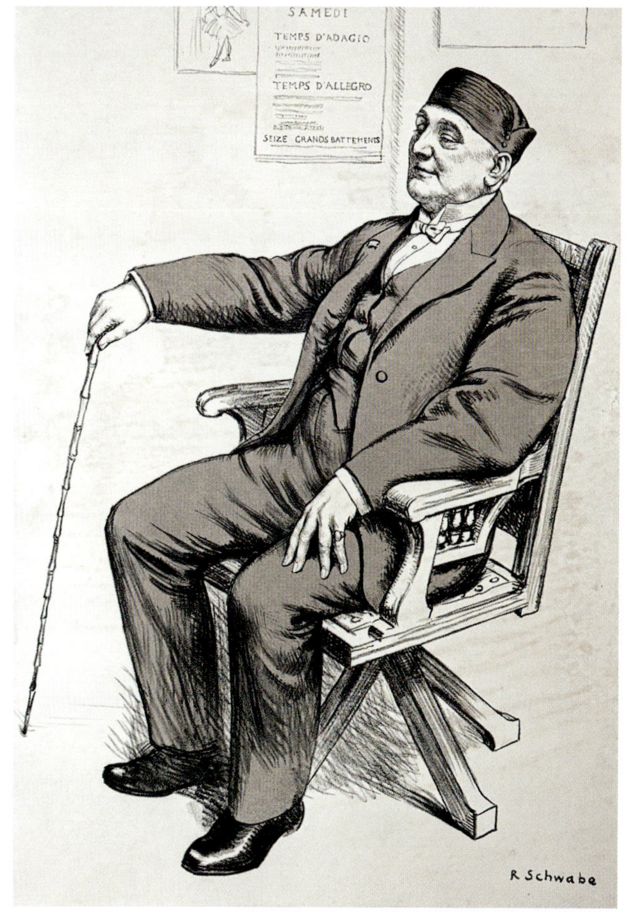

Enrico Cecchetti, The Maestro
lithograph | 45.1 x 31.9 cm

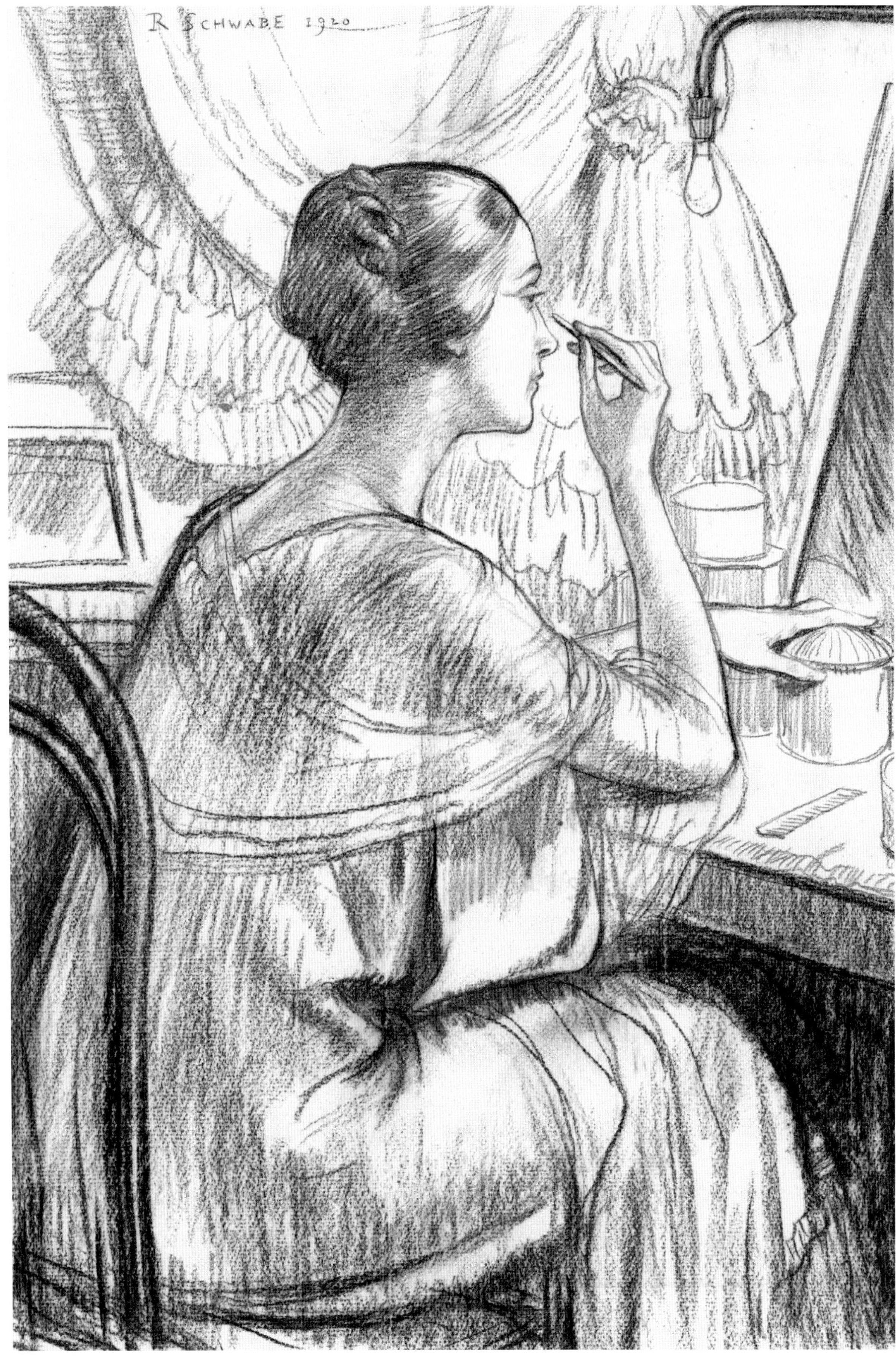

Tamara Karsavina making up in her dressing room
1920 | charcoal | 47.9 × 32 cm
© VICTORIA AND ALBERT MUSEUM, LONDON

Cecchetti's reputation as a pedagogue.'[31] The manual, which took two years to complete, was divided into two parts, the first concerned with theory and the second with practice which contained exercises and precise detail as to their execution. Schwabe undertook the laborious task of producing the numerous line diagrams for these. 'Lopokova demonstrated pointe steps and Cyril posed for head movements.'[32] Cecchetti, although over 70, also posed for some of the steps but as he was 'rather Pickwickian in contour… Schwabe… adjust[ed] the drawings accordingly, once they had been passed as technically correct by Cecchetti himself.'[33] The drawings were undertaken during a particularly cold winter in Cecchetti's flat in Wardour Street. The procedure adopted was as follows:

> [the] Maestro donned a fur-lined coat. Schwabe marshalled a row of sharpened pencils on the table. We lit the fire, applied the lid, the flames roared upwards, whereupon Cecchetti threw off his coat and took the desired pose for a short period, while Schwabe recorded it.

Beaumont found it absorbing watching Schwabe and Cecchetti:

> two individuals so diametrically opposed: the expansive maestro and the grave bespectacled, scholarly-looking artist, each a master of his profession, collaborating in perfect accord. Schwabe revelled in drawing positions and poses so far removed from those normally taken by a professional art school model. It was a fascinating experience to see his pencil and probing eye trace the bone structure beneath Cecchetti's skin, and clothe it with idealized flesh.

Schwabe undertook a portrait of the Maestro (c.1921–23) seated in his swivel chair, malacca cane in right hand, ready to instruct his pupils; the lithograph was

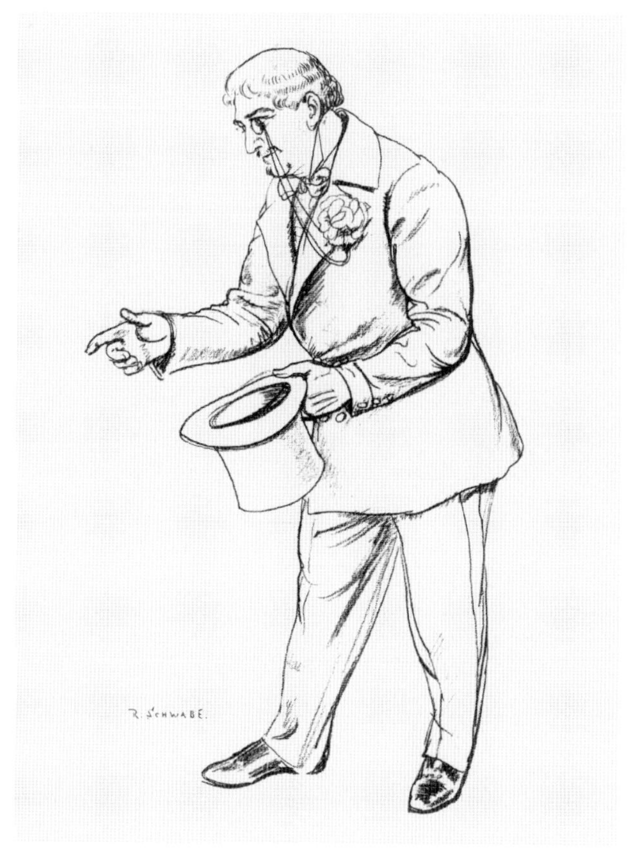

Sketch of Cecchetti as Pantalon in Carnaval
COLLECTION JANET AND DI BARNES

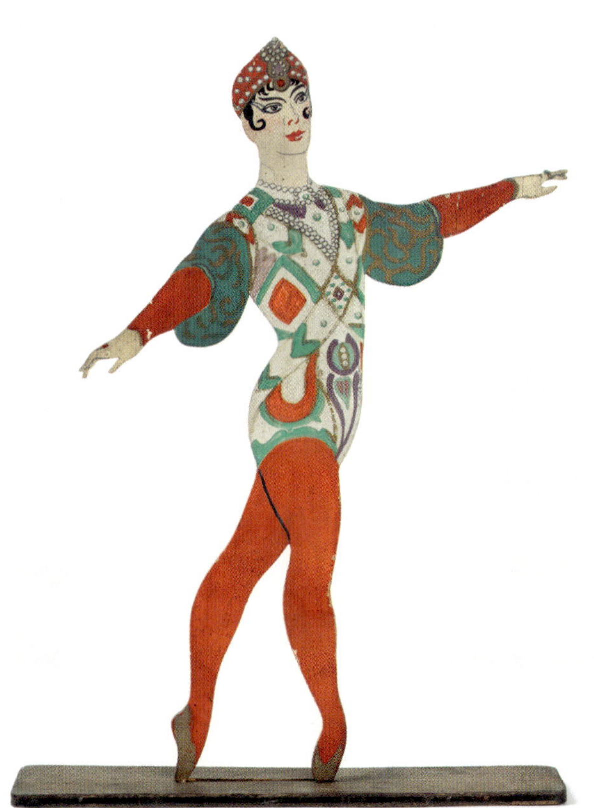

Stanislas Idzikowski as Bluebird
c.1928 | wood and gouache

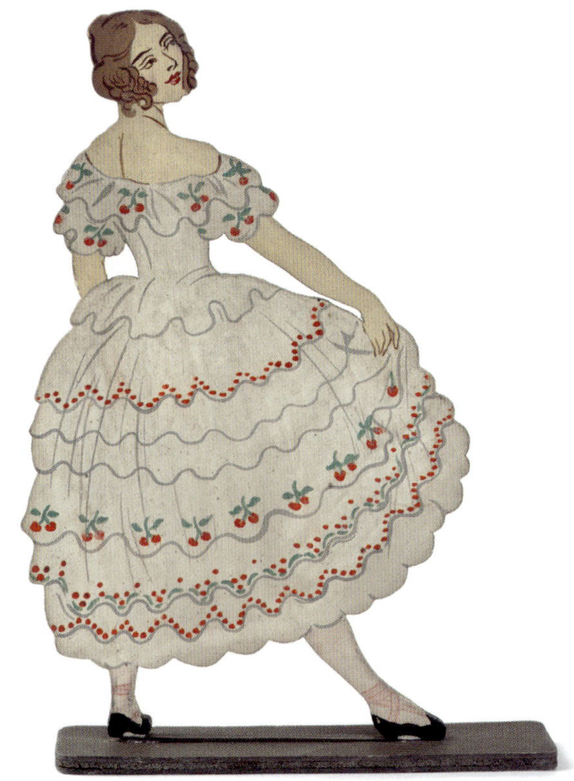

Lopokova as Columbine in Carnaval
c.1928 | wood and gouache

'displayed at all centres of the Cecchetti Society to remind students of Cecchetti's methods, which was governed by strict principles of discipline.'[34]

Beaumont produced with Margaret Craske a sequel to the manual, *The Theory and Practice of Allegro in Classical Ballet* (Cecchetti Method) (1930). Schwabe undertook the illustrations for which Edna Tresahar posed, herself a former pupil of Cecchetti.

1922 was a busy year for Schwabe as he also completed a full-length portrait of Lydia Lopokova as Columbine in *Le Carnaval*, which was reproduced in grey and pink in Beaumont's album *Lydia Lopokova* alongside ten camera portraits of Lopokova in sepia. Schwabe's next undertaking was to make drawings of Tamara Karsavina (1885–1978) for *Thamar Karsavina* by Valerien Svetlov. The Russian text was translated by H. de Vere Beauclerk and Nadia Evrenov and edited by Beaumont. Karsavina 'who was noted for her artistry rather than her virtuoso technique'[35] gave special sittings for Schwabe at which her husband, the diplomat Henry Bruce, would attend so as to make his own sketches. Schwabe contributed drawings of Karsavina in *Les Sylphides*, *Le Spectre de la Rose*, *Le Carnaval*, *Schéhérazade*, *The Three Cornered Hat*, *Le Astuzie Femminili* and in her dressing room, a head- and tail-piece and a decorative cover in orange with a repeat pattern of a tiny dancer. There were in total seventeen hand-coloured and other illustrations by Glyn Philpot, V. Seroff, John J. Sargent and Adrian Allinson amongst others. The text was decorated by Claud Lovat Fraser.

The growing interest in and demand for souvenirs of the Diaghilev Ballet led Beaumont to embark on the making of small two-dimensional, wooden figures of some of the principal dancers. Allinson collaborated

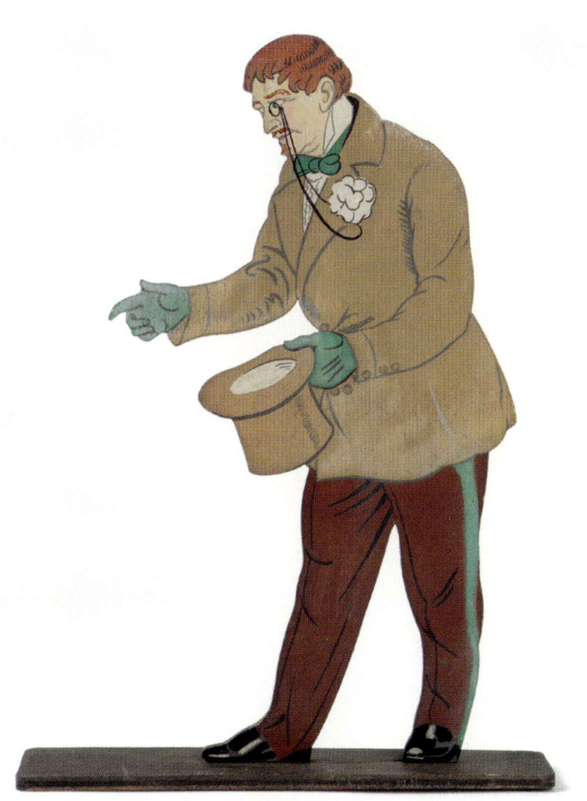

Enrico Cecchetti as Pantalon in Carnaval
c.1928 | wood and gouache
© VICTORIA AND ALBERT MUSEUM, LONDON

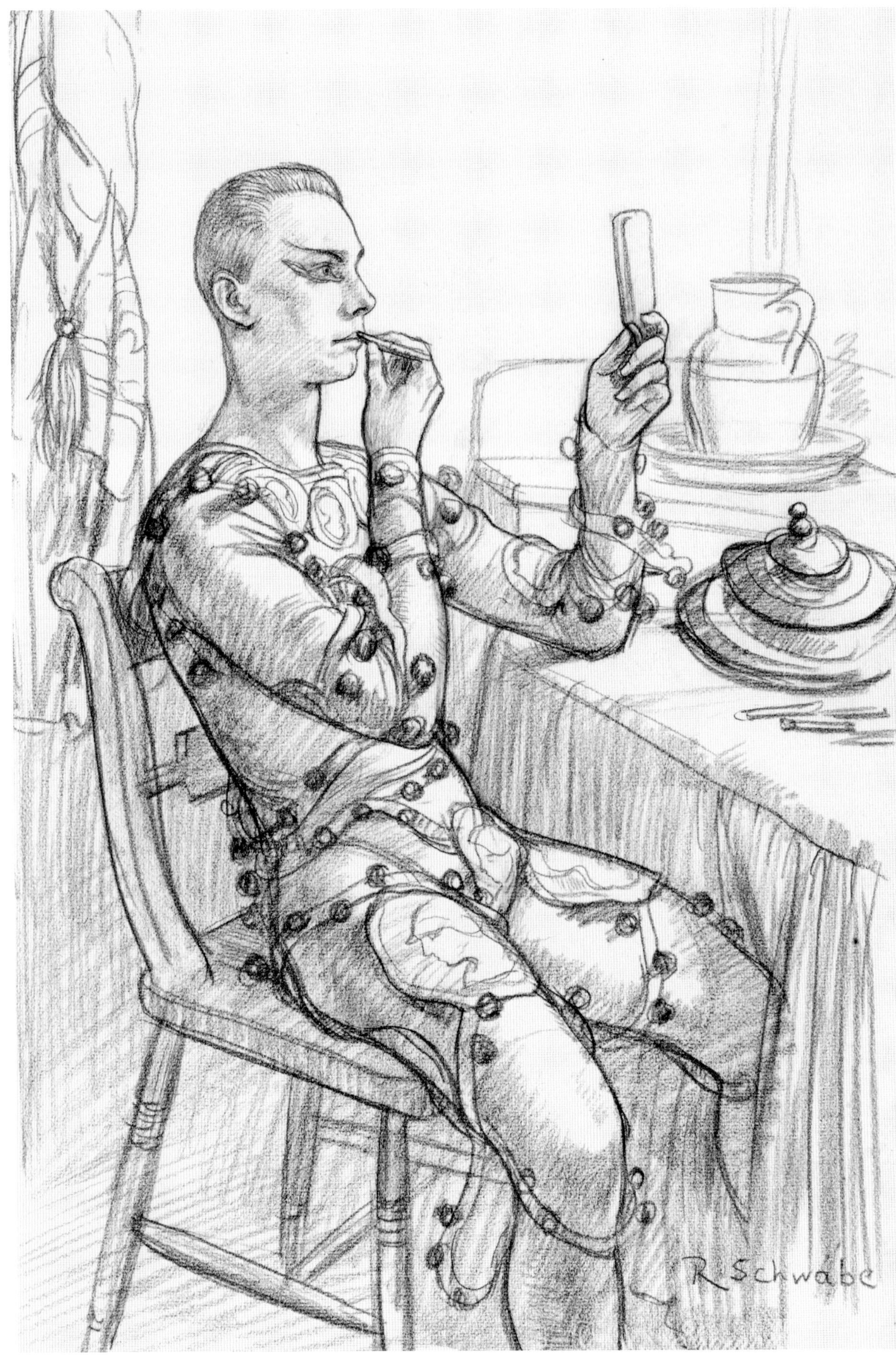

Stanislas Idzikowski applying make up
c.1925 | pencil on paper | 43.2 × 29.8 cm
© VICTORIA AND ALBERT MUSEUM, LONDON

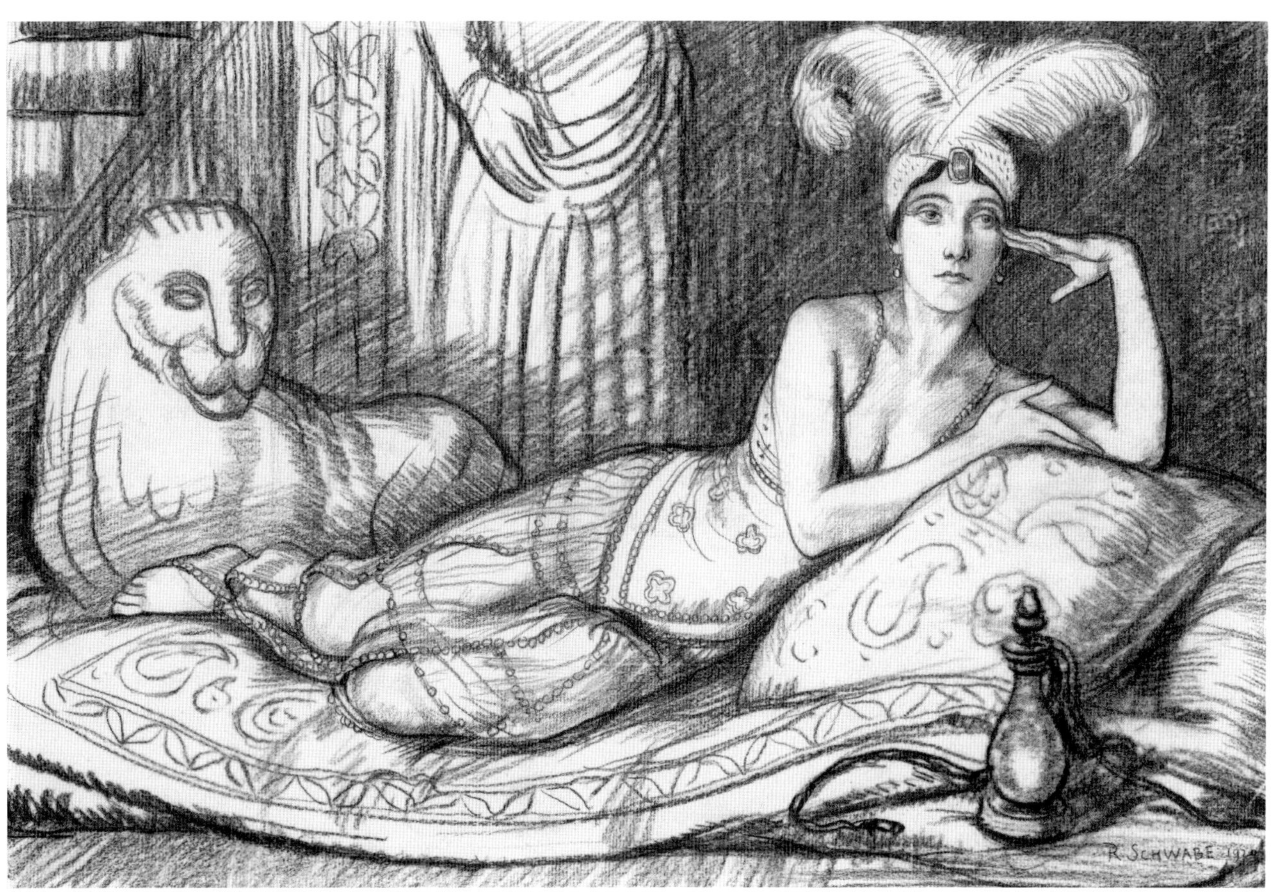

Tamara Karsavina as Zobeide in Schéhérazade
1920 | charcoal | 37 × 48 cm
© VICTORIA AND ALBERT MUSEUM, LONDON

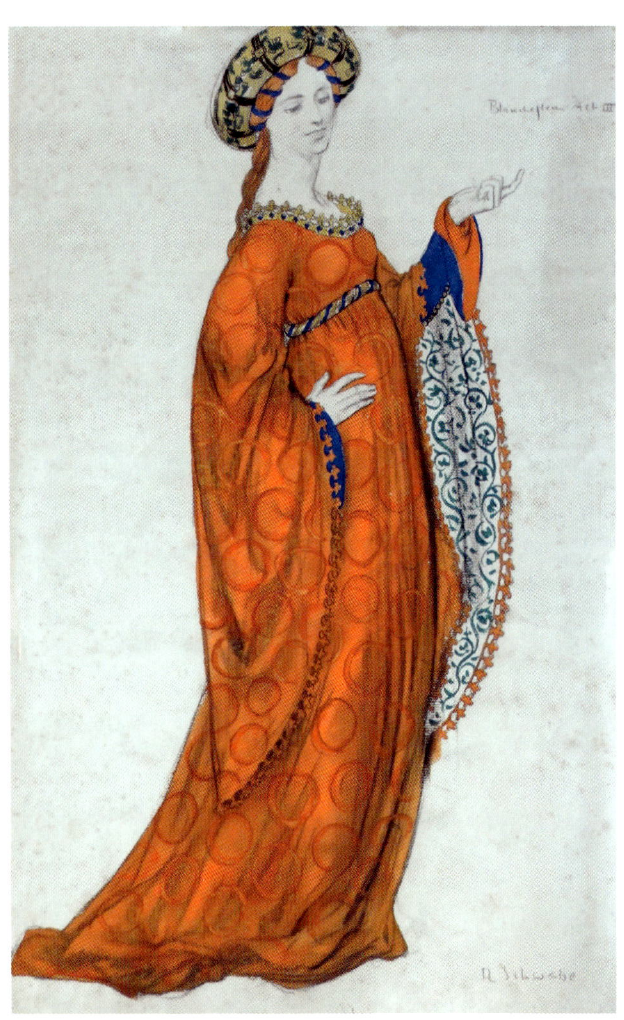

Costume design for Muriel Pratt as Blanchefleur,
The Loving Heart
1918 | watercolour

with Beaumont to produce nineteen 10-inch-high costumed figures, including Pavlova and Nijinsky, in two-ply wood mounted on detachable stands in a characteristic pose from the ballet. 'The wooden figures were cut by the Aldon Studios and then hand-painted by the artist who had done the design.'[36] Limited to fifty copies they were sold for *7s. 6d.* each. They proved so popular that after the war Beaumont 'developed the figures, the features and costumes being treated in greater detail'[37] and employed other artists,[38] including Schwabe to design these. Three figures from Marius Petipa's *The Sleeping Princess* are attributed to Schwabe – *Stanislas Idzikowski as Bluebird*, *Lydia Lopokova as Princess Aurora* and *Lubov Tchernicheva as Ariana* and two from Mikhail Fokine's ballet *Le Carnaval* – *Lydia Lopokova as Columbine* and *Enrico Cecchetti as Pantalon*. The 'sittings' or more accurately 'standings' for these created a challenge for Schwabe and the dancers as they took place 'in all kinds of odd corners, on a stair landing, in a dressing room, behind the back-cloth… Sometimes the pose was difficult to hold for the required length of time'[39] and Beaumont had to assist by holding the dancer's foot or waist. This was not necessary when Schwabe sketched Cecchetti wearing a monocle and frock coat and holding his top hat in the mime role of *Pantalon* he had created. 'As a performer [he was] revered for stunning interpretations and constant innovations in his mime roles.'[40]

Schwabe's final ballet contribution was a drawing *of Stanislas Idzikowski applying make-up* which appeared in Beaumont's *The Art of Stanislas Idzikowski* (1926). Philpot contributed a portrait, Vera Willoughby four colour plates and Beaumont an essay; the volume also included a series of twelve camera portraits of *Idzikowski* in parts associated with him.

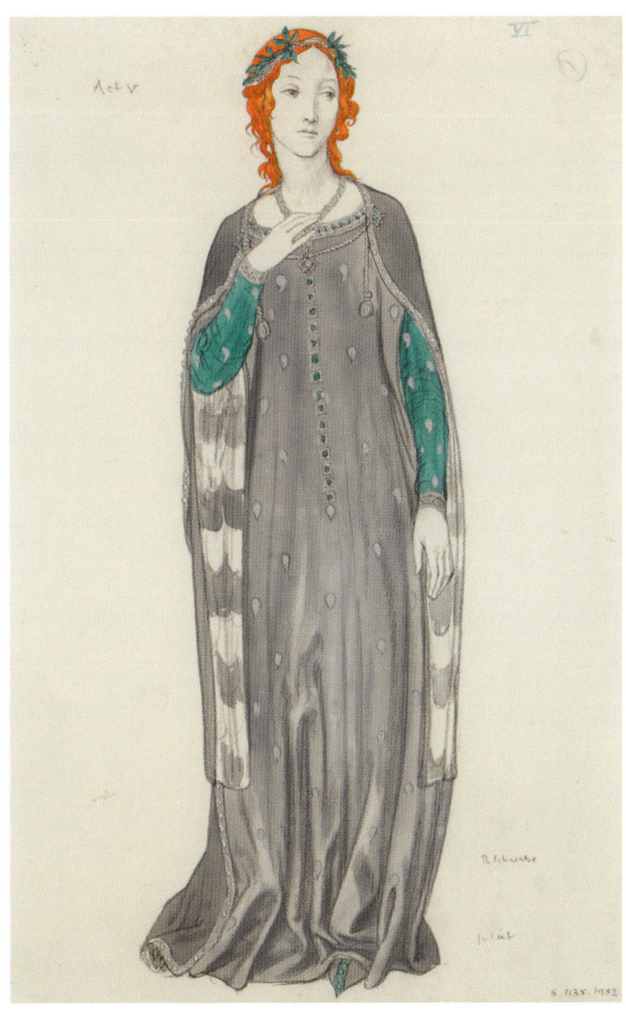

Costume design for Doris Keane as Juliet,
Romeo and Juliet
1919 | watercolour
© VICTORIA AND ALBERT MUSEUM, LONDON

COSTUME

Schwabe's longstanding interest and intimate knowledge of historical costume enabled him to move smoothly into the challenge of designing costumes for the Boccaccio period play *The Loving Heart* 'adapted from two of the more famous "Decameron" stories, with trimmings from others, by Henrietta Leslie and John Dymock'[41] and produced by William Bridges-Adams (1889–1965) at the Duke of York's Theatre in June 1918. Schwabe thought it a 'rotten play' – he was not alone in his verdict, the critic for *The Times* opining that 'Quite the happiest feature of the production is Mr Bridges-Adams's scenery'.[42] The costumes of medieval Italy were described as being quite exquisite – Schwabe had designed the dresses for Muriel Pratt who gave a 'spirited performance'[43] as the heroine Blanchefleur and the costume for Russell Thorndike who played Miles, the magician's ill-treated son. Schwabe's costumes also received hearty congratulations from Charles Rutherston who wrote to him from the Langham Hotel, London 'before retiring to rest' after having been to the play.[44] Rutherston subsequently purchased the costume designs and lent them to the Birmingham Repertory Theatre 5th Foyer Picture Exhibition (c.1919) as part of a show of *Paintings and Drawings* by Schwabe and Sylvia Gosse.

In April 1919 Schwabe produced designs for *Romeo and Juliet*, produced by Basil Sydney and Doris Keane at the Lyric Theatre, Hammersmith. It was Keane's first appearance as Juliet; Romeo was played by her husband Sydney; and Ellen Terry returned to the stage to take the part of the Nurse. The reviews were mixed but there was unanimous praise for the beautiful scenery and the original and gorgeous costumes. Schwabe's attention to detail was likened to that of the Italian renaissance painter Benozzo Gozzoli.[45] He also carried out designs for another *Romeo and Juliet* production by Norman Macdermott at the Everyman Theatre, Hampstead in November 1920.

The period costumes for *The Enchanted Cottage* by the dramatist Sir Arthur Pinero (1855–1934) were designed by Schwabe and executed by Alfred Blackmore. These included costumes for a 'Tudor Lady and Gentleman', a 'Lady and Gentleman of the Time of Charles II', and a 'Lady and Gentleman, 1820.' The play opened on 1 March 1922 and ran for six weeks at the Duke of York's Theatre. The costumes and 'Costume Design for Ballet, "Marie Antoinette" produced at the Coliseum, 1922' were exhibited at the International Theatre Exhibition at the Victoria and Albert Museum during June and July.

Alongside these commitments Schwabe was busy collaborating with Francis Kelly, his old friend from his Slade student days and fellow costume *aficionado*, on what Kelly referred to in April 1914 as 'our opus'. Kelly was referring to their proposed book on *Historic Costume* in which they sought to envisage the subject from a fresh angle to that of the writers whose work they thought had 'been little more than [that of] camouflaged copyists'[46] of the early pioneers. Accordingly they spent over a decade on painstaking research in the Bodleian Library, the British Museum and in the principal museums in France, Holland and Germany for their *opus* based 'on contemporary witnesses, pictorial and literary'[47] so as to add something of value to past treatises on costume. As Kelly remarked 'Give me three months uninterrupted at the Bodleian & B.M. & I venture to believe I could get chapter & verse for nearly every detail I want.'[48]

They wanted the book to be compact, reliable and in a handy form for the artist, actor, costumier, film producer and the like, such as those who might organise pageants and historical tableaux. In short they wanted it to be 'the standard book within its limitations.'[49]

The result of Schwabe's and Kelly's extended and extensive labours was *Historic Costume: A Chronicle of Fashion in Western Europe, 1490–1790* published by Batsford in late 1925 and priced 25s. It contained a number of plates in colour and seventy photographic reproductions of historic pictures, portraits and scenes, together with over a hundred sketches closely copied and placed throughout the text by Schwabe of typical groups, figures and details. For example, in the final chapter *Paniers, Powder and Queue (1715–1790)* in the section *Head-Gear* the reader is informed that 'towards 1790 the broad wide-awake shake shape, of felt or beaver, with tall crown decorated with buckles and bows of ribbon, was adopted by sporting ladies'.[50] Among the pictures (and old brasses) Schwabe used was George Morland's (1763–1804) *The Squire's Door* painted c.1790. In the later section on *Hair* he drew on a portrait of the actress *Elizabeth Farren* painted by Sir Thomas Lawrence (1769–1830) to show how 'For undress in the 'eighties a full curly crop over the crown and very long hair behind were fashionable and for informal occasions powder was more often discarded or sparingly employed.'[51]

The scholarly explanatory commentary by Kelly ('he was a stickler for precise and correct nomenclature'),[52] 'amplified by Mr Schwabe's spirited and lucid drawings'[53] was highly acclaimed by a plethora of critics from *The Burlington, Connoisseur, Artwork, Queen, The Cinema*, the *Manchester Guardian* through to the *Yorkshire*

From *Historic Costume: A Chronicle of Fashion in Western Europe, 1490–1790* by Francis Kelly and Randolph Schwabe
1925

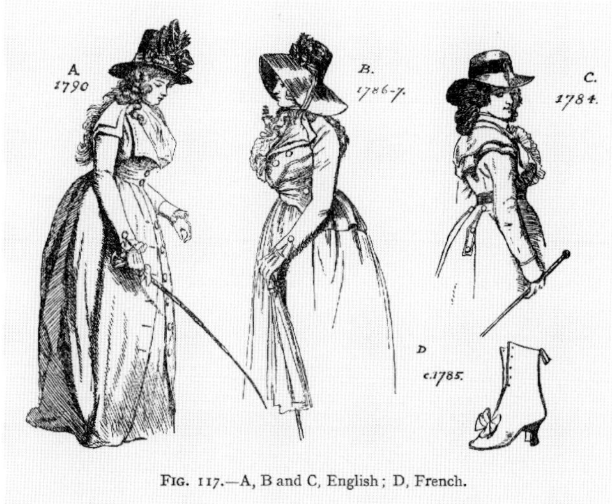

FIG. 117.—A, B and C, English; D, French.

Weekly Post. The reviewer in the *Times Literary Supplement* drew attention to a number of minor weaknesses in the book, including the severe compression in places due to the authors' quest to make the book compact and thought 'the omission of reference to tippets an oversight.' He concluded that such details as these were slight and that the 'book is the most informing guide to costume which has appeared in English.' The final section on *Patterns* added to the practical utility of the book by giving diagrams of how to cut out and make various items of costume; this was welcomed by the critic for *Eve* who commented 'even though we may no longer wear a peasecod doublet and trunk-hose, we may learn the solution of how they were made…Briefly, not only an historically valuable, but a very fascinating volume.'[54] The book sold well both at home and in America and as a result in 1929 a revised and enlarged edition was published which included a number of new illustrations. That too sold well. Kelly wrote to Schwabe in December 1930 about their next book and also to tell him that:

> *The fact is in the USA the second edition of our old K. & S. is selling it seems like hot cakes & Scribners [based in New York City] have ordered a further batch. We've had a topping press & B.T.B. [Batsford] are anxious to take advantage of the boom while it lasts. Apropos, Lucarotti [Production Manager] who gives most encouraging reports of 'Historic Costume' hints that a solid dollop of royalties should shortly be coming along. If, as I understand, the USA have already accounted for 600 copies of the 2nd ed. that should mean £90 odd coming to you…*

> *Hope the new era at the Slade shaping even better than the last…*

Kelly and Schwabe published in 1931 *A Short History of Costume and Armour, Chiefly in England*, Volume 1 covered the period 1066–1485 and Volume II 1485–1800. The principle underlying it was essentially the same that governed its predecessor, namely 'the primary importance of contemporary art, *rightly apprehended*, to the proper understanding of the evolution of human clothing in past ages.'[55] The reviews were less fulsome but nonetheless positive as to the scholarship and thoroughness of the research and the view that it would doubtless earn a place as a standard work of reference. The critic for *The Burlington* pointed out, though, that 'its very fullness of detail sometimes makes it difficult for the reader to see the wood for the trees.'[56]

Schwabe as a leading authority on matters of costume and armour was on occasion asked to assist with identifying paintings such as the disputed portrait of *Henry VIII*, attributed to Holbein and part of the collection of Castle Howard, near York, which when exhibited in London in November 1933 provoked much controversy. His advice was also sought over the designs for plays including *The Hundred Days* by Mussolini and Forzano, translated by John Drinkwater, which dealt with Napoleon's return from Elba, for which Schwabe asked for a fee of 10 guineas. Fellow artists also sought his advice, including Stephen Gooden (1892–1955) who wanted advice about costume drawings on postage stamps and Enid Marx (1902–98), who was compiling a book with her long-time friend Margaret Lambert on traditional art in England (*English Popular and Traditional Art*), wanted information for the textile section about the pearlie shirts costers wear.[57]

OF HUMAN BONDAGE

In 1935–36 Schwabe received a major commission to supply twenty four full-page collotype plates for

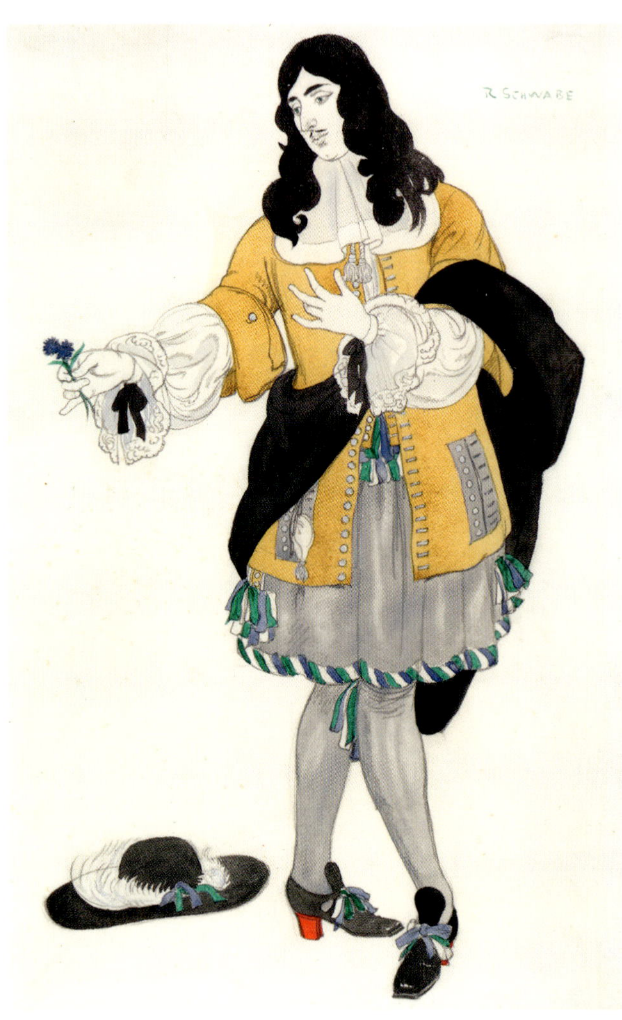

Costume design for *The Enchanted Cottage*
*c.*1922 | pencil, colour washes and silver | 56 × 40 cm
© UCL ART MUSEUM, UNIVERSITY COLLEGE LONDON

a special edition of W. Somerset Maugham's auto-biographical novel *Of Human Bondage* (1937) for the Literary Guild of America. *Of Human Bondage*, a mixture of fact and fiction, was written when Maugham was twenty three years of age, having spent the previous five years at St Thomas's Hospital, London studying medicine. Published in 1915, it received mixed reviews; the *Athenaeum* reported that it was too long and the hero (Philip Carey) so handicapped (he had a 'club-foot') that he was removed out of the category of the average, and thus the values he accords love, realism, and religion 'are so distorted as to have no interest beyond that which belongs to an essentially morbid personality.' Theodore Dreiser, writing for the influential American magazine *The New Republic* described it as 'novel or biography or autobiography or social transcript of the utmost importance.'[58]

Gerald Kelly (1879–1972), a friend of Somerset Maugham, had asked Gwynne-Jones for advice as to a suitable person to illustrate the novel; he recommended Schwabe. In pursuance of the commission, at the end of May 1935 Schwabe called on Kelly, to leave some half dozen books he had illustrated for the Beaumont Press between 1924-31 so that he could form some idea as to whether Schwabe was suitable. At that stage Schwabe had not read the novel. He thought it might be rather an interesting job if he got it.

Kelly also made overtures to Barnett Freedman who went so far as to design a title-page and to John Farleigh (1900–65) about illustrating Maugham's novel. However, on 12 July 1935 Schwabe met Nelson Doubleday (1889–1949) of the publishing company Doubleday, Doran & Company, at 6 Robert Street, Adelphi, to discuss his undertaking illustrations to

Dust-jacket for *Of Human Bondage*
1937

Maugham's book and terms for the commission. Three months later Schwabe met Maugham at the Café Royal where over moules à la marinière and partridge, accompanied by claret, they discussed *Of Human Bondage*.[59] Maugham was inclined to let Schwabe have 'a pretty free hand' and was in favour of his asking a fairly good price from Nelson Doubleday. Schwabe asked for £10 a drawing. He found Maugham amiable and they had much in common, including the fact that both stammered. Schwabe noted in his dairy 'It is this infliction, of course, transmuted into a club foot, which makes him so sensitive in the autobiographical parts of the novel. Kelly told me this.'

Schwabe began his first drawing for *Of Human Bondage* on 8 November 1935 when he worked in Hampstead all day. As part of his research, he visited the seaside town of Whitstable in Kent where he was particularly interested to see the harbour and the old Vicarage where Maugham's uncle used to live and thereby get some ideas about 'Blackstable' for the novel. On his return he stopped at King's School, Canterbury where Maugham had been a pupil, with a view to using it for his illustrations. By March 1936 he was working on his thirteenth illustration – 'a complicated drawing of a staircase'.[60]

The following month Schwabe took the drawings he had completed to show Kelly and Maugham, who told Schwabe that they made him want to read the book again. Maugham had not opened it for 20 years.[61] Schwabe's research for the remaining illustrations took him to Hampton Court and later he made a brief note of some details in Peter Robinson's shop-window, when he was asked rather offensively what he was doing by a shop-worker thinking Schwabe was pirating some

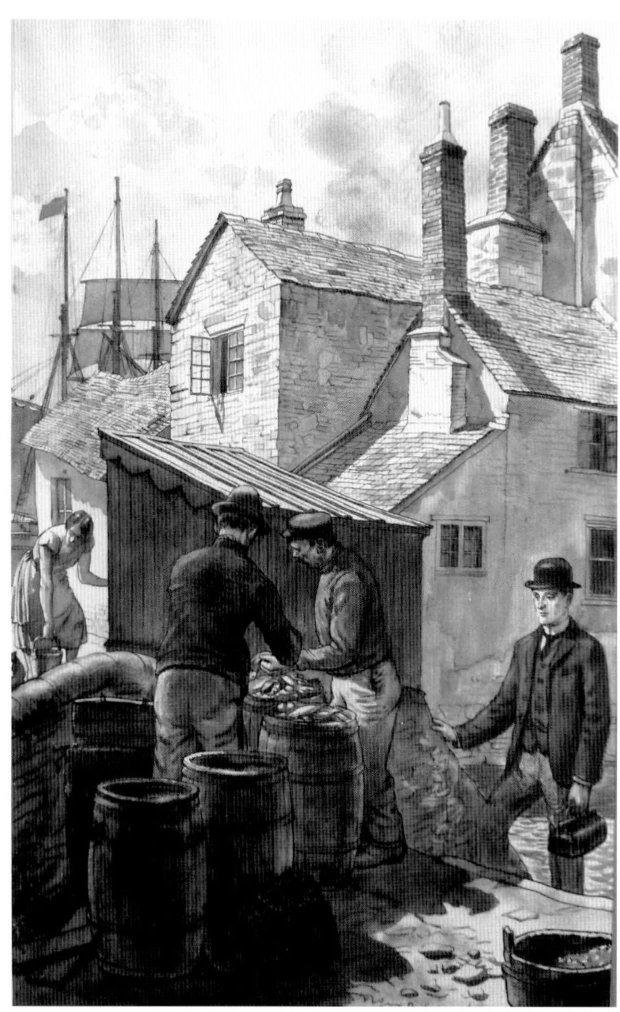

'Down below, by the harbour,
the little stone houses of a past century were clustered'
for *Of Human Bondage*
c.1935 | collotype | 69.5 x 48 cm

of their dress designs. Schwabe then spent 15/- in Wardour Street on fashion plates of the early 1900s, again with an eye to *Of Human Bondage*.[62] Such was the thoroughness of his research that in the summer he also went to see an operation at University College Hospital, having the scene in mind for another illustration. Schwabe observed the operation for about an hour, the result being the illustration *On certain afternoons in the week there were operations*. By 1 September he was able to arrange for the complete set of drawings for *Of Human Bondage* to be despatched to America.

In December Schwabe once again met Maugham in London, this time to do a drawing of him at Kelly's suggestion. He thought he had a very mobile face and had to ask him, at intervals, not to talk. Maugham expressed himself 'pleased with the drawing, using the word "distinguished" (of his own appearance under my hands), and said that it made him look like a writer, not a stockbroker. He stammered very little indeed, but referred again to that subject.'[63] The following month Schwabe received a cheque from Maugham, for his portrait. He had made a slip in writing the figures – £10-0-0 instead of guineas, but Schwabe could not be bothered to send it back to him at Cap Ferrat.

THE OXFORD ALMANACK

With the outbreak of the Second World War, commissions dried up. For Schwabe the demands of running the Slade in its evacuated premises in the Ashmolean Museum were so considerable that there was little time or opportunity for private work. However he was able to accept a commission from the Clarendon Press to undertake a drawing for *The Oxford*

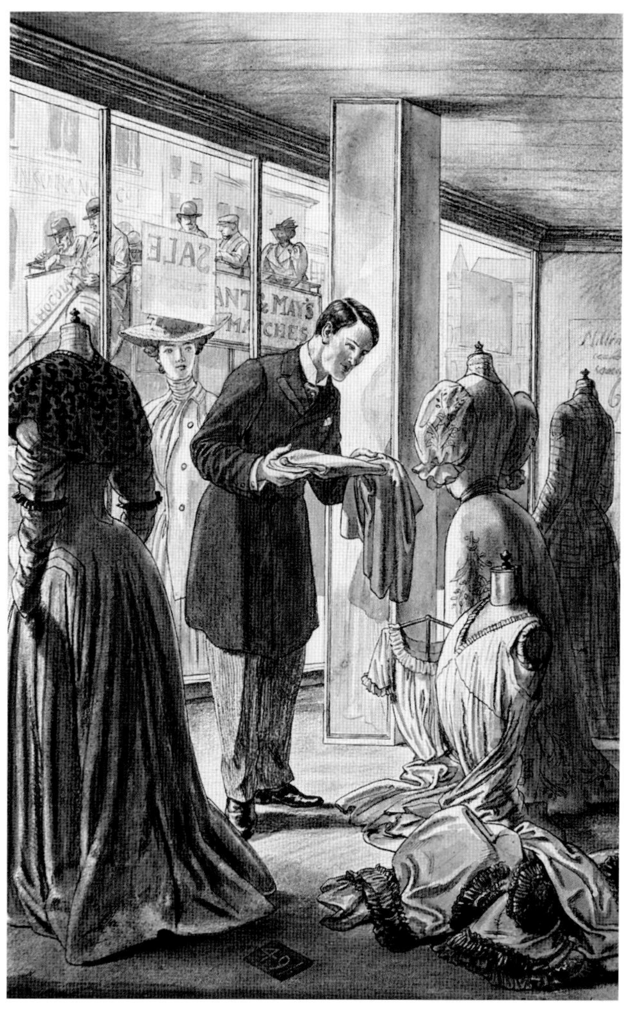

'He dreaded Friday morning,
on which the window was dressed'
for *Of Human Bondage*
c.1936 | collotype | 69.5 x 48 cm
COLLECTION JANET AND DI BARNES

Almanack for publication in 1941. Muirhead Bone had recommended Schwabe. *The Almanack* had been published since 1674 and the designs were of 'a scholarly and literary approach rather than a creative one'[64] which suited Schwabe well. He had been approached by Kenneth Sisam of the Clarendon Press to supply a drawing of Oxford in the Blackout with moonlight. Schwabe started before term began by 'making notes in the afternoon and then studied the moonlight (which was very clear) in the evening, after the 9 o'clock radio.'[65] He decided on Magdalen Tower as it was important that the subject matter was at once recognisable as Oxford. The result of his studious approach, *Oxford in the Full Moon, September 1940* complemented earlier designs admirably. Schwabe in early 1942 was asked to supply for the almanack something topical and 'connected with the University as a whole rather than any particular college'.[66] At the beginning of July he accompanied Arthur Norrington, Assistant Secretary of the Press, to London to examine their offices in Amen House with a view to making a drawing of them. There was devastation all around the building, following heavy bombing raids and fires which had hit many of the nearby publishers and booksellers under the shadow of St Paul's. The house and a few of its neighbours stood as a small group amid the partially cleared ruins of others. Schwabe commenced work *in situ* on 19 July and by 11 August it was nearly complete.

Following completion Schwabe took his charcoal and watercolour drawing *Warwick Square, London E.C.4, August 1942, with Amen House in the Middle Distance* to be censored by the Ministry of Information. He received £40 for his drawing which graced the cover of the *Times Literary Supplement* in the New Year. William Rothenstein wrote

'Oxford in the Full Moon, September 1940'
for The Oxford Almanack
black chalk, with areas scraped out | 29 x 41 cm
© ASHMOLEAN MUSEUM, UNIVERSITY OF OXFORD

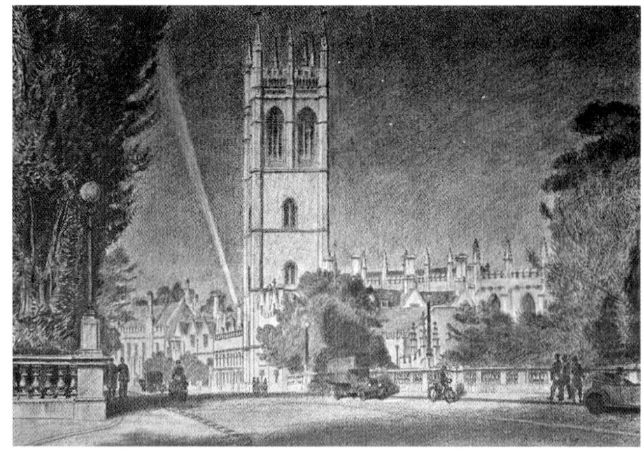

to Schwabe saying 'What a fine drawing that is of yours… Your drawings get better and better – this one is an impressive example, and addition to the fine series of Oxford Almanacs. The reproduction is, also, a happy one.'

SHOOTING TO LIVE

In 1942 Schwabe illustrated *Shooting to Live with the One-Hand Gun* by his brother, Captain Eric (Bill) Sykes (1883–1945) and Captain William E. Fairbairn (1885–1960). Eric had changed his surname to Sykes by deed poll in 1917. By that time he had been working in the International Settlement in Shanghai for about a decade. His friend Fairbairn was Assistant Commissioner of the Shanghai Municipal Police (SMP) and had established a Sniper's Unit in December 1925 which Sykes, a reserve unpaid sergeant, took charge of. The Sniper's Unit 'was a reserve unit of civilians particularly skilled in the use of telescope equipped rifles, chambered for high-velocity ammunition. Far from being a vigilante group, members… were made to undergo extensive training, and were made to periodically qualify as marksmen, under a severe set of standards.'[67] In May 1940 Sykes and Fairbairn returned to England and offered themselves to the Government 'for services of a special nature.' At the end of December Sykes received a call from the War Office to serve as an Instructor, with the rank of Acting Captain, on the Staff of the Special Training Centre at Lochailort in Scotland, where he was to work as a close combat instructor within the newly formed SOE (Special Operations Executive).

Schwabe observed that his brother and Fairbairn did not get on as well together as they had previously done.

'Fairbairn hates this country, and grumbles and is miserable: Bill likes his job and thrives on it. The Hythe Gunnery School, after sending a representative to inspect the doings at Lochailort, has adopted a good part of the method of shooting taught by Fairbairn and Bill. Their design for a lethal knife has been taken up and manufactured in thousands by the Wilkinson Sword Company: it is stamped F. & S.: Fairbairn & Sykes.'[68]

On 17 October 1941 Sykes received a letter from the War Office returning the manuscript and granting permission for the publication of *Shooting to Live*. Schwabe had been working on diagrams for Bill's book since July 1941. He did the headpiece after getting material from a copy of Samuel Meyrick's (1783–1848) *A Critical Inquiry into Ancient Armour* and Joseph Skelton's engravings in a book in the Ruskin School. By the end of the month he had finished his twelfth diagram and a fortnight later he completed the twenty-seventh and last diagram. These diagrams, for which Bill insisted on paying him £20, included precise drawings of firing positions and loading and unloading a pistol. It was not until the end of November that Schwabe finished the book-jacket.

Sykes, now promoted to Major, was obliged to retire with heart trouble in early 1945. The many letters of thanks he received all commented on his expertise in unarmed combat and weapon training and his great influence in the field. The Director of SOE, Major General Colin McVean Gubbins, in expressing his appreciation of his valuable work said 'there are many of our friends who owe their lives to you, and many of our enemies who have been satisfactorily dealt with as the result of your training'.[69] Sykes died suddenly in his sleep on 12 May 1945. Schwabe placed a brief notice

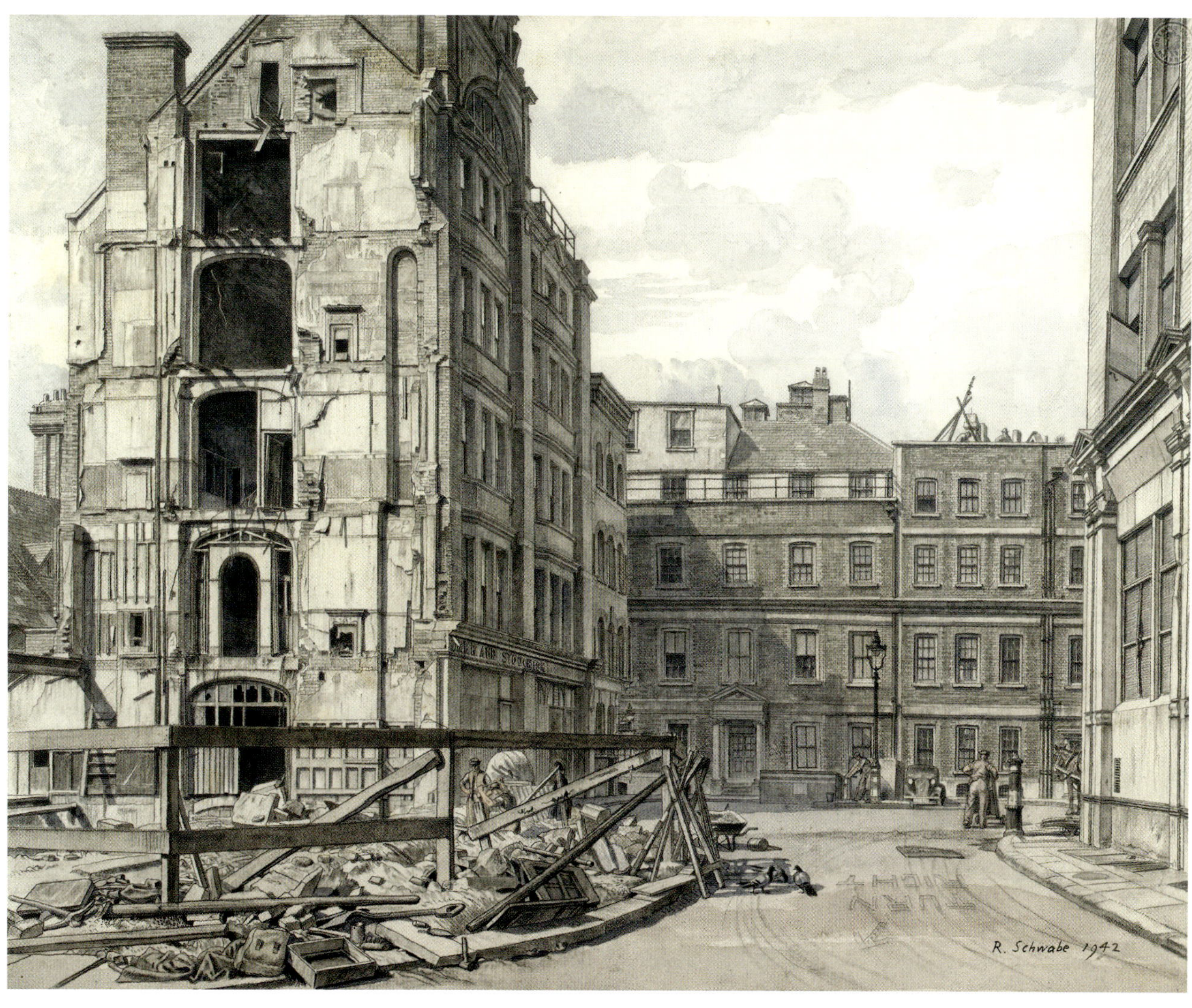

'Warwick Square, London EC4, August 1942, with Amen House in the Middle Distance' for *The Oxford Almanack*
black chalk with stump and tinted with watercolours, on London drawing board | 42.2 x 52.8 cm

in *The Times* announcing his death, likening him to Chaucer's Knight in *The Canterbury Tale*, 'A Verray Parfit Gentil Knight'. The day after his death Schwabe took the train to Bexhill to Bill's lodgings; he 'broke down when landlady Mrs. King uncovered his face: it was peaceful'. He was cremated at Charing, Kent five days later. Representatives of his army unit attended, including six sergeants, and an officer. Schwabe did not feel that he could give up his job for the day.

'A BATSFORD BOOK'

The term 'a Batsford book' became a household name under Harry Batsford (1880–1951), the chairman and managing director of the well-known publishers. Schwabe continued his association from his student days with Batsford and, having collaborated with Kelly on the well received books on costume, he was an ideal choice for a number of book jackets. He was, like Batsford, deeply 'rooted in England and English life.'[70]

Batsford called on Schwabe in November 1941 asking him to design the book jacket for Gerald Cobb's *The Old Churches of London*, bringing with him a large volume of Kip's (1653–1722) copper-plate engravings. The following month Schwabe started tracing Kip's view of London of the towers and steeples of the City churches shortly after their completion for the book jacket. Batsford thought 'it perfectly adorable' and said 'we are proud to put it round our book. If the author carps at positions and proportions, he can go boil his head!'[71] Charles Collins writing in the *Chicago Daily Tribune*, in his column 'Line O' Type or Two', was also effusive; in a paragraph of book gossip he praised the jacket and nominated it for a Pulitzer Prize in America as the best of the year. However, there was no such

honour and Collins was forced to write to Mrs Batsford on 14 June 1943 to explain that this comment was intended humorously, explaining 'Pulitzer prizes are given for almost every other activity of the book and newspaper businesses.'

Schwabe also undertook in colour the frontispiece of the Batsford shop in High Holborn, he recalled old B.T. Batsford and how he had quite a noticeable Cockney accent. He received £20 for the watercolour of *Batsfords in 1893*. It was a reconstruction of the premises by Schwabe as it had been destroyed. He did not relish his next job for Batsford in September 1945, describing it as 'a piece of hack-work' – it was a drawing of a monument from a photograph. He found his next task of completing a set of four line drawings from photographs, for one of Batsford's books on sculpture, exacting but far more agreeable as it had interest for him.

The last commission Schwabe undertook for Batsford was the book jacket for Katharine Esdaile's *English Church Monuments 1510–1840* (1946) the research for which involved a 'Delightful day with Harry Batsford and his Mr. Wells' who made the blocks and reproduced the jacket. The three went by car from the office in North Audley Street, Mayfair to inspect 'Harefield Church, still in its setting of fields and trees: the very rich collection of monuments to the Newdegates and others.' Schwabe 'was attracted to the Grinling Gibbons work without knowing who the sculptor was. Batsford is very good on these occasions, having great knowledge.'[72] They went next to Bisham which Schwabe found just as it used to be 30 years before, when Alice was small, and he and Birdie walked there from Marlow. At the Church of All Saints, parts of which dated from the twelfth century, Schwabe made detailed colour

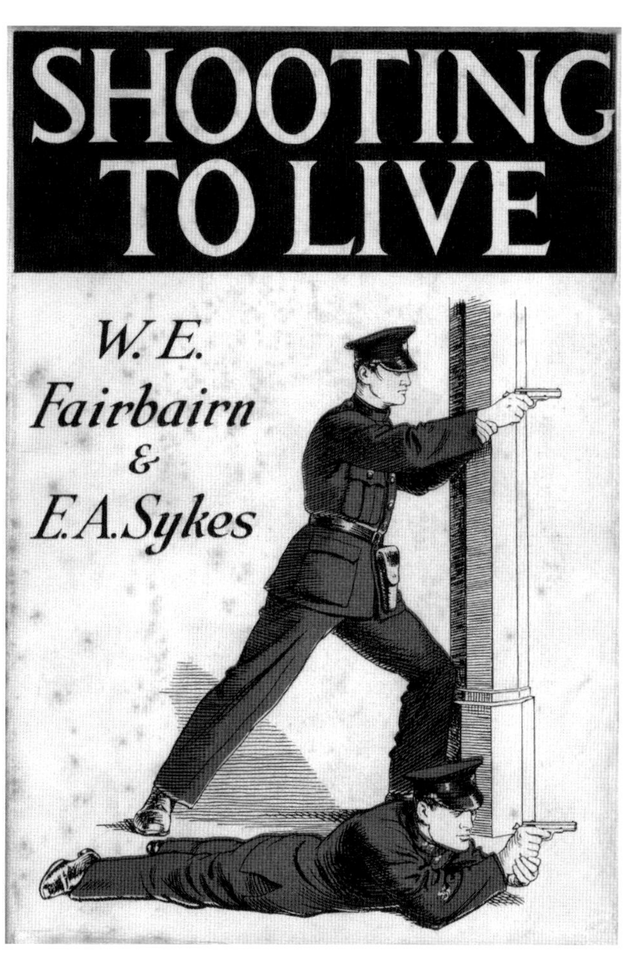

Dust-jacket for *Shooting to Live*
1941

notes of the Hoby tombs for the book jacket which Batsford later asked him to extend so that there was a 'turnover' to the jacket. The 'turnover' was of Sir Thomas Hoby, whose feet rest against hobby hawks, a play upon the name of Hoby. Schwabe faithfully reproduced the detail of his armour together with the arch above the tomb and the Swan Monument commemorates Hoby's son. The tomb by the sculptor Cornelius Cure (d.1607) on the front of the jacket is of Elizabeth, Lady Russell, formerly Hoby, kneeling at a prayer desk, with a coronet above her coif. Behind her kneel her three daughters who predeceased her and her two sons; facing her is her only surviving daughter in peeress's robes and wearing a coronet.[73]

ARTICLES AND ARTWORK

'Schwabe lived up to his reputation as a scholarly man,'[74] regularly contributing articles and reviews of exhibitions and books to various art periodicals including *The Burlington Magazine*, *The Studio* and *The Print Collector's Quarterly*. The articles contributed to *The Burlington* ranged from 'Expressionism' in October 1918 to a decade later 'A drawing ascribed to van Dyck.' For *The Studio* he wrote a lengthy treatise on 'British Book Illustration: Change and development in Present Day Technique' and for *The Print Collector's Quarterly* he wrote on fellow artists Rushbury, Dodd and Unwin and on one of his great interests 'Fashion-Plates'. Schwabe also designed the cover for *Fanfare*, the short-lived musical *causerie*, during its run from October 1921–January 1922 and contributed a drawing of Lydia Lopokova.[75] The fortnightly periodical was noted for its 'very short original compositions entitled "fanfares", written by leading composers of the early 1920s.'[76] In addition Schwabe was art critic for the *Saturday Review*.

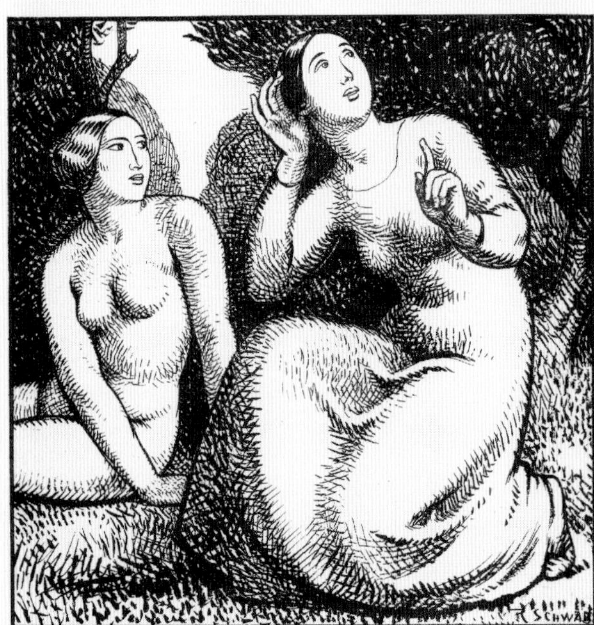

Cover for *Fanfare*
c.1921–22

Autumn 1930 saw Schwabe, newly in post as Head
of the Slade School, become editor of *Artwork*, an
international quarterly of arts and crafts magazine
for 'artworkers and artlovers'. *Artwork* was 'intended
as a rallying-point for all modes of expression, and
to give publicity to views of practising artists on their
various arts'. Its contributors reflected 'the spirit of the
age' and included 'reactionaries and rebels'.[77] In his
new role, Schwabe who had been assistant editor from
summer 1929 to D.S. MacColl (1859–1948) was assisted
by Leonard Elton, MacColl's nephew with R.A. Walker
as sub-editor. George Clausen in a congratulatory letter
commented that 'the mantle falls on you… – it is a
heavy kind of garment!'[78] It was indeed a heavy mantle
for shortly after Schwabe took over *Artwork* it was 'on
the rocks' – the finances were in a 'rotten' state and
J.M. Dent, its publishers, were losing money on the
magazine. Priced at 2/6d. a single copy or 11/- for
an annual subscription it was becoming increasingly
difficult to sell. MacColl in a confidential letter to
Schwabe said, 'If it would help Dent at all to give it a
longer chance I would be prepared to contribute at the
ordinary rate, & if the summer number were to be the
last, cooperate with you in any other way to go down
with flag flying.'[79] The terms paid were generally £12
for 1,500–1,700 words, with illustrations. The following
month MacColl suggested to Schwabe that he consider
the possibility of combining with Desmond MacCarthy's
Life & Letters which had been established in 1928 in
a jointly edited monthly to be called *Art and Letters*.
Schwabe made a 'graceful retirement from the field
of Art magazines'[80] after receiving a memorandum
from Dent on 2 October 1931 'to say we must definitely
look forward to giving it up after the next issue.'[81]

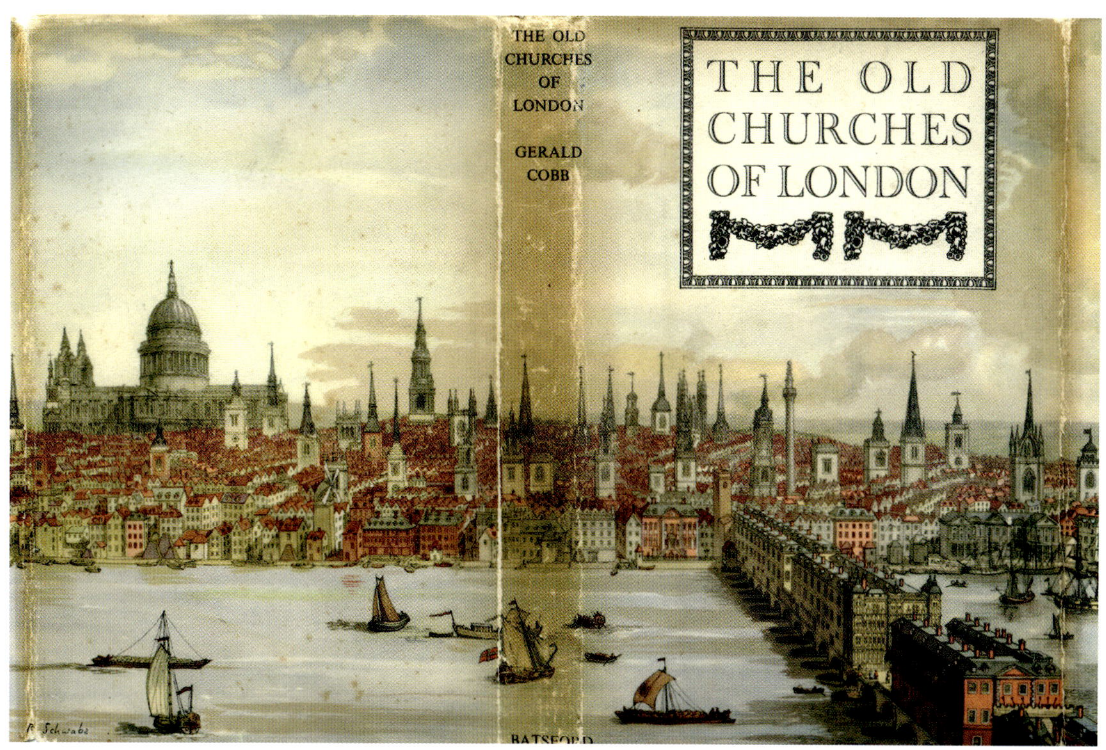

Dust-jacket for *The Old Churches of London*
1941

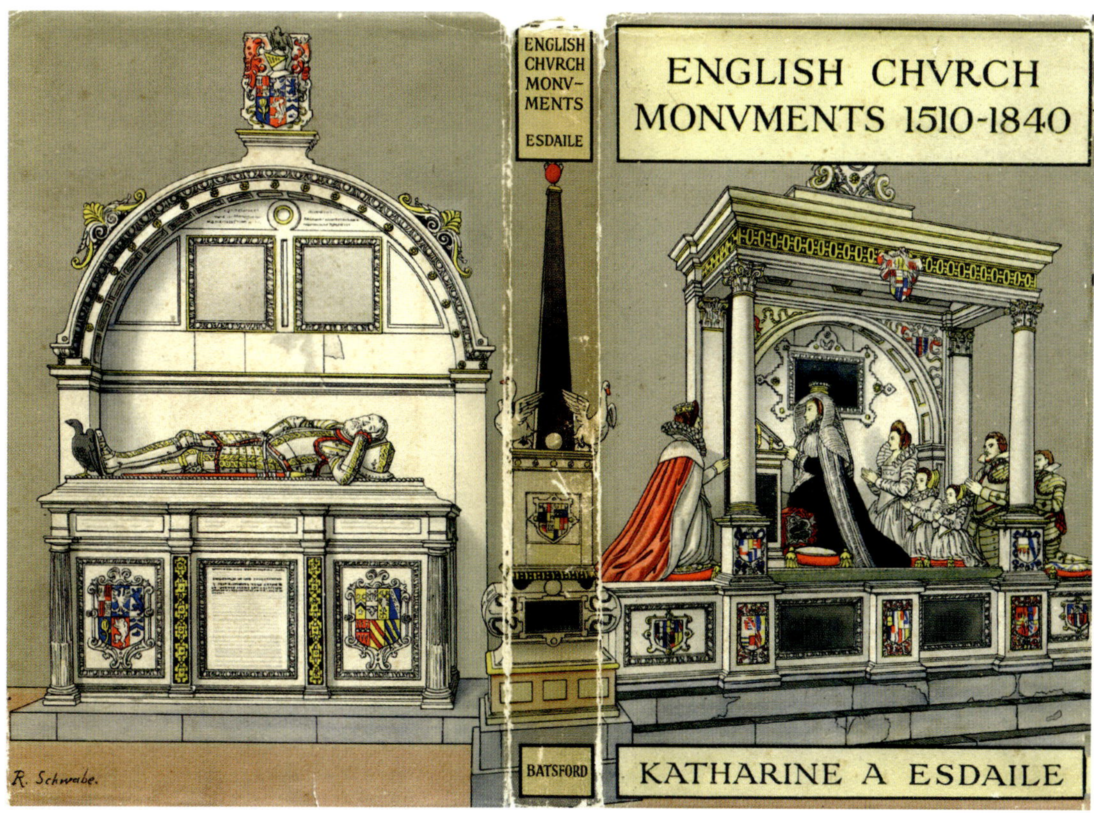

Dust-jacket for *English Church Monuments 1510–1840*
1946

1 Beaumont, C. (1927/1980) *The first score. An account of the foundation and development of the Beaumont Press and its first twenty publications*, p.76. *The first score* was dedicated to Randolph Schwabe.
2 Horne, A. (1995) *The dictionary of 20th century British book illustrators*, p.383.
3 Beaumont, C. (1975) *Bookseller at the ballet: Memoirs 1891 to 1929*, p.262.
4 Beaumont (1975) Ibid., p.287.
5 Beaumont (1927/1980) Op. cit., p.72.
6 Anon (1948) 'Prof. R Schwabe. An appreciation', *The Manchester Guardian*, 12/10/1948, p.3.
7 Tennyson, C. (1957) *Stars and Markets*, pp.196-7.
8 Allinson, A. (unpublished) *Painter's Pilgrimage* cited by The Court Gallery www.courtgallery.com/artwork/allinson_caferoyal.html (accessed 27/4/2012).
9 Hooker, D. (1986) *Nina Hamnett: Queen of Bohemia*, p.42.
10 Schwabe letter to Beaumont, 24/9/1923. Schwabe was staying at The Lodge, Dunford, Midhurst. V & A Theatre & Performance Archives.
11 'The agricultural sequences are portrayed with great charm especially the group of girls taking a risk in July-August by bathing in the nude with nothing but a hedge between them and a man riding on a reaper and binder.' See H. Simon (1973) *Song and Words: A history of the Curwen Press*, p.172.
12 Beaumont (1927/1980) Op. cit., p.81.
13 Beaumont (1975) Op. cit., p.328.
14 *The Actor. A poem by Robert Lloyd* (1926) was 'embellish'd with Theatrical Figures' by Schwabe. Jackman (1975) argues that this is not part of the series nor is *The history of the harlequin* (1924) by Constantini for which Schwabe did the cover (see 'The Beaumont Press 1917–1931: The story of a collection', *The Private Library*, 8, 1, pp.4–37).
15 Claudia Guercio married Barnett Freedman in 1930.
16 See Wilfrid Owen's memorable poem 'Anthem for Doomed Youth' written in 1917.
17 Schwabe letter to Beaumont, 6/3/1930. V&A Theatre & Performance Archives.
18 Schwabe diary 1930.
19 Schwabe diary 1930.
20 Schwabe diary 1930.
21 Blunden letter to Parker at the Ashmolean following his donation of the original drawings to the museum, 19/10/1937. Ashmolean Museum, University of Oxford.
22 Beaumont letter to Schwabe 18/8/1930. Private collection.
23 Beaumont letter to Schwabe 13/8/1930. Private collection.
24 Beaumont letter to Schwabe 19/9/1930. Private collection.
25 Schwabe diary 1943.
26 Webb, B. (1990) *Edmund Blunden: A biography*, p.196.
27 Schwabe diary 1933.
28 'One of the links between the Schwabe family and the Mackintoshes was Margaret Morris, wife of the Scottish artist J.D. Fergusson, who started teaching Alice… to dance at the age of three. When Alice left Bedales at the age of 15 it was to return as a teacher for Margaret…' (Weyers, J. (1982) The little girl who made friends with Toshy…, *Glasgow Herald*, Dec. 4, p.7.)
29 Alice, Lady Barnes interview with the author November 2009, Scotland. Beaumont was very fond of Alice and dedicated his first children's book *The mysterious toy shop: A fairy tale* published in 1924 and illustrated by his friend Wyndham Payne to Alice Schwabe.
30 Beaumont (1975) Op. cit., p.280.
31 Poesio, G. (1995) 'The maestro' in L. Brillarelli (Ed.) *Cecchetti: A ballet dynasty*, p.80.
32 Sorley Walker, K. (2002) 'Cyril Beaumont: Bookseller, Publisher, and Writer on Dance Part One', *Dance Chronicle*, 25, 1, p.68.
33 Beaumont (1975) Op. cit., p.254.
34 Kodicek, A. (1996) *Diaghilev: Creator of the Ballets Russes; art, music, dance*, p.146. The Cecchetti Society was founded in 1922.
35 Pritchard, J. (2004) *Tamara Platonovna Karsavina*, ODNB.
36 Kirk, A. (2011) 'Beaumont souvenirs' in J. Pritchard (Ed.) *Diaghilev and the golden age of the Ballets Russes 1909–1929*, p.184.
37 Beaumont (1975) Op. cit., p.168.
38 The other artists included Eileen Mayo, Michel Sevier, Ethelbert White and Vera Willoughby who also worked under the name of Vera Petrovna.
39 Beaumont (1975) Op. cit., p.227.
40 Brillarelli, L. (Ed.) (1995) *Cecchetti: A ballet dynasty*, p.47.
41 Cutting 'The Loving Heart', n.d. Schwabe's Scrapbook, p.89.
42 *The Times* 13/6/1918, p.9.
43 *The Times* 13/6/1918, p.9.
44 Rutherston letter to Schwabe 12/6/1918. Private collection.
45 See respectively *The Observer* 13/4/1919, p.12 and *The Times* 14/4/1919, p.16.
46 Kelly, F.M. & Schwabe, R. (1925) *Historic costume: A chronicle of fashion in Western Europe, 1490–1790*, Preface, p.v.
47 Kelly & Schwabe (1925) Ibid., p.v.
48 Kelly letter to Schwabe, 7/4/1915. Private collection.
49 Kelly letter to Schwabe, Ibid., 1915. Underlined in the original.
50 Kelly & Schwabe (1925) Op. cit., p.228.
51 Kelly & Schwabe (1925) Op. cit., p.226 & pp.230-31.
52 J.G.M. (1945) Obituary, *The Burlington*, July, p.179.
53 *Times Literary Supplement*, 26/11/1925.
54 *Eve*, 4/10/1925.
55 Kelly, F.M. & Schwabe, R. (1931) *A Short History of Costume and Armour, Chiefly in England*, Volume 1, Preface p.v.
56 Holmes, M.R. (1932) 'Costume through the ages', *The Burlington*, October, p.185.
57 Gooden letter to Schwabe, 12/5/1933. Marx letter to Schwabe,

1946. Private collection.

58 Reviews from Sanders, C. (Ed.) (1970) *W. Somerset Maugham.*
An annotated bibliography on writings about him, p.55.

59 Schwabe diary 1935.

60 Schwabe diary 1936.

61 Schwabe diary 1936.

62 Schwabe diary 1936.

63 Schwabe diary 1936. The whereabouts of the portrait is not known.

64 Petter, H.M. (1974) *The Oxford Almanack,* p.4.

65 Schwabe diary 1940.

66 Petter, H.M. (1946) *The Oxford Almanack 1674–1946,* p.18.
Schwabe diary 1940.

67 Cassidy, W.L. (1978) *The Shanghai experiments: Historical origins of the
special weapons and tactics concept,* January, pp.49–50.

68 Schwabe diary 1941.

69 Gubbins letter to Sykes, 18/1/1945. Private collection.

70 Batsford, H. (1943) Preface in H. Bolitho (Ed.) *A Batsford century.
The record of a hundred years of publishing and bookselling 1843–1943,* p.vi.

71 Schwabe diary 1942.

72 Schwabe diary 1945.

73 See *A brief survey of the history of Bisham Church, Berkshire* compiled
by H.A. Jones, c.1945.

74 Eva, R. (1994) Introduction Randolph Schwabe catalogue,
Bourne Fine Art.

75 Other covers were designed for example by Ethelbert White,
William Roberts and McKnight Kauffer.

76 See RIPM Journal Information www.ripm.org/journal_info.
php5?ABB=FAN (accessed 24/1/2012).

77 *Artwork.* 1,1, 1924, p.iv, edited by Herbert Wauthier (b.1881).

78 Clausen to Schwabe, 26/5/1930. Private collection.

79 MacColl letter to Schwabe, 17/12/1930. Private collection.

80 Schwabe letter to MacColl, 13/12/1930. University of Glasgow
Library Special Collections.

81 Schwabe diary 1931.

DRAWING TO THE END

In the early hours of Sunday 14 March 1948 Schwabe had a serious heart attack without pain, but marked by breathlessness. He recorded in his diary that he thought he could not live and how 'he struggled from his room to Towner's door along the hallway and asked him to fetch Dr Plowright, who came and injected something into his arm'. Schwabe found everyone sympathetic – the Hutchinsons, the Ayrtons, the Charltons. Rutherston telephoned, and Maureen, from D.S. MacColl. Charlton called to assure him that the Slade could carry on. Schwabe was told to take quite a long rest. Three days later he was taken in an ambulance to University College Hospital. He found he had lost the desire to smoke. He had given it up a week previously, after having rationed his cigarettes for some time to 11 a day. Schwabe thought it 'a resource to keep this Diary going', especially as a means of preventing boredom while confined to his bed. He was mightily relieved when Birdie came for a whole hour having been fearful that she might not be able to get away from the Towners.

Three weeks later Schwabe had his tea sitting up in a chair for the first time since he had been in hospital. On 15 April he left by taxi with Birdie for Hill House, a nursing home with a long-distance view over south London. The next day Birdie brought him drawing materials. They discussed plans for the future. He wrote in his diary on 21 April 'no doubt Birdie is right about 8 Church Row [Towner's house] being now thoroughly unsuitable for us. But what are we to do?' The following evening he had 'a heart collapse' and while not as bad as the first it meant a return to what he called the 'tied-to-one's bed regime'. Birdie's visit was much welcomed; she was 'A cheerful oasis in an afternoon of torpor.'[1]

On 4 May Schwabe was visited by Pye, the Provost – the conversation was mostly about arrangements for running the School but Pye did inform Schwabe that he had been made a Fellow of the College. Gerrard, being an established Professor, was in Schwabe's absence to be the nominal head. Through-out his stay at the nursing home Schwabe received regular visits from his friends and colleagues from the art world who would bring him news and reading materials.

On 29 May his brother-in-law Dr Tom Cobbe came from Dover to collect him – he was allocated a special petrol allowance for the occasion. While in Dover Schwabe finished writing the forty-four captions for the Degas drawings for his book *Degas: The Draughtsman* which was the first in a series of books for students of draughtsmanship.[2] Schwabe also started a drawing of a group of buildings behind the Maison Dieu. He returned to his pitch on a number of occasions before suffering another slight attack on 7 July. He was again confined to bed where he read and wrote letters.

On 23 July he returned to London by car and two days later he went with Cobbe by train to Glasgow. His son-in-law Harry Barnes collected them and drove them to Helensburgh to his home to join the large family party: Professor and Mrs Barnes who had moved from Sheffield to join their son; Alice and her two children Janet and Diana; Birdie's sister Dora and her daughter Margaret on holiday from London University; and Birdie. Schwabe was given a bed in the library on the ground floor in the old house; he admired the iron hand-rail of the stairs bowed out to accommodate crinolines and remembered the various rather grotesque neo-Gothic features from a previous visit.

Schwabe now revised and completed as far as possible the drawing of *Maison Dieu* and to commence a drawing in the hay-field of *Wood-End Farm* across the road at the back of Auchenteil. Birdie carried his things so as to enable him to begin a new drawing of the farm from the cabbage field. On 6 August he started a drawing of an oak from the laundry at the back of the house. Schwabe took his young grand-daughters Janet and Diana for a walk to the farm to look at the animals and found to his discomfort that a hay trolley which he had drawn from memory had different wheels from those in his drawing – much smaller. On 12 August Schwabe was taken ill again. His son-on-law helped him by typing some of his Slade letters, among them a testimonial for Percy Horton, who was applying, with Rutherston's approval, for his post of Ruskin Master.

The Tennysons arrived on 20 August. Schwabe, who was 'many sided in his conversation',[3] had much discussion with Charles about art and architecture and other matters of mutual interest. Tennyson in his auto-biography *Stars and Markets* recalled at length and with much affection the visit:

> one warm day during his last illness he was able to sit out and begin a beautiful drawing of the kitchen garden, in the course of which he was observed to be making an accurate record of a row of cabbages, treating each plant as an individual study. When asked whether he thought this really necessary, he replied in evident astonishment, 'Why, surely every c–c–cabbage is as different from every other c–c–cabbage, as every man from every other man.'[4]

Schwabe recorded their departure on the morning of Sunday 5 September 1948 as Ivy wanted to see her doctor in London. It was Schwabe's last diary entry.

He died on 19 September without returning to the Slade which he so deeply loved and which had been so much a part of his life. It was a mark of Schwabe's standing in the art world and the respect accorded to him that his death did not pass unmarked, with fulsome obituaries in the national newspapers and glowing tributes in learned journals. The Professorial Board at UCL resolved:

> to place on record its sorrow at the death of Randolph Schwabe, for eighteen years a distinguished Head of the Slade School of Fine Art. It was not only in the Slade School that his influence was felt. His wide humanity and kindness endeared him to all and the impact of his gentle personality was felt throughout the College.

> The Professorial Board, in expressing its grief at the death of a loved and revered colleague, wishes to offer to Mrs Schwabe its deepest sympathy in the loss of her husband.

A Service in Schwabe's memory was held in St Pancras Church on 12 October, 1948. A small statue carved by one of Schwabe's oldest friends, Alan Durst, stands against the wall of the churchyard of Hampstead Parish Church where his ashes are interred. Wrapped around the figure is a banner on which is written:

> Randolph Schwabe in whose life we have seen such excellence in beauty.

His was a life devoted to art.

---

1 Schwabe diary 1948.
2 Published by Rockcliff Publishing and The Art Trade Press in 1948.
3 Tennyson, C. (1957) *Stars and Markets*, p.196.
4 Ibid

SELECTED REFERENCES

Aitchison, D. (1989) 'The Slade School of Fine Art at the Ashmolean Museum, 1939–41', *The Ashmolean*, 15, Christmas 1988 & Spring 1989, pp.3–5

Aitken, C. (1926) 'The Slade School of Fine Arts', *Apollo*, 3, 13, January, pp.1–11

Arnold, B. (1981) *Orpen: Mirror to an age*, London: Jonathan Cape

Beaumont, C. (1927/1980) *The first score. An account of the foundation and development of the Beaumont Press and its first twenty publications*, New York: N T Smith

Beaumont, C. (1975) *Bookseller at the ballet: Memoirs 1891 to 1929* incorporating The Diaghilev Ballet in London. A record of bookselling, ballet going, publishing, and writing, London: C.W. Beaumont

Beetles, C. (1985) *S.R. Badmin and the English landscape*, London: Collins

Bertram, A. (1951) *A century of British painting 1851–1951*, London: The Studio Publications

Binyon, H. (1983) *Eric Ravilious: Memoir of an artist*, London: Lutterworth Press

Bolitho, H. (Ed.) *A Batsford century. The record of a hundred years of publishing and bookselling 1843–1943*, London: Batsford

Bowness, A. et al. (1991) *British Contemporary art 1910–1990: eighty years of collecting by the Contemporary Art Society*, London: The Herbert Press in association with the Contemporary Art Society

Brillarelli, L. (Ed.) (1995) *Cecchetti: A ballet dynasty*, Toronto: Dance Collection

Brown, F. (1930) 'Recollections (II) The early years of the New English Art Club', *Artwork*, 24, pp.269–77

Buckman, D. (2006) *Artists in Britain since 1945*, volume 1 (A to L) & volume 2 (M to Z), Bristol: Art Dictionaries Ltd.

Campbell, L. (1996) *Coventry Cathedral: Art and architecture in post-war Britain*, Oxford: Clarendon Press

Carrington, N. (Ed.) (1965) *Mark Gertler. Selected letters*, London: Rupert Hart Davis

Chambers, E. (2004) *Student stars at the Slade 1894–1899 Augustus John and William Orpen*, London: UCL Art Collections

Chaplin, S. (1998) *A Slade School of Fine Art archive reader: A compendium of documents, 1868–1975, in University College London, contextualized with an historical and critical commentary, augmented with material from diaries and interviews*, Slade School of Fine Art

Clarke, G. (2006) *Evelyn Dunbar: War and country*, Bristol: Sansom & Co.

Clarke, G. (2008) *The Women's Land Army: A portrait*, Bristol: Sansom & Co.

Cross, T. (1992) *Artists and Bohemians: 100 years with the Chelsea Arts Club*, London: Quiller Press

Daintrey, A. (1963) *I must say*, London: Chatto & Windus

Dunstan, B. (2006) *The paintings of Bernard Dunstan*, Newton Abbott: David & Charles

Everett, K. (1951) *Bricks and flowers. Memoirs of Katherine Everett*, Bungay: Richard Clay & Company

Fehrer, C. (1994) 'Women at the Académie Julian in Paris', *The Burlington*, 136, 1100, November, pp.752–77

Forge, A. (1961) 'The Slade (3): to the present day', *Motif* , 6, Spring, pp. 42–65

Forge, A. (Ed.) (1976) *The [William] Townsend Journals. An artist's record of his times 1928–51*, London: Tate Gallery

Fothergill, J. (Ed.) (1907) *The Slade. A collection of drawings and some pictures done by past and present students of the London Slade School of Art*, MDCCCXCIII–MDCCCVII.

Freeman, J. (1979) *Made at the Slade. A survey of mature works by ex-students of the Slade School of Fine Art, 1892–1960*, Brighton: Brighton Polytechnic, Faculty of Art & Design

Gardiner, J. (2010) *The Blitz. The British under attack 1939–1945*, London: Harper Press

Gardner, J. (1983) *Elephants in the attic. The autobiography of James Gardner*, London: Orbis

Harries, M. & S. (1983) *The war artists. British official war art of the twentieth century*, London: Michael Joseph in association with the Imperial War Museum & Tate Gallery

Hobhouse, J. (1989) *Everybody who was anybody: A biography of Gertrude Stein*, New York: Anchor

Holroyd, M. (1974) *Augustus John, volume 1: The years of innocence*, London: Heinemann

Hooker, D. (1986) *Nina Hamnett: Queen of Bohemia*, London: Constable & Company

Horne, A. (1995) *The dictionary of 20th century British book illustrators*, Woodbridge: Antique Collectors' Club Ltd.

Horne, J. (1939) *The life of Henry Tonks*, London: William Heinemann

Janet, Sister (1972) *Mother Maribel of Wantage*, London: SPCK

Jenkins, D.F. & Stephens, C. (Eds) (2004) *Gwen John and Augustus John*, London: Tate Publishing

John, A. (1962) *Chiaroscuro: Fragments of autobiography*, London: Grey Arrow

Kelly, F.M. & Schwabe, R. (1925) *Historic costume: A chronicle of fashion in Western Europe, 1490–1790*, London: Batsford

Kelly, F.M. & Schwabe, R. (1931) *A short history of costume and armour, chiefly in England*, volume 1 & 2, London: Batsford

Kodicek, A. (Ed.) (1996) *Diaghilev: Creator of the Ballets Russes*, London: Barbican Art Gallery/Lund Humphries

Laffitte, F. (1940/88) *The internment of aliens*, London: Libris

Llewellyn, S. & Liss, P. (2010) *The unknown artist: Stanley Lewis (1905–2009) and his contemporaries*, Cecil Higgins Art Gallery & Bedford Museum, lissfineart.com

Lindsay, D. (1963) *The Felton Bequest: An historical record 1904–1959*, London & Melbourne: Oxford University Press

Macdonald, S. (2004) *The history and philosophy of art education*, Cambridge: Lutterworth Press

McConkey, K. (2006) *The New English. A history of the New English Art Club*, London: Royal Academy of Arts

MacDougall, S. (2002) *Mark Gertler*, London: John Murray

MacLeod, M. (1988) *Thomas Hennell: Countryman, artist and writer*, Cambridge: Cambridge University Press

Malvern, S. (2004) *Modern art, Britain and the Great War*, London: Yale University Press

Meyrick, R. (1996) *The etchings and engravings of Edgar Holloway. A catalogue raisonné*, Aldershot: Scholar Press

Milner, J. (1988) *The studios of Paris. The capital of art in the late nineteenth century*, London: Yale University Press

O'Keeffe, P. (2000) *Some sort of genius: A life of Wyndham Lewis*, London: Jonathan Cape

Peppiat, M. (1982) *Raymond Mason: Coloured sculptures, bronzes and drawings 1952–82*, London: Lund Humphries

Petter, H.M. (1974) *The Oxford Almanack*, Oxford: Clarendon Press

Picard, B. (2005) *A life's work*, Redruth: Great Atlantic Publications

Pritchard, J. (Ed.) *Diaghilev and the golden age of the Ballets Russes 1909–1929*, London: V & A Publishing

Reynolds, M. (1971) *The Slade. The story of an art school, 1871–1971*, unpublished, Slade Archives

Robertson, P. (Ed.) (2001) *The Chronycle: The letters of Charles Rennie Mackintosh to Margaret Macdonald Mackintosh 1927*, Hunterian Art Gallery, University of Glasgow

Rothenstein, J. (1929/1970) *A pot of paint. The artists of the 1890s*, New York: Books for Libraries Press

Rothenstein, W. (1931) *Men and memories: Recollections of William Rothenstein 1872–1900*, London: Faber & Faber

Rothenstein, W. (1932) *Men and memories: Recollections of William Rothenstein 1900–1922*, London: Faber & Faber

Rothenstein, W. (1939) *Since fifty: Men and memories, 1922–38. Recollections of William Rothenstein*, London: Faber & Faber

Ruck, B. (1959) *A smile for the past*, London: Hutchinson

Russell, J. (2004) *England eats out: A social history of eating out in England from 1830 to the present*, Harlow: Pearson

Rutter, F. (1933) 'The art of Randolph Schwabe', *The Studio*, June, pp.374–79

Sanders, C. (Ed.) (1970) *W. Somerset Maugham. An annotated bibliography on writings about him*, De Kalb. Northern Illinois University Press

Schwabe, R. (1926) 'Francis Dodd', *Print Collector's Quarterly*, 21, 2, April, pp.143–64

Schwabe, R. (1934) 'Francis Sydney Unwin, etcher and lithographer', *Print Collector's Quarterly*, 21, 1, pp.59–69

Schwabe, R. (1943a) 'Reminiscences of fellow students', *The Burlington*, January, pp.6–9

Schwabe, R. (1943b) 'Three teachers: Brown, Tonks and Steer', *The Burlington*, June, pp.141–46

Shone, R. (1975) 'The Friday Club', *The Burlington*, 117, 866, p.279–84

Simon, H. (1973) *Song and words: A history of the Curwen Press*, London: Allen & Unwin

Skidmore, I. (2008) *Kyffin, a figure in a Welsh Landscape, the biography of Sir Kyffin Williams, RA, told through conversations with the artist and his friends*, Bridgend: Seren

Sorley Walker, K. (2002) 'Cyril Beaumont: Bookseller, publisher, and writer on dance Part One', *Dance Chronicle*, 25, 1, pp.51–94

Spalding, F. (2003) 'John Piper and Coventry, in war and peace', *The Burlington*, July, CXLV, pp. 488–500

Spalding, F. (2009) *John Piper. Myfanwy Piper. Lives in art*, Oxford: Oxford University Press

Speaight, R. (1962) *The portrait of an artist in his time William Rothenstein*, London: Eyre & Spottiswoode

Spencer, G. (1974) *Memoirs of a painter*, London: Chatto & Windus

Spencer, R. (Ed.) (2000) *Eduardo Paolozzi: Writings and interviews*, Oxford: Oxford University Press

Steen, M. (1943) *William Nicholson*, London: Collins

Stevenson, J. (2007) *Edward Burra: Twentieth-century eye*, London: Jonathan Cape

Summerfield, A. (1989) *The artist at war, Second World War paintings and drawings from the Walker Art Gallery's collection*, National Museums and Galleries on Merseyside

Tennyson, C. (1957) *Stars and markets*, London: Chatto & Windus

Tennyson, H. (1984) *The haunted mind*, London: André Deutsch

Thornton, A. (1935) *Fifty years of the New English Art Club*, London: Pitman & Sons

Thornton, A. (1938) *The diary of an art student of the nineties*, London: Pitman & Sons

Tonks, H. (1929) 'Notes from "Wander-Years"', *Artwork*, Winter, 5, 20, pp.213–35

Towner, D.C. (1979) *Recollections of a landscape painter & pottery collector, an autobiography*, New York: Born-Hawes Publishing

Webb, B. (1990) *Edmund Blunden: A biography*, London: Yale University Press

Williams, K. (1993) *Across the Straits an autobiography*, London: Duckworth

Wright, H.L. (1931) *The etchings, drypoints and lithographs of Alphonse Legros 1837–1911*, London: The Print Collector's Club

INDEX

Académie Julian 9, 22–25, 41
Airy, Anna 16, 60
Alexander, Margaret 106
Allan, Griselda 101, 105
Allan, Rosemary 76
Allinson, Adrian 54, 65, 143, 160
Anrep, Boris 25, 28, 33
Artists Aid China 101
Artists Aid Russia 101
Artists' General Benevolent Institution 82
Arts League of Service (ALS) 47, 87
Artwork 9, 45, 55, 87, 148, 157–158, 161
Ashmolean 85, 86, 91, 93, 94, 95, 96, 98, 99, 100,
    101, 102, 108, 110, 117, 137, 152, 160
Athenaeum, The 74, 85, 88, 111
Ayrton, Max 82, 91, 162
Ayrton, Tony 82, 91

Badmin, Stanley 46, 87
Barker, Margaret 43–44
Barnes, Alice Lady (née Schwabe)
    6, 8, 31, 32, 33, 35, 40, 41, 51, 73, 84, 85, 99, 117,
    134, 139, 156, 160, 162
Barnes, Diana (Di) 6, 8, 112, 162, 163
Barnes, Harry 6, 99, 162, 163
Barnes, Janet 6, 8, 40, 108, 162, 163
Bateman, H. M. 92
Batsford Book 148, 149, 156–157
Bawden, Edward 46, 47, 76
Bayes, Walter
    37, 43, 44, 45, 54, 57, 58, 61, 64, 65, 87, 88
Baynes, Tony 93, 94
Beaumont, Cyril
    54, 131–134, 136–139, 141, 143, 146, 160
Beaumont Press 9, 131–138, 150, 160
Beaumont Street 86, 92, 96, 101
Bedales School 134, 160
Bell, Clive 35
Bell, Robert Anning 45, 47
Bell, Vanessa 35, 65
Berry, Ana 47, 49
Bevan, Robert 38, 51, 65
Binyon, Helen 46
Birdie (Gwendolen Rosamund Schwabe née Jones)
    31, 32, 33, 35, 37, 49, 51, 55, 58, 60, 68, 73, 79, 80,
    82, 84, 85, 92, 100, 102, 105, 108, 112, 131, 132,
    136, 138, 156, 162, 163
Birrell, Augustine 54, 55
Blaikley, Ernest 17, 21
Bland, Beatrice 16, 102
Bliss, Douglas Percy 46, 112
Blue Cockatoo, The 35

Bone, Muirhead
    8, 29, 91, 99, 102, 103, 108, 115, 123, 153
Bone, Stephen 92, 102
Borenius, Tancred 94, 106
Bragg, Sir William Henry 74
British Independent Society 44
British Museum 15, 19, 24, 52, 68, 74, 148
British Restaurant 100, 112
British School at Rome 59
Brockhurst, Gerald 28
Brooker, Peter 62, 76, 106, 110
Brown, Frederick
    9, 16, 17, 18, 19, 20, 21, 29, 43, 44, 52, 60, 73, 75
Brown, Philip 6, 108–109, 113
Burn, Rodney 59, 106
Burra, Edward 46

Cadbury 92, 120
Café Royal 131, 132, 151
Camberwell School 8, 43–44, 49, 59, 60, 61, 68
Camden Town Group 38, 45
Carline, Sydney 84
Carrington, Dora 84
Carrington, Noel 80
Carrington, Mrs Noel 80
Cashelnagore 24, 108
Cassel Hospital 65
Cecchetti, Enrico 139, 141, 143, 146
Cecchetti Society, The 143, 160
Central Institute of Art and Design 103
Cercle International des Arts 25
Cerne Abbas 80, 81, 82, 85, 86, 91, 92, 94, 101
Cézanne 26, 62
Charlton, Daphne 79, 80, 82, 84, 85, 94, 162
Charlton, George 64, 74, 75, 79, 82, 84, 85, 94, 98,
    100, 105, 106, 110, 162
Chelsea 9, 29, 31, 32, 35, 38, 60, 73, 116, 124
Chelsea Arts Club Ball 33, 35
Chelsea Manor Studios 73
Cheston, Charles 65, 91
Cheyne Row 32, 51
Cheyne Walk 29, 35, 46, 66, 69, 79, 116
Church Row 46, 68, 82, 86, 105, 162
Clarendon Press 152, 153
Clark, Kenneth 86, 87, 91, 99, 103, 112, 120, 123, 124
Clarke Hall, Edna 16, 52
Clause, William (Willie)
    43, 44, 45, 60, 64, 65, 79, 102, 129
Clausen, George 55, 62, 64, 88, 158
Cobbe, Dora 31, 73, 136, 162
Cobbe, Tom 73, 96, 136, 162
Coldstream, William 106

Collins Baker, Charles H. 28, 79
Colquhoun, Ithell 65, 77, 92
Connard, Philip 28, 54, 58, 65, 66, 68, 102
Contemporary Art Society (CAS) 49, 52, 68, 91, 99
Costume 147–149
Council for the Encouragement of Music and the Arts
    (CEMA) 99
Coventry Cathedral 117, 120, 121, 122
Coxon, Raymond 44, 46
Cundall, Charles 65, 81, 102, 129

Dalton, William 43, 49
Daumier, Honoré 26, 28
Davies, Randall 38, 60, 94
Davy, Leo 108
Degas 80, 162
Dennis, Celia 93
Dennison, Daphne 101, 102
Dent, Hugh 46
Devas, Anthony 91, 102
Diaghilev 76, 138, 143
Dickey, E.M. O'Rourke 65, 117, 120, 122, 123, 126, 130
Dodd, Francis 6, 8, 29, 55, 60, 68, 74, 75, 115, 129, 157
Dodgson, Campbell 74
Doubleday, Nelson 150, 151
Douie, Charles 77, 88
Dover 57, 65, 73, 82, 83, 84, 96, 111, 136, 162
Dowling, Walter 11, 12, 13, 15
Doyle, Camilla 41, 100, 103
Dunlop, Ronald Ossory 98, 102
Dunstan, Bernard 93, 101, 102, 105
Durst, Alan 47, 84, 163
Duval, Miss 93
Duveen, Sir Joseph 54, 104

Eastbourne School of Art 46
Elder, Eleanor 49
Elton, Leonard 85, 86, 88, 89, 91, 92, 158
Emerson, Keyna 6, 113
Engels family 11
Enwonwu, Benedict (Ben) Chuka 104, 112
Epstein, Jacob 28, 54
Ermen, Cuthbert 115
Ermen, Godfrey 11, 115
Ermen, Godfrey Anthony van 115
'Ermen & Roby' 40

Farleigh, John 65, 150
Feiler, Paul 6, 75, 76, 94, 95, 104
Felton Bequest 99, 112
Fergusson, J.D. 47, 56, 160
First Edition Club 137

Fisher Prout, Millie 81, 94, 102
Fiztalan, Lord 55
Foster, Gregory 59
Fothergill, John 33, 37, 40
Friday Club 8, 35, 43
Fry, Roger 28, 29, 35, 41, 54

Gabain, Ethel 64, 66
Gerrard, A.H. 61, 77, 79, 92, 106, 110, 112, 162
Gertler, Mark 29, 38, 65, 80, 93
Gill, Colin 29, 80, 110
Gill, Eric 45, 55, 82
Ginger (Dr Joseph Bramhall Ellison) 82, 88
Ginner, Charles 23, 49, 51, 52, 82, 99
Glasgow 56, 73, 74, 88, 162
Glasgow School of Art 51, 112
Glass, Rhoda 'Dodie' (later Masterman) 76, 85
Gleadowe, Reginald Morier Yorke 74, 123
Gooden, Stephen 149
Gosse, Sylvia 38, 147
Grant, Duncan 22, 49, 80, 101
Greenham, Peter 101, 105
Gregory, Robert 25, 26
Grillion's Club 55
Grimmond, William 66, 86
Guercio, Claudia 134, 160
Gwynne-Jones, Allan
    33, 46, 47, 49, 59, 60, 61, 64, 65, 66, 74, 76, 92,
    93, 94, 99, 101, 105, 110, 116, 150

Hagedorn, Karl 66, 80, 84, 129
Hamnett, Nina 38, 65
Hampstead 9, 12, 46, 68, 84, 86, 103, 148, 151, 163
Harmar, Fairlie 64, 82, 108
Hartington, Marquis of 55
Havard Thomas, George 64
Haward, Lawrence 129
Heath Brow Chronicle 12, 13, 14
Heath Brow School 11, 15, 40
Hemel Hempstead 11, 12, 13, 14, 15, 24, 25
Hennell, Thomas 81, 108, 113
Hind, Arthur Mayger 55, 74
Holland, George 44, 81
Holloway, Edgar 77, 112
Holmes, Sir Charles John 58, 59, 65
Home Front Heroes 124–129
Horton, Percy 46, 47, 93, 99, 163

Idzikowski, Stanislas 139, **142**, **144**, 146
Innes, James Dickinson 21, 28, 29, **31**, 33, 84

Jackson, Ernest 86, 101, 110
Janes, Norman 77, 106
Japp, Darsie 31, 116
John, Augustus 16, 18, 20, 21, 26, 28, 32, 33, 37, 54,
    84, 87, 98, 101, 104, 132
John, Gwen 16, 37
Johnston, Edward 108
Jones, David 45
Jones, Gwendolen Rosamund (see Birdie)
Jones, Herbert and Elizabeth 31
Jowett, Percy 65, 86, 87, 99

Karsavina, Tamara 140, 143, **145**
Kelly, Francis 9, 15, 123, 148, 149, 156
Kelly, Gerald 150, 151, 152
Kennedy, George 24, 25
Kestelman, Morris 44
Koe Child, Charles 61, 64, 89
Konody, Paul G. 57, 88
Koring, Patricia (Pat) 93

Lamb, Euphemia 26, 31
Lamb, Henry 25, 26, 28, 29, 31, 55
Lamb, Lynton 43

Laver, James 76, 88
Leaf, Dr Walter 55
Lee, Rupert 65
Leeds, Edward Thurlow 100
Legros, Alphonse 16, 55, 65
Lehmann, Olga 64, 77
Lewis, Neville 56, 77
Lewis, Stanley 47
Lewis, Wyndham 17, 21, 45, 47
Lindsay, Daryl 81
Londoners' England Scheme 103–104
London Group 8, 38, 43, 54, 65
Lopokova, Lydia 139, 141, **142**, 143, 146, 157
Lowinsky, Ruth 32, 84, 92
Lowinsky, 'Tommy' 32, 84, 92, 94, 95, 99

MacColl, Dugald Sutherland
    21, 56, 58, 59, 60, 65, 89, 102, 158, 162
Macdonald, Margaret 8, 33, 35, 51, 55, 73, 160
Mackintosh, Charles Rennie
    8, 33, 35, 51, 54, 55, 73, 88, 160
Macnamara, Francis 84
Mahoney, Charles 47, 87
Maison Dieu 162, 163
Maitland, Helen 28
Manchester 11, 49, 111, 115, 129
Manchester Academy of Fine Arts 129
Manson, James Bolivar 65, 68, 88, 108
Marriott, Charles 65, 66
Marsh, Ernest (Eddie) 56, 64, 66, 82, 92
Marx, Enid 149
Mason, Raymond 108
Maugham, W. Somerset 150, 151, 152
Mayer, Katherine 78, 79, 80, 88
Mawer, Allen 61, 77
McKnight Kauffer, Edward 38, 47, 161
Medworth, Frank 43, 68
Mellor, Hugh Lyell 96, 112
Meninsky, Bernard 24, 45, 54, 65
Menzel 98, 112
Meo, Luigi Innes 21
Miles, June 102, 105, 109
Modern English Watercolour Society 51, 52
Moira, Gerald 45
Monnington, (Walter) Thomas 46, 59, 60, 61, 86, 109
Moore, Henry 44, 45, 47, 65, 76
Morrell, Lady Ottoline 33
Morris, Margaret 47, 54, 160
Morse, Enid 46
Moynihan, Rodrigo 65, 106

Nash, John 49, 51, 99
Nash, Paul 49, 92, 95, 99
National Gallery 19, 43, 74, 86, 99, 123, 124
Nevinson, C.R.W. 35, 38
New English Art Club (NEAC) 8, 20, 26, 29, 32, 43, 44,
    52, 54, 65, 66, 68, 80, 94, 96, 99, 102, 108, 111
Newbery, Francis (Fra) 51
Newbery, Jessie 51, 54, 73, 74
Nijinska, Bronislava 139
Nuttall-Smith, Ralph 92, 104, 105, 106

Ormrod, Frank 64, 85, 94
Orpen, William 16, 20, 21, 26, 28, 54, 88, 98
Oxford 6, 9, 15, 16, 21, 29, 55, 74, 84, 85, 86, 91–106,
    108, 109, 110, 122, 129, 137, 153, **154**
Oxford Almanack, The 152–154, 155

Paolozzi, Eduardo 110
Paris 9, 16, 22–26, 28, 29, 38, 41, 47, 88
Parker, Dr K.T. 91, 95, 96, 160
Parker, Stanley 101–102
Pearce, Maresco 24, 31, 51
Pettiward, Roger 77, 88
Philpot, Glyn 143, 146

Picard, Biddy 6, 92, 96
Picasso 26, 110
Picture Post 44, 90, 98, **99**
Piper, John 45, 99, 100, 120
Piranesi 26, 37, 87
Pissarro, Lucien 51, 80
Pite, Beresford 45, 46
Polunin, Vladimir 64, 76, 100, 101, 106
Porter, Frederick 25, 65
Post-Impressionism 54
Poynter, Edward 16, 18
Pringsheim 95
Pullée, Edward 46
Pym, Roland 84

Ravilious, Eric 46, 99
Raverat, Gwendolen 65
Riley, Cecil 6, 88, 94, 96
Riley, Joan (née Batty) 6, 94, 98
Rome 26, 59, 60
Rome Scholarship 47, 87, 109
Ross, Robert 115, 131
Rothenstein, Albert (see Albert Rutherston)
    21, 29, 31, 35, 37, 40
Rothenstein, John 96, 99
Rothenstein, William
    8, 21, 37, 45, 49, 58, 74, 91, 108, 153–154
Rough, Maribel 21, 41
Royal Academy 19, 24, 29, 101, 108
Royal College of Art (RCA)
    8, 9, 15–22, 43, 44, 45–47, 55, 58, 59, 61, 129
Royal Society of Painters in Water-colours (RWS)
    74, 81, 82, 87, 94, 96, 99, 100, 108
Rushbury, Henry 52, 60, 68, 115, 130, 157
Ruskin Master of Drawing 9, 84, 93, 163
Ruskin School of Drawing
    9, 84, 85, 89, 91–106, 110, 126
Russell, Walter 17, 19, 75, 99, 112, 123
Russian Ballet 76, 132, 138–146
Rutherford, Sir Ernest 55, 74
Rutherston, Albert (see Albert Rothenstein)
    8, 9, 33, 40, 52, 58, 65, 74, 81, 84, 85, 91, 93, 94,
    95, 96, 99, 100, 101, 102, 104, 105, 106, 110, 111,
    137, 162, 163
Rutherston, Charles 40, 147
Rutter, Frank 8, 9, 57, 68

Sandby, Paul 8
Schwabe, Eric (see Eric 'Bill' Sykes) 11, 12, 13, 88
Schwabe, Lawrence 11
Schwabe, Octavie Henriette (née Ermen) 11
Schwabe, Randolph
    costume designs for
        Muriel Pratt as Blanchefleur, *The Loving Heart* 146
        Doris Keane as Juliet, *Romeo and Juliet* 147
        The Enchanted Cottage 150
    illustrated books
        After Berneval: Letters of Oscar Wilde to Robert Ross 131
        The Art of Stanislas Idzikowski 146
        The Café Royal 131, 132
        Crossing: A Fairy Play 131
        The Curwen Press Almanack 133
        Of Human Bondage 149–150, 151–152, 153
        The Letters of J. E. Flecker to Frank Savery 134
        Madrigals and Chronicles 133
        *A Manual of the Theory and Practice of
            Classical Theatrical Dancing* 139, 141
        Masks of Time 133, 134
        To Nature 131, 132
        Shooting to Live with the One-Hand Gun 154–156, 157
        *The Slade. A Collection of Drawings and Some Pictures
            of the London Slade School of Art* 33, 40, 86
        The Sleeping Princess 138, 146
        A Summer's Fancy 134, 136, 137
        Thamar Karsavina 143

The Theory and Practice of Allegro in Classical Ballet 143
The Tinkers of Elstow 130
The Wet Flanders Plain 134, 135
To Themis-Poems on Famous Trials with Other Pieces 138
books by Schwabe
 Degas: The Draughtsman 162
 Historic Costume: A Chronicle of Fashion in Western Europe,
  1490–1790 (with F.M. Kelly) 148, 149
 A Short History of Costume and Armour, Chiefly in England,
  Vols. I & II (with F.M. Kelly) 123, 149
other books and magazine
 The Old Churches of London 156, 159
 English Church Monuments 1510–1840 156, 159
 Fanfare 157, 158
list of works
 The Armchair 57
 The Artist's Wife 101
 AUK 128, 129, 130
 Bank Holiday – The Swings 36, 37, 38
 The Barn, New College, Oxford 108
 The Basilica of Constantine 26, 37
 The Bath 30, 31
 Batsfords in 1893 156
 A Beach Scene 63, 64
 Augustine Birrell 54
 Sir John Rose Bradford 84
 Braunton, Devon 54
 Cashelnagore 108
 Sketch of Cecchetti as Pantalon in Carnaval 141
 Enrico Cecchetti as Pantalon in Carnaval 143
 Enrico Cecchetti, The Maestro 139
 Cerne Abbas 81
 Cerne in Winter 94
 Chelsea Backs 57
 Chelsea Old Church 56, 57
 Clerkenwell Green, with the Church of St James's 103
 43A Cheyne Walk 66, 69
 Cocking Mill-Pond, Cottages, Dunford-Front View 51
 La Conciergerie, Paris 23
 The Confession 29, 34, 37
 Cottages, Dunford-Back View 51
 Coventry Cathedral 121
 Danbury 65
 Mr Randall Davies 94
 Dedham Churchyard 65
 Les deux Andronnes at Sisteron 82
 Francis Dodd 75
 Dover, Alexandra House 57
 Dover: the Basin from Above 65
 Camilla Doyle 103
 Enwonwu 104
 Esch–sur–Sûre 82
 Everett's Shop, Cerne Abbas 86, 101
 Exotic Dance 35
 Family Group 81
 Farm Buildings, Pont 68, 71
 Farm Carts, Lanteglos 68, 72
 Farningham, Kent 103
 Figure Standing 22
 From Finavara 37
 Mrs Sargant Florence 51
 Fructidor 66, 88
 Giants Head Farm, Cerne Abbas 94
 The Girl and the Lamb 49
 Grave Diggers 35, 37
 Hall Farm, Bodinnick 68
 Head of an Old Woman 38
 Miss Hollyer GM 123
 Hotel de Paris, Dover 82, 83
 House in Cheyne Walk 29
 In Bed 37
 Stanislas Idzikowski as Bluebird 142
 Stanislas Idzikowski applying make up 144
 Interior-Lanteglos Church 68
 Janet 108

 Judge's Walk, Hampstead 103
 Keddle Bridge 94
 Kings Lynn 81
 The Lake on the Plateau, Donegal 65
 Landscape in Devonshire 38
 Lanteglos Church 68
 Leghorns 38, 39
 Lopokova as Columbine in Carnaval 142
 The Mausoleum 37, 38
 Katherine Mayer 78
 The Mill, Heyshott 51
 Mill, Penpol 68
 The Moustiers-Aiguines Valley 101
 Musidora 52
 Near Matravers 42, 51
 Oxford in the Full Moon, September 1940 154
 Pastoral 54
 Peeling Potatoes 48
 Pembroke Street, Oxford 94
 Petersfield, the Square 52
 Piccadilly Circus 37, 52
 Pin-Riveting a Lancashire Boiler 129, 130
 Police Constable F.H. Dart BEM 127
 Pont Neuf 24, 25
 Ponte Fabrico 26, 27
 Portrait 38
 Portrait of J.D. Innes 31
 Port St Michael, Paris 29
 The Postman 50, 51
 The Quadrant 37, 52, 53
 The Radcliffe Observatory 104, 106
 No. 14, Regent-street 37
 Ringwould 101
 St James's Church, Dover 111
 St James's Square 68
 St Thomas's Street, S.E.1 103
 Mrs Randolph Schwabe 38
 Sewing 65
 Sheep Dipping 68, 70
 Ship Street Backs 99
 Sisteron, Provence 94, 95
 Stacking Turf 29
 Standing Nude 57
 The Stour at Dedham 65, 67
 Study of a Child 65
 Study for The Women's Land Army and German Prisoners 117
 Suffer Little Children to Come Unto Me 10, 20
 Tamara Karsavina making up in her dressing room 140
 Tamara Karsavina as Zobeide in Schéhérazade 145
 Thatching Flax for Aeroplanes 118
 The Turl, Oxford 100
 The Unprepossessing Child 51
 V.2 Damage at the Chelsea Pensioners' Hospital, London, SW3
  124, 125
 Vanbrugh House 96, 97
 Voluntary Land Workers in a Flax-Field, Podington,
  Northamptonshire 114, 116
 Warwick Square, London E.C.4, August 1942,
  with Amen House in the Middle Distance 155
 West Mersea Regatta 51
 Whitby 32
 Woman in a Long Coat 37
 The Women's Land Army and German Prisoners 119
 Wood-End Farm 163
Shaw, Evelyn 59, 60
Sheppard, Sydney 100, 101
Short, Sir Francis (Frank) 45, 87
Sickert, Walter 37, 45
Sisteron 82, 94, 95
Slade, The 8, 9, 15–22, 23, 24, 26, 29, 31, 32, 33, 41,
 43, 44, 51, 55, 56, 57, 58–89, 91–113
 Cabaret & Dance 76, 110
 Dinner 64, 94
 Picnic 85, 96, 104, 110
 Sketch Club 21, 74, 98

 Society 74, 94, 96, 100, 102, 110, 111
 Summer Composition 20, 62, 64, 80
Society of Print-makers 51
South London Group (SLG) 49, 68, 80, 87
Spencer, Gilbert 43, 47, 66, 74
Spencer, Stanley 31
Squirrell, Leonard 81, 99
Stage Painting 76
Steer, P. Wilson 16, 19, 21, 40, 61, 66, 75
Stein, Gertrude 25, 26
Strang, David 24, 41
Strang, Ian 20, 22, 24, 43, 84
Strang, William 24, 37, 137
Swaisland, Hettie 35, 41
Sykes, Eric (Bill) 88, 154, 156
Symons, Arthur 131, 132, 133
Syrett, Kate 28

Taylor, Diana Yeldham 85, 101
Tennyson, Charles 60, 73, 84, 92, 103, 105, 106, 163
Tennyson, Ivy 60, 73, 84, 92, 101, 103, 105, 106, 163
Thomas, Margaret 6, 76, 88
Thornton, Alfred 44, 54
Thorogood, Stanley 43, 44, 49, 80, 81
Tonks, Henry 8, 9, 16, 17, 18, 19, 21, 24, 54, 57, 58,
 60, 61, 62, 73, 75, 76, 77, 79
Towner, Donald 44, 46, 47, 66, 105, 162
Townsend, William 62
Tunstall, Edward A. 100, 112

Underwood, Leon 44, 46, 52
Unwin, Francis 8, 26, 28, 29, 37, 38, 52, 157

Van Gogh 26, 38, 62
Venice Biennale 28
Victoria and Albert Museum 19, 62, 76, 89, 108, 148
Villiers, Margaret de 6, 8, 41, 46, 88, 112
Violinist, The 24
Vyse, Charles 44

Wadsworth, Edward 47, 52
Walker, Ethel 16, 65, 66, 101, 102
Walker, Rainforth Armitage 58, 64, 158
War Artists' Advisory Committee (WAAC)
 8, 105, 108, 117, 120, 123, 124
Wellington, Hubert 20, 47, 58, 80, 87
Westminster School of Art
 8, 16, 18, 19, 22, 43, 44–45, 130
Whistler, James McNeill 16, 32, 79
White, Ethelbert 52, 66, 160, 161
Williams, Kyffin 94, 98, 99, 102, 104, 112
Willoughby, Vera 146, 160
Women's Land Army, The 116–117, 119
Wynter, Bryan 96, 101, 105, 112

Yockney, Alfred 115, 116